WHAT OTHERS ARE SAYING

If you have a pet, don't just feed it. Listen. Dr. Monica can help you how. She's a born teacher, alternating between clear instructions and real-life examples. I'm especially enthusiastic about her view of "The Energy Imprint Process." Thank you, Dr. Monica, for another book imprinted with your distinctive qualities of compassion and insight.

— Rose Rosetree, author of *Let Today Be a Holiday:*
365 Ways to Co-Create with God

Dr. Monica takes animal communication to a whole new level in *Pets Have Feelings Too!* She offers advice on how to tell if an animal has reincarnated or is doing "energy imprinting" — following in the footsteps of a previous family pet. She explains how animals can actively direct their own healings. She touches upon pets as soulmates and healers of themselves, their human companions, and other animals. Her ability to relate case studies about her experiences and include details that enable others to emulate what she does makes this book an invaluable contribution to the literature.

— Linda and Allen Anderson, founders of Angel Animals Network and
authors of *Angel Dogs: Divine Messengers of Love* and *Rainbows & Bridges: An*
Animal Companion Memorial Kit

WHAT OTHERS ARE SAYING
ABOUT DR. MONICA'S FIRST BOOK

Through her captivating stories, Dr. Monica proves that animals can think and feel and that they experience lives not so different from our own. This courageous account of her psychic exploration will help you understand the power of your own mind and open your heart to the inner world of your animals. Bravo, Monica, on a job well done!

— Amelia Kinkade, author of *Straight from the Horse's Mouth: How to talk to*
animals and get answers

This book reveals animal thoughts, feelings and motivations. When it is time to let your pet go, Dr. Monica's stories, advice, and wisdom will provide you with courage, compassion and validation.

— Dan Poynter, author of *The Older Cat*

If you care, as I do, about your animals, this is one book you'll want to keep nearby. Learn that your animals are trying to communicate with you and how you can communicate back to them. You will be better able to care for your animals and help them live a better life.

— Jim Donovan, author of *Reclaim Your Life*

Your book is great. I enjoyed the many photos and stories. Like you, my favorite pastime is working with animals. They are so honest and so willing to communicate. The more books that are out on animals, the better it is. One of our missions on this earth is for people like us to teach as many people as we can how to communicate with animals and plants. We are doing just that. Keep up the good work.

— Patricia Murphy, author of *Cats/Canines Can Communicate*

I thoroughly enjoyed this book! Skeptics may scoff, but sooner or later, animal communication will be recognized as a valid phenomenon. And when that happens, it will be thanks to books like *What Animals Tell Me*. Dr. Diedrich's humanity, modesty, and integrity shine forth on every heart-warming page. Three paws up!

— Helen Weaver, author of *The Daisy Sutra: Conversations with my Dog*

Many people swear that their pets try to 'talk' to them. Through the psychic skills of animal communicators like Diedrich, it is possible to know exactly what they are saying. The author describes the techniques she uses to get in touch with the minds of dogs, cats, birds, horses, rabbits, and even a wolf. She discovers their complaints and preferences, their affection and fears. Directly quoted conversations reveal pets' intelligence, devotion, and sense of humor. The author also works to heal sick animals and contact and guide lost creatures. Charming color photographs of an assortment of animals, plus snapshots of Diedrich with contented animal clients further enliven the chatty accounts of the sessions. Most books on animal communication concentrate on describing body language and vocalizations animals use to relate to one another as opposed to humans. (This one) stresses psychic communication and spiritual qualities of animal life.

— *School Library Journal*, New York, N.Y

What Animals Tell Me is a collection of testimonies from an animal communicator. Dr. Monica Diedrich has been speaking with animals since the age of eight. Chapters recount her experiences with the strong wills of living animals, as well as the spiritual essence of animals that have crossed over to the other side. Pictures illustrate this heartwarming and spiritually uplifting anthology, sure especially to touch the hearts of devoted pet owners.

—*Wisconsin Bookwatch/ The Metaphysical Studies Shelf*

PETS HAVE FEELINGS TOO!

UNDERSTANDING YOUR PET'S PHYSICAL, EMOTIONAL AND SPIRITUAL NEEDS

DR. MONICA DIEDRICH

TWO PAWS UP PRESS
ANAHEIM, CALIFORNIA

PETS HAVE FEELINGS TOO!
UNDERSTANDING YOUR PET'S PHYSICAL, EMOTIONAL AND SPIRITUAL NEEDS

DR. MONICA DIEDRICH

Copyright © 2005 Monica Diedrich
Published 2005

ISBN: 0-9713812-3-2
Library of Congress Control Number: 2005909643

Published by:
Two Paws Up Press
PO Box 6107
Anaheim, CA 92816-6107
Phone: (714) 772-2207
Email: drmonica@petcommunicator.com
Website: www.petcommunicator.com

PRINTED IN THE UNITED STATES OF AMERICA

Table of Contents

ACKNOWLEDGEMENTS

When my first book was finished and my editor, Tony, told me he would see me again during the editing of my second book I laughed out loud. "No," I said. "I've already written what I need to say."

But time continues to teach us lessons and I felt compelled to write these lessons down as I learned them. Then I realized that many people could benefit from them — hence this second book. I'd like to thank the following people for lending their vital gifts:

I thank my husband for putting up with my long explanations and readings of material as I requested his input on this new project. His patience and genuine encouragement gave me the confidence I needed to include a lot of important subjects.

I extend my most sincere thanks to Colleen Fox, a client who not only became my friend, but also my first editor. She took my material and helped me keep it organized, pouring so much devotion, love and wisdom into this project that my work was enhanced by her loving touch. I thank her from the bottom of my heart for the many late night hours and months she put into this book. I could not have done it without her.

I thank my second editor, Sue Cramer, for putting up with us, our schedule changes, months of e-mails, and finally keeping up with a strict deadline. She graciously extended her efforts beyond the normal scope of an editor's work and for that I'm grateful.

With sincere gratitude, I also thank —

Victoria Jennings for allowing me to use her words for Life Assignment and make them part of me.

Cyd Tanimura, my client and friend, for hours of reading my material and for her comments and invaluable suggestions.

Tony Stubbs, final editor of my first book and now this one; because I can always count on him.

Dr. Leonard A. Sigdestad, DVM, for being one of those rare veterinarians who's open to listening to everything that's in the best interest of the animal he's trying to heal.

Dr. Jacqueline DeGrasse DC, my friend and colleague, who continues to assist me in finding other ways to help and heal our pets.

To each of these people — my gratitude and blessings.

Of course, I'm most grateful to all of my clients and friends who have given me the privilege of translating for their pets, and for the animals themselves whose stories will surely touch the hearts of many.

INTRODUCTION

It's the Fourth of July weekend in the United States and everyone's busy making plans for the holiday. Thousands of people will go to ball games, beaches and amusement parks, all places sure to have fireworks displays, along with entertainment, fun and relaxation for the whole family. Independence Day is always an occasion for celebrating!

But the plans I've made for the weekend are now long since forgotten because I'm lying on a gurney just outside the operating room waiting for the doctor to arrive for emergency surgery. I've been in pain for more than 48 hours and it's become unbearable.

Thinking it was just a tummy ache, I didn't seek professional advice until I couldn't walk, and now I'm afraid it may be too late for them to save me. My husband and younger son are with me and I can see the anguish on their faces. I fear the worst and ask for pen and paper because, weakened by the unrelenting pain, I'm no longer able to talk.

I'm barely able to move my hands as I try to make a list of all the important things I'd so hoped to accomplish before I died. I'm thinking it would be a sad ending for my life to leave now without first sharing so many of the wonderful teachings I've received. I also wanted to compile all the many fascinating experiences animals have related to me during my numerous talks with them that weren't included in my first book. Only vaguely aware of what I'm doing, I hand the notes to my husband as a "Honey Do" list, hoping that maybe he can finish my work if I don't make it through surgery.

They wheel me into the operating room and I'm suddenly aware of tears rolling down the sides of my face as they wet my neck and shoulders. The pain is too much to handle. A nurse leans over and tells me, "I'll take good care of you, don't worry," and the anesthesiologist instructs me to start counting backwards from ten. "Ten . . . nine . . . eight . . . ."

It took the next three months for my body to recuperate from coming so close to death, but this recovery period allowed me precious time to think. I reflected on why my life had been spared, and reviewed what I'd written on that piece of paper before surgery. I knew I needed to write a second book which would give people hope, especially for those times when their animals needed healing. There was so much more I wanted to share than what I'd been able to include in my first book.

But how did I come to have such a wealth of information to write about in the first place? That's a story in itself.

It's true that ever since I was eight years old, I've been able to receive pictures from animals which tell me what they're thinking and feeling. Yet, for many years, I didn't know exactly what to do with those pictures and feelings. Consequently, I'd never used that information in any practical way to help animals.

Happily, though, I would eventually learn how to use my intuitive gift to communicate effectively with them, and also bring healing to them, but that would come about only after I'd embarked on a spiritual quest which started some time before the emergency surgery.

My life changing journey began when I met my spiritual teacher, Master Tam Nguyen at the Center for Research in Metaphysics in Westminster, California (now located in Garden Grove). The course he was teaching about Cosmic Healing was my first introduction to the concept of Universal or Life Force Energy. At the end of my fourth class with him, I had a profound experience of *vibrantly feeling* this Life Force Energy flowing through me. I can only describe it as a feeling of being hugged and loved unconditionally!

At the time, I didn't understand exactly what had happened, but that event was the beginning of the transformation of my life. After class, Master Tam encouraged me to visit his Center often. He told me I'd find many opportunities there to learn how to let this healing energy flow through me as a loving gift to others.

I'd now intensely experienced this unconditional love for myself, but would I ever be able to let It flow through me to do Its healing work? I couldn't blindly believe in anybody else's ability to bring healing energy to others. Why should I? And if I couldn't readily believe that others had this ability, how could I believe it about myself?

Still, just to satisfy my curiosity, I decided to study and observe further, often doubting, yet at the same time wondering if I was also meant to help others in this special way. My time of spiritual study was filled with challenges as well as abundant opportunities for growth. And gradually, joyfully, I did develop and nurture the ability to let this healing energy flow through me for the benefit of others.

Master Tam taught that the Life Force Energy was there to bring comfort and healing to *every* living being. It wasn't just for people. My spirit leapt for joy as I grasped the full meaning of what he was saying, because my passion for working with companion animals was even stronger than my desire to work with people.

While volunteering at the Center, I regularly began offering my help to people who were concerned about their pets. They were surprised and delighted at the precise answers I was able to give them in response to their questions. What they wanted to know confirmed again and again that everyone was eagerly searching for answers which no one else seemed able to provide — not even their trusted veterinarians, or professionals who trained animals. Their continual requests for my help with their pets showed me that there was definitely a need to be met.

It wasn't long before I learned that by using all of my senses I had the ability to translate an animal's thoughts, feelings, wishes, and needs so that their human companions could better understand them. And, now I also realized that I could let the loving healing energy flow through me to the benefit of every animal I met!

My volunteer work at the Center was the first step in bringing together my love for animals and my desire to let the healing energy flow through me to help them. I didn't know, that in the very near future, I'd discover there was already a well-defined profession in which I could use my gift for communicating with animals, but whether I knew it or not at the time, the experiences during my spiritual journey provided just the preparation I needed for what would become my Life Assignment.

Life Assignment! What is that you might ask? Victoria Jennings wrote a book titled, *God as Mother*, based on the teachings of Maria Bauer Hall, wife of the late Manly P. Hall.* She described it like this:

"A person's Life Assignment is an obligation to life that must be fulfilled. It is our true purpose, somewhat like a ship designed to take us to our destiny. There is no peace unless you are fulfilling your Life Assignment, for there is an unquenchable thirst - an emptiness and longing - that only it can fulfill. Though it may not yet be revealed, your Life Assignment lies waiting in the innermost recesses of the human spirit. Its drama, this histo-tragic-comedy of Life, waits to unfold.

"Its presence is undeniable, its patience unlimited until you take your first humble step, and then with that step, the pattern within you is ignited. You are filled by a sudden thrust of energy and stamina to complete the task at hand, for this is the 'Divine Energy of Life' that molds our being, as we are swept away, driven to our destiny."

Isn't that beautiful? When I read this in Victoria Jennings' book, I felt as if those words were written especially for me. I'd never before referred to my gift as being my Life Assignment, but I just knew at some deep intuitive level that I was supposed to do something special with that gift somehow, someday!

And so, not long after my life transforming experiences at the Center, I began my private practice as an animal communicator.

One day, while I was actively living my Life Assignment, I received a call from a new client requesting an appointment. Our meeting would lead to so much more than just that single consultation. It would quickly open up a whole new world of animal healing for me.

---

*   Manly P. Hall was the founder of the Philosophical Research Society. In over 75 years of dynamic public activity, he delivered more than 8,000 lectures in the United States and abroad, and authored countless books, essays, and articles.

As I do every morning, I was answering e-mails on my computer when the phone rang. The voice on the other end seemed extremely surprised and pleased to have made a connection with a real person instead of an answering machine.

As requests go, this one was a little out of the ordinary because she wanted to see me in person at her home. Considering Southern California freeways and the fact that she lived in another county more than 50 miles away, this trip could easily take me up to two hours, depending on traffic, but her tone of voice told me that our meeting was important. I knew intuitively that this was something I was supposed to do, so we made an appointment for me to talk with her five dogs.

When I arrived, I was boisterously greeted by three very impressive Dobermans and two Manchester Terriers, all of whom were barking their heads off. One dog in particular, Calamity, firmly let me know she was in charge. Standing there, I momentarily reconsidered whether or not I wanted to go in! But I knew without a doubt that I was supposed to be there and I had work to do. The consultation lasted several hours until the client's questions had been answered and she was satisfied.

As we visited afterwards, she told me that her sister had given her a copy of my first book, *What Your Animals Tell Me.*** Reading it, and knowing that I was also in Southern California, inspired her to call and request an appointment. She'd decided that if we were supposed to meet, she'd reach me directly. Since she did, she was confident that our meeting was meant to be.

I next learned that she was a chiropractor who treated both people *and* pets. We talked about her work with animals, and then about mine, and decided to hold a seminar at her office so people could learn how they, too, can communicate with their pets.

On many occasions after our first visit, she also consulted with me about some of her clients. Because we realized that the information I

** Originally, my first book, published by Two Paws Up Press, was titled, *What Your Animals Tell Me*. In the summer of 2005, the same book, under the title, *What Animals Tell Me,* was released by Llewellyn Worldwide Publishing Co.

received from the animals often provided her with important insights about the chiropractic adjustments she needed to make, I began devoting one day a week to working with her at the clinic. When X-ray and veterinarian input confirmed what we were both seeing and feeling, we knew the circle of care was complete, and we were witnesses to some incredible healings and even small miracles, some of which you'll soon be reading about.

My chiropractor associate constantly had me ask the animals an abundance of questions. I found that the more questions I asked, and the more specific they were, the better we functioned as a team in our goal to help the animal. At her request, I asked the pets questions like: Do you have a headache? Are you short of breath? How well can you see? Do you have difficulty hearing? Is it hard for you to chew or swallow? Do you have a tummy ache? Does it burn when you pee, or do you have to strain when you have a bowel movement? If you're in pain, can you tell me how sharp it is and exactly where it's located? Does the pain come and go or is it steady? How did you feel after receiving an adjustment from the chiropractor?

These are questions you may not think to ask your pets since you're probably accustomed to the conventional, *but incorrect*, idea that they're unable to communicate their specific needs. As you'll discover while reading this book, we need to make a major adjustment in our thinking when it comes to what animals *can* tell us and how much they understand about what we're saying.

After working so closely with my chiropractor colleague, my respect and admiration goes out all the more to our veterinarians who, without being able to obtain the simplest of answers directly from their animal clients, are still able to pinpoint most of their ills and prescribe the appropriate remedies.

Wouldn't it be wonderful, though, if the animals themselves, through a translator, were able to tell their veterinarians where it hurts, or how an injury happened, and what would make them feel better? Or better still, what if veterinarians themselves learned to communicate directly with their pet patients? And what if they also actively understood that healing often takes place on more than one level? Maybe that day will come.

After working with so many pets, I realized that when animals exhibit behavioral problems or display symptoms of a diseased body, sometimes the origin of their discomfort is emotional or spiritual, or associated with a past event. Physical problems are sometimes healed when the emotional or spiritual causes are addressed. In the case of behavioral problems, often the only thing that needs to be corrected is a pet's misperception. And a lot of healthy animals with behavioral problems can happily be re-trained once everyone understands the nature and origin of the problem.

The health or attitudes of the people they live with may also significantly affect how a pet feels or behaves. That's because animals often reflect exactly what's happening in a person's own state of physical, emotional or spiritual health, much like a mirror reflects the image before it.

Occasionally, pets even try to take on our emotional problems or physical ailments themselves. Their reasons for doing so range from wanting to empathize with us, trying to show us how we need to change our thinking, or hoping to relieve us of those problems altogether so that *we'll* feel better. Most of the time in these situations, a pet requires spiritual healing, rather than medical treatment, in order to let go of any physical or emotional condition he or she has apparently taken on.

In the following chapters, I'd like to share with you some very interesting case studies which will help you understand not only the physical problems, but also some of the emotional and spiritual challenges our pets face as well. You'll see how they can play a very active role in healing themselves when they have someone to translate for them, and how they themselves can also act as very effective healers for people.

Their stories will help you view animals and their feelings in an entirely new light. Hopefully you, too, will come away with a new appreciation for their needs, and a much deeper empathy for their feelings!

— Dr. Monica
Anaheim, CA

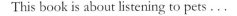

AN IMPORTANT NOTE BEFORE YOU BEGIN

This book is about listening to pets . . .

. . . and talking to pets . . .

. . . about how to help pets heal . . .

. . . and about how they help us to heal.

It's about my Life Assignment . . .

. . . and possibly about yours.

It's about the Universal Truths of Spirit, Life, and Love.

Whether a person believes in God, a Supreme Being, or the Big Bang, there is always a philosophical expression we live by.

Regardless of your philosophy, religious faith or creed, each of you should bring to this book your own favorite words to express these Universal Truths which help convey your idea of God.

As I wrote these chapters, I used expressions for God, Spirit, Life and Love with which I'm most familiar, those which touch my heart. My hope is that the expressions which I've used will touch your heart, also, or that you'll be able to freely adjust them in your own mind to those which are your chosen favorites.

Regardless of the specific terms I may have used in order to keep the presentation simple, my desire is that each of you will find your own sense of spirituality in this book.

It matters little to our animal friends what our religious or philosophical preferences are. Their only purpose in life is to give us Unconditional Love and teach us how to Love Unconditionally. Love is their religion, their philosophy. And through the deep Love you and your pet share, I know that you'll be able to joyfully speak to each other's hearts!

On a very practical note, for ease of expression, there are places in this book where I've chosen not to follow one of the regular rules of grammar. I've mixed a singular noun with plural pronouns, or vice versa, knowing full well that I'm taking the liberty of not matching singular with singular or plural with plural. I do so with apologies to editors, teachers, and anyone who loves exactness of expression.

Also for ease of both writing and reading in several examples, I've sometimes referred to a pet only as "he," or only as "she." However, in your own mind as you read, please feel free to use the pronoun that best represents your own beloved pet.

— Dr. Monica
Anaheim, CA

CHAPTER 1

COMMUNICATION
HAPPENS IN MANY WAYS

P eople have been relying on the spoken word for thousands of years. But before we developed language skills, was there any other form of communication? Of course!

People communicated with each other over great distances using telepathy to send messages back and forth. They were either person to person messages much like a phone call, or broadcast messages relayed to an entire group. *Telepathic communications are simply messages sent without using any spoken words.*

Even today we find living examples of such communication. The Aborigines of Australia are able to send telepathic messages while on their walkabouts. The Bushmen of the South African Kalahari Desert, the tribesmen of the southern Sudan and the Celts of the Scottish Highlands all use their telepathic abilities over great distances to communicate with each other. Their experiences have all been studied and documented.

Over time, however, this skill has generally been replaced by verbal and written communications. Yet, there are some people who are so sensitively attuned to each other that they, too, communicate telepathically, though they don't typically use that word to describe what they do. They finish each other's sentences or they hand their mate an item like a cup of coffee or a blanket before it's even requested. One strongly wishes the other would call, and within minutes the phone rings. Even before answering, it's understood that it's their spouse calling, and not someone else. These messages are telepathic because they're conveyed without spoken words.

Animals also communicate telepathically. In what may be one unique example of animal telepathy, researchers noted that monkeys on an isolated island engaged in a similar, but very uncharacteristic, behavior. Scientists placed sweet potatoes in the sand and then observed the monkeys washing them in the ocean before eating them. The monkeys on one island seemed to learn it from observing the very first monkey who ever did it. In the beginning, only a few monkeys washed the sweet potatoes, but gradually the practice spread to almost all the inhabitants of that island. Then, to their amazement, the researchers discovered that monkeys on far-distant islands started doing the very same thing without ever having had any direct contact with the inhabitants of the first island. It seems that when enough of the population engaged in the same behavior, it became part of the consciousness of the entire species. The message about washing the sweet potatoes may very well have been communicated from island to island telepathically.

All members of the animal kingdom communicate extensively among themselves using telepathy. In addition, some species, like whales, dolphins and elephants, employ sounds or body language as well. Members of the animal kingdom also *try* to communicate with humans who are often either not receptive or are oblivious to this fact.

Our domesticated pets are excellent examples of animals who try to communicate telepathically with humans. Any caring person who's ever been on the receiving end of intense shining eyes, alert ears, and wagging tails can comprehend the message that's being communicated — *I want a treat; let's go for a walk; let's play; let's go for a ride in the car.* Or in other telepathic ways, a pet may communicate that he or she needs to go outdoors, wants dinner, or wants an ear or body massage. In every case, our pets are sending us a telepathic message, *a message without spoken words*. However, they also find it necessary to use some form of body language for emphasis because, otherwise, most people would fail to receive their pet's messages at all.

People actually communicate telepathically all the time, too, but it's often done unconsciously. Whether we're aware of it or not, we, like the animals, send out a multitude of messages every day *without using spoken words*. We communicate both with other people, and with pets, by sending them sensory information through our thoughts and body language.

Perhaps you recall an occasion when you thought about taking your dog for a walk at an earlier time than usual because you were going to be away from home at the regular walk time. Before even getting up from your chair, and without saying a word, your dog is sitting by the front door, wagging his tail, absolutely SURE that the two of you are going out right now. How can this be? You didn't say anything, yet the dog knew exactly what you were thinking because you'd created a very specific picture in your mind. Your pet, who is always receiving information from you, knew exactly what your intentions were.

Or perhaps you were upset or crying. Our pets pick up on the feelings of distress or sadness we're sending out, and if we've allowed them to do so, they've communicated their understanding and sympathy to us by lying silently at our side, offering their paws as a condolence or resting a sympathetic chin on our lap. We've conveyed to them that we're sad or distressed and, in return, they're empathetically trying to communicate to us that they want to ease our pain in the best way they know how. These communication exchanges usually take place without any words being spoken.

For most of our lives, we and our pets rely on body language to send our messages without words, but there's another much more effective way in which we and our animals can communicate with one another.

In my previous book, *What Your Animals Tell Me,* I talked about how animals use what I call "picture telepathy" to send information to us. I've been using this form of telepathy with animals since I was eight years old and I've listened to countless species tell me things that amuse, surprise, delight and touch me deeply.

You'll learn about my many experiences communicating with animals as you read the case studies in this book. It would probably help if I explain something about *how* I receive communications from animals. I'll be talking about a new language — the language of pictures. It's probably the easiest one you'll ever learn!

From the time we're born, we're taught to communicate with each other by speaking in words and sentences. This is a natural and easy process when learned in childhood. But if we try to learn another language as an adult, we generally find it much more difficult.

In order to master a new language, you have to learn to "think" in it. You can never translate what you want to say directly from one language into another, because of the differences in grammar and syntax. Therefore, you first need to *think the thought* in the language you now want to speak.

When it comes to language translations, I have firsthand experience. I moved to the United States from Argentina when I was 18 years old and quickly learned that you cannot translate Spanish into English, word for word. It simply doesn't work. I first had to learn to think, in English, about what I wanted to say, before saying the English words. That took me a couple of years, a lot of practice, and countless tears of frustration.

My husband still remembers our first trip to McDonald's. At that time, more than 30 years ago, we made only very simple choices — ones that could be expressed very easily in as few words as possible. We walked up to the counter and in our best English we said, "Two hamburgers with potatoes fried." Then, remembering my English grammar, I quickly said to my husband, "Wait! You have to put the adjective before the noun in English."

He smiled at me, then turned to the girl behind the counter again and said, "Fried potatoes, please." She still had a puzzled look on her face. I can't remember exactly how the conversation went, but I remember a lot of hand signals and pointing up at the sign behind the counter. "French

Fries?" we repeated in unison. Why the heck are they called French Fries? To this day, we don't know the answer to that question, but we learned our lesson. We have to *think* in the language we're going to use before we *speak* it, otherwise we may not be understood.

That's also going to be true for you if you want to communicate in a more effective way with your pets. *You must first think, and then speak, in the one language that nearly everyone can recognize — the language of pictures.*

A picture indeed is worth a thousand words. I've seen this firsthand when animals of different species living in the same household have used pictures to tell me things about other animal family members. And this is not only *my* experience. Today, there are hundreds, maybe even thousands, of professional animal communicators, as well as ordinary people, who've shared experiences similar to mine.

Maybe because we think of ourselves as being more evolved, we believe that communication is something that can only occur at the human level. More likely, we've been incorrectly taught since childhood that this is so.

I was taught that, too, but, of course, I couldn't believe it. Animals had been communicating with me from the time I was very young. They told me things I didn't already know about them, or in some cases, things I didn't want to know because they were particularly sad or painful.

People around me didn't understand my gift. I was often told I had too vivid an imagination or that I was just crying "crocodile tears" over what they considered foolish things, like seeing a dog left alone tethered to a tree. They thought the dog didn't care one way or the other, but I knew better because the pet could send me pictures telling me how lonely and distressed it was. Animals could communicate with me and I could communicate with them because we both used pictures.

Temple Grandin, who has a Ph.D. in Animal Science from the University of Illinois, uses her unique gift for communicating with animals through pictures even though she's autistic. Unlike other autistic persons who are unable to speak and seem to be cut off from human interaction,

Temple works as an associate professor of Animal Sciences at Colorado State University, and frequently lectures throughout the country.

She's designed one third of all the livestock handling facilities in the United States, as well as designing many in other countries. She's not only been able to understand and manage her limitations, but has also written a book entitled *Thinking in Pictures*. A quote from her book hit home with me as it describes exactly what happens in my head and how I feel about my gift.

She writes: "I THINK IN PICTURES. Words are like a second language to me. I translate both spoken and written words into full-color movies, complete with sound, which run like a VCR tape in my head . . .. Language-based thinkers often find this phenomenon difficult to understand, but in my job as an equipment designer for the livestock industry, visual thinking is a tremendous advantage . . .. I value my ability to think visually, and I would never want to lose it."

Amen to that, Temple! She combines her visual abilities with her love for animals and observes cattle and sheep, looking at the world from their point of view. She tries to "become" them in order to see what they see and feel what they feel. That's what I do, and with my help, when you finish this book, you'll have a better understanding of the process as well.

With this foundation, many of you will no doubt begin communicating with your own animals. For those who'd like additional guidance, I'm currently putting the finishing touches on my next book entitled *For Pet's Sake, DO SOMETHING! Tools for Healing your Pets*. That book will provide specific examples showing you how to develop an even closer bond with your beloved pets through the art of communication. Be sure to check the Epilogue for more information.

For the purposes of this book, however, we'll focus on the fascinating talks I've had with some of the many animals who've confided in me. It's time now to check out the next chapter and see what pets really have to say!

CHAPTER 2

LISTENING TO YOUR ANIMALS

Animals do the best they can to convey their thoughts to us using their eyes, ears, tails, body language, or even sounds when necessary. It seems to us that those are the only means they have to capture our attention. But they can also communicate very effectively with us in other ways. When we listen quietly, with love, we can receive messages from our pets in our mind's eye and have a real conversation with them.

When I'm listening to animals, I usually receive a pet's messages as a series of pictures. I believe our exchange takes place this way because animals think and communicate using sensory images. Many times, their pictures look like the clip of a movie that lasts for only a few seconds. Other times they send one or more snapshots, similar to what you might see in a photo album.

When I "tune in" to pets, I open up all of my senses so I can receive their feelings and emotions, as well as the images they send. Their visual images provide sights, smells, tastes and sounds. Since I'm listening to them from the energy center of my heart, their feelings are also able to come through loud and clear. I see what they see and feel what they feel. I pay close attention to the energy of the animal and to his or her emotions. I don't have any expectations since I'm merely the vessel through which their messages are transmitted. I simply sit and wait, eyes closed with hands relaxed in my lap, until I receive a response. Then I translate the pet's pictures and feelings into sentences that make sense to the client.

Once I start translating, the clips or pictures come easily. Pictures don't imply or reference a time frame so I don't always know at first whether the pet is showing me an event from the past, present, or future. The pet may even be using the picture to make a request.

To determine the approximate time of the event, I establish a link between the picture I receive and the animal's response to a specific question. This may be a question I choose to ask, or one which the client wants me to ask the pet. To get the most out of each session, I always suggest that my clients bring a written list of questions they'd like to address during the consultation. If they have all of their concerns written down, they won't forget something important which they wanted to cover. As the pet and I continue to talk, I also ask many questions of my own to clarify the information they're sending me.

When I first get in touch with the animals, I always allow them to tell me anything they want before I ask them any questions. Many times they'll start by telling me the very same things their humans want to know. To me, this affirms that they're acutely aware of what is on their humans' minds and therefore they know what needs to be addressed first.

Quite often, pets have definite requests. They may need a different kind of food, more time together with their humans, better sleeping arrangements, or they may want to be allowed to do what they perceive to be their job, without being scolded, like barking when strangers approach their home or taking care of a specific person or animal.

There are many everyday reasons to listen to our pets, but one of the most important times to listen to them is when they're sick or dying. It's on these occasions when they often need to have us follow their wishes more than at any other time, even though this is usually very painful and difficult to do.

The most important thing I can suggest to my clients is to learn to listen thoughtfully to what the animals are saying every time, and then find a way to meet the needs they've expressed. Once a pet's needs are understood and met, most life situations work themselves out satisfactorily for both the person and the pet.

Although this type of listening takes practice, I find that many people are able to master the art of communicating with their pets over time. When they haven't been able to do so, or when they're too emotionally invested, those are the occasions when the help of an animal communicator can be invaluable.

———

In this first case study, you'll see how active listening can bring about emotional release and inner healing for both person and pet. Lori raises and trains puppies for the Guide Dogs of America. Her story describes someone who willingly responded to what her dog was telling her, even though it wasn't what she wanted to hear. Because of her selflessness, Lori was even able to give her dog permission to do whatever it was Grady needed to do.

GRADY

I considered it a privilege to meet Lori and her seeing-eye dog trainee, Grady. Grady had been with Lori since she was eight weeks old and every day of her young life she'd been in training to be a service dog. Lori heard through a co-worker that I was available for consultations, so she dropped everything she was doing to come see me.

With pain in her voice, Lori said, "It's going to be so difficult to see her go. I love her so much." She was preparing herself for the final phase of Grady's training which would require her to leave Grady for a week long tryout and test to make sure she was a good candidate for the program. After that, Grady would live as a service dog with another family.

There was only one problem. "I don't want to be a service dog," Grady said as soon as we started our conversation. "It's so boring. All I do is walk very slowly and then sit and wait, sit and wait. I don't want to do that! I need to do something exciting! I'm smart and I want to learn new things. I love to retrieve things and my sense of smell is very good! Couldn't I be doing something more active?"

Lori understood Grady's pleading very well. Somewhere in her heart she knew Grady didn't want to be a service dog. Grady had growled once at another dog two weeks prior and that was a definite no-no. Lori had hoped against all hope that it was a one time thing, but two days before seeing me, it happened again. It was a low growl, no barking, no snapping, just a message, "I'm *not* happy. Don't get close to me."

Although Lori was disappointed, she understood the message. She was hoping that all her hard work over the last 13 months would give Grady a chance to be with someone who really needed her, but she had to admit that Grady was not enjoying this type of life.

Lori then told Grady that she'd have to go for her test anyway. Grady then asked Lori, "Do I have to be really good there?"

"No, Grady, you can be and do whatever you want. I'll still love you," Lori replied.

That's all Grady needed to hear. She told me she was very happy that she'd be free to express her feelings.

Two weeks later I checked with Lori to see how Grady had fared. After a week of tests and practice, on the last day at a routine tie-down under a table, Grady suddenly growled. She was dropped from the program that day.

There's a long list of people waiting for service dogs, which makes it all the more heartrending when, for some reason or another, a dog doesn't make it through the intense training program. Because of their wonderful dispositions and extensive training, there's even a three year waiting list for those choosing to adopt dogs who *don't* successfully make it through the program.

Lori's co-worker and friend had already fallen in love with Grady's playfulness and spirit, and was excited at even the remote possibility of getting Grady if she happened to be dropped from the program. Because of Lori's relationship with this co-worker and the opportunity for her to visit Grady often, Lori's superiors in the program made an exception and granted placement of Grady with Lori's friend. It was also beneficial for Grady because she'd been around her potential new family often during her thirteen months of training. They weren't strangers and the adjustment time went smoothly.

Grady enjoys her new family who has given her the freedom she so much desired, and she delights in being able to still see Lori with whom she has such a loving bond. Both families often plan trips to the park together!

Seldom do I have the opportunity to provide continued follow-up for a family so willing to listen to their pet, as in this next case study. My experience with them gave me a profound sense of understanding that my Life Assignment, as an animal communicator, is well worth the effort I put forth when I'm relating to an animal's innermost feelings.

PANDORA

Pandora is a nine-year-old female English Staffordshire Terrier. It was just several days before Christmas when her lifelong male partner had to be euthanized. What was equally distressing was that four days later, she was seemingly "abandoned" by her human family. In actuality, Pandora's parents went to South Africa to spend the holidays with family, but as far as Pandora was concerned, they were gone — gone forever, just like her best friend and companion of many years.

His name was GB. He had several cancerous tumors which were growing and advancing rapidly throughout his weakened body. I'd seen him two months earlier when he'd told Mom exactly how to know when it would be time for him to be put down. He was as stoic as they come, but I knew it wouldn't be long.

It was still a very difficult decision, and Mom waited until the last minute. However, she knew that he wouldn't survive while she was gone for the holidays, so with a heavy heart she followed GB's instructions to the end. She also allowed Pandora to go to the vet with them to say her final goodbye.

This is something I recommend every person should do because it allows the animal who remains in the family to have a last smell and to understand that the other pet won't be coming back home, thus minimizing the mourning period. This time, however, it didn't work quite as planned.

During the following four days, Pandora clung to Mom every minute, but other than being a little down and eating less, there were no major complaints or outward signs of her distress.

On Friday, the family packed their bags and left Pandora with a house sitter who knew the house and daily routines because she'd taken care of Pandora and GB before. No problem, right?

Five days later, I received a call from the house sitter. Pandora, who hardly ever barks, had been howling almost continuously day and night. She repeatedly searched the entire house looking for her family. She wouldn't eat, wouldn't calm down no matter how much attention she received, and what's worse, she wouldn't sleep or let anyone else in the neighborhood sleep either. In a last ditch effort to restore sanity, the pet sitter had even taken Pandora to the vet who prescribed Valium for her. Unbelievably, there was still no change.

I went to see Pandora who was now at the hospital under observation. "These past two weeks have been very difficult for me," she said pitifully. "No GB and no Mom. I can't bear it!"

It took a lot of "picture talking" on my part to convince her that her parents were coming back and she'd soon be with them again. Pandora said she didn't want to go home again until they returned. It was just too difficult without her family around. She asked me to let her stay where she was since the hospital is also a vacation kennel.

Pandora's mom called me from South Africa. She was willing to forego her vacation, her holidays, and time with her family if necessary just to see her grieving dog well again. When we checked back with the kennel, two days after my first conversation with Pandora, they told us that she no longer appeared anxious. In fact, she was off the Valium and hadn't howled or barked once since I left.

By then, her mom understood that Pandora simply needed to get away from the home she'd shared with GB while the rest of her family was also away. She decided to let Pandora stay at the kennel and she continued with her original holiday plans. I was to remind Pandora daily, through telepathic communication, that her parents were coming back for her.

After they returned, Pandora slowly regained her sense of well-being. Her family helped by giving her extra attention and taking her along on car rides. Friends and neighbors often stopped by to say hello, and in time she was back to her normal self.

Each of us, humans and animals, mourn in our own unique way. By listening to our pets and following their wishes to give them the time they need to heal, we help them to sort things out so that they once again can become the happy, healthy companions we love so much.

On a side note, please don't think that by bringing a new puppy home right away, your pet's grieving or loss would be lessened. Think of your own feelings about losing a spouse or a child and how you wouldn't be ready to welcome a new member into the family very soon! We worry about our animal friends and want them to be happy and well-adjusted quickly, but sometimes, *all* they need is time.

In Pandora's case, her relationship with GB was very special, and a new friend or addition to the home wouldn't have relieved her stress or her feelings of loss. On the contrary, it could very well have backfired, making it unclear about the love Pandora's family had for her, and the future pet's hierarchy in the home. The old adage "Time heals all wounds" clearly applies here, and time is what Pandora needed.

———

We have to remember that our beloved animal friends have their own ideas and can clearly express what they need or want when it comes to their own well-being and their future. We only need to listen to them with an open mind and heart, and then respond to their requests or needs in every reasonable way possible.

Most clients who come to visit me are very open to hearing from their pets, but often even skeptics contact me as a last resort, though usually without the same openness of mind and heart. Sometimes when clients don't hear what *they* want to hear during a consultation, instead of listening to their pets, they respond by insistently trying to convince their animals to do what the human feels is best — *for the human*. They have only their own agendas in mind and sometimes they totally *ignore* the importance of what their pet has just told them. The following is a classic example of *not* listening.

SHEBA

Every Wednesday, my chiropractor colleague would join me as we drove from her home to her clinic. But early one morning, she called to request that I meet her at the animal hospital instead.

When I walked inside to let her know I'd arrived, I could see, through the open door, that she was still attending to her emergency patient. A large female Rottweiler, who'd been sedated, was lying on the floor on a mat and the chiropractor was kneeling down beside her manipulating the dog's upper spine and neck. Trying not to interrupt, I stood quietly by the door observing her work.

Because of the affinity we have and the working relationship we've developed, my colleague thought nothing of saying to me in front of the patient's human, "Jump in at any time with any information, Dr. Monica."

From my vantage point in the doorway, all I could see was my colleague and the dog, but I knew someone else must be sitting nearby. I hesitate to say anything until I know a person is open to what I do, but I'd been tuning in to the patient for several minutes. What I "heard" sounded so funny I was compelled to share it.

The dog said to me, "Why is she pulling on my neck? Tell her that's not where it hurts. Tell her it's my leg that hurts!" I proceeded to tell my friend exactly what the dog had relayed to me.

"I *know* it's her leg, but while she's under sedation, I want to work on her neck and spine, too!" she said laughing out loud.

The vet then came into the room and my colleague said, "There's something wrong with her right leg and I don't think I can fix it. We need to take some X-rays."

At that moment, I was called out of the room by the receptionist, and when I returned, my colleague was ready to go. As it happened, we never had an occasion to discuss this case again.

Several weeks later, a couple came to see me with a 6½-year-old female Rottweiler named Sheba. Their discomfort, mannerisms and eye contact with me indicated that they were both very skeptical. I suspected that my colleague had suggested they talk with me and they were probably doing it just to please her.

They were very careful not to give any clues when they asked questions. They suggested only general inquiries for me to discuss with Sheba such as, "Ask her if she has any friends at home," or, "Ask her if she has any pain." I encounter many people who begin a consultation like this and I always honor their requests.

I asked Sheba to describe her home environment. She said, "There's another dog at home. He's bigger than I am but the same. He's kind of crazy. He thinks he's the boss and I have to do what he says!"

Dad verified for me that there was another Rottweiler at home, a male, who drives Sheba crazy. By now Dad was smiling, and looked somewhat curious. Mom, however, remained impassive.

"What's wrong with her?" asked Mom. "Ask her to describe it."

Sheba had been standing next to Dad until now. Her leash was tight and she was unable to move about. Sheba said to me, "I'm in a lot of pain. My leg hurts. It feels like the bones are fused together and it's hard to walk. I'm very independent and this makes me feel very uncomfortable."

Mom then informed me that Sheba had been diagnosed with bone cancer and would have to have her right leg amputated. When I told Sheba this she said, "No way! I can't function with three legs. If you cut it off, I won't be able to balance my big body. I don't want you to do that!" Sheba was very overweight and it would, in fact, have been very difficult for her to be able to pull her body around with only three legs.

Mom became visibly upset and I wasn't sure at that moment, if she was upset with me or with the answer Sheba had given. After a difficult silence, she said, "Tell her that if she doesn't have the operation, she'll die."

Sheba took a single breath and responded vehemently, "I don't care! I'd rather die with all my legs!"

Mom didn't seem to hear what Sheba said and continued to tell Sheba what *she* thought would be best for her. She promised she'd feel better after having the surgery. Mom also said she wouldn't allow the male close to her until she recuperated fully. She didn't ask Sheba to reconsider her position and she spoke as if Sheba had no choice in the matter. In resignation, Sheba stopped listening to me, stood on all four's next to the door, and indicated that she was ready to go home.

I felt much empathy for the woman because I could feel her pain. She wanted Sheba to go through the amputation, have radiation and chemotherapy, and continue to live a semi-normal life. It frustrated me to sense that she felt I was just making things up. What I observed was a lack of resolution between a determined Rottie and an unwilling listener.

I must confess that I was a little hurt later when I heard that the woman thought the consultation was very vague. To me, Sheba was anything *but* vague! "I'd rather die!" she'd said. Not until later was I to find out that this was the same dog I'd seen under sedation two weeks prior.

Several weeks later, I learned that while making preparations for surgery, the vet found that the cancer had spread to Sheba's left leg. With no possibility of a cure or rehabilitation, the vet suggested the only appropriate course of action. She needed to be euthanized.

Because of my conversation with Sheba, I have no doubt that she was relieved by the outcome of her situation. I couldn't help but think however, how wonderful it would have been if her humans could have said their goodbyes over time and told her how much they loved her. They could have spent their last weeks enjoying each other's company and doing Sheba's favorite things instead of being consumed by a course of action Sheba neither wanted nor approved of. By dragging her all over town to see different specialists, and having her poked and prodded, her last weeks were filled with pain and anxiety rather than with the calm company and affection of those closest to her. But in the end, the Universe was listening, and Sheba's request was granted.

In this last case study, you'll experience the wonderful benefits of pet communication when a person *does* actively listen, even though it's a particularly difficult time in both their lives.

GUNNER

Cyndi is a young lady in her late twenties. Ever since she'd been on her own, she'd shared her life with her constant companion, Gunner, now a 13-year-old male German Shepherd. He was very athletic, running with Cyndi three miles every day and accompanying her as she bicycled several times a week.

A beautiful girl with long blond hair who's smart and witty, Cyndi loves the outdoors. She not only needed company, but a big dog who would care for her and keep strangers at bay. It was one of those relationships made in heaven. Gunner lived for Cyndi and Cyndi was in love with her Gunner.

One day Cyndi was stunned to find that Gunner couldn't finish running the first mile. He collapsed in the middle of the road and waited for her to come to his rescue. After weeks of tests and agonizing over what could be wrong, Gunner was diagnosed with cancer. Surgery wasn't an option because his body was already shutting down a little bit at a time. The cancer had spread to all his vital organs.

Cyndi came to see me with Gunner, not once, but several times. She was comforted to find that he was willing to stay with her for as long as he could. He said he'd stay until the pain was severe enough for him to have to leave.

We saw each other many times over the next six months. At first, Gunner would walk in and greet me, but soon enough, because the cancer was taking its toll, he'd walk in very slowly needing help to get up and down. On his final visit, he had to be carried in and out. But each time he came to see me, Gunner basically had the same thing to say, "No, I'm not ready to leave yet."

During his last visit, Cyndi told me she could see how difficult it was for Gunner to continue. He could no longer control his bladder or bowel movements. He had to be supported with the use of a towel when he moved around and he often shifted his position to alleviate pain or to improve his circulation.

Cyndi was devastated, but she summoned up her courage to ask him, "How will I know when it's time? I don't want to do it, but if you can somehow tell me that you're suffering too much I'd do whatever you ask of me, even if my heart rips apart."

I translated for Cyndi what Gunner said in response. "Tell her I'll let her know when the pain is too much; I'll make a noise, like a whimper. Tell her to wait until the last minute."

Cyndi was confused by his answer. She told me that Gunner had never, ever uttered a sound before, other than barking at someone who would come too close to her without her permission. Never in all the years they'd been together, nor during his year-long battle with cancer, did she ever hear him growl, whimper, moan or cry. She wasn't sure he could do it. Still, after so many conversations with me, she trusted me to translate Gunner's wishes, although not without some reservation.

Fortunately, her vet also went through a list of signs she needed to look for. We parted ways that day and I didn't see her for another three months. That's when she told me her story.

When it came to Gunner's last days, Cyndi would lie on blankets on the floor and sleep with him every night. Her room was upstairs, so she had to come downstairs to be with him. On Halloween morning, while she was sleeping, he nudged her arm, then laid his head in her lap. He also gave out a long, deep throaty sigh. He was telling her that he was tired of the struggle and ready to go. At that moment, she promised she'd take him to the vet that day. He perked up at the very mention of the idea.

But first, Cyndi wanted to take him for one last visit to a favorite place. They went to the mountains near a small picnic area known as Mill Creek. Since Gunner could no longer walk or chase the birds as he'd done in the past, Cyndi parked her truck and opened the tailgate. Gunner watched the birds with his ears perked up, tasted the air with his beautiful wet nose, and kept an eye on any hikers passing by. He was savoring the beauty of that day as if he knew he was going to be a part of it again tomorrow — in spirit.

It was a memorable day and they spent several hours enjoying the view, breathing the fresh air, and savoring the smells. Gunner was so excited he didn't even sleep. Instead, Cyndi could see the happiness in his eyes. They had a fun-filled day, even though her very heart was breaking.

On the way out of the park, since Gunner now seemed to feel better than he had that morning, Cyndi thought quietly to herself, maybe today *isn't* the day. Maybe we should just go home — and as soon as that thought crossed her mind, Gunner unexpectedly made a whimpering sound. He'd read her thoughts! It was as if he was saying to her, "But you promised!" Shaken to the core and momentarily unable to think straight, Cyndi remembered our conversation. It *was* time! So she drove straight to their veterinarian's office though it was the hardest thing she'd ever had to do.

Cyndi was still crying when she recalled the events of that day, and with a heavy heart and tears running down her face, she shared with me, "I wish he was here to keep me company — especially in the lonely times and when I want to hike! I sometimes feel his spirit with me and I wish he'd come to visit me in my dreams! I'd love to see his fabulous furry face agan! I cherish every moment I ever had with that hero."

Then she concluded, "But I did what I promised I'd do. I did it for Gunner, even though it was the most difficult thing I ever did in my life. If he wouldn't have made the whimpering sound when he did, and if I hadn't remembered what you'd told me, I probably would have waited longer. Thank you for translating that!"

Cyndi had truly listened!

CHAPTER 3

TALKING WITH YOUR ANIMALS

Over and over again, I see animals experiencing distress because they're unaware of your plans or the reasons why things are suddenly so different in their lives. To alleviate their worry, I can't stress enough how important it is to talk to your animals *out loud*. Talk to them just as if they understand every single word and detail you're telling them. This is especially necessary if you're making a sudden or major change in one of their routines, or if you're going away for a few hours, a few days or a few weeks.

If you leave the house without saying anything to them, they don't know where you're going or *if* you're coming back. They don't know who that stranger is who's coming in to feed them, or why Mom or Dad isn't there anymore. This kind of confusion causes anxiety for animals just as it would for a child.

If you make a change in one of their routines, tell them what you're going to be doing differently and why it's necessary. Say it out loud! Explain everything. Why? Because when we talk, we simultaneously visualize what we're saying and we also send out energy. This is a form of telepathy which pets are able to sense and understand. If you say something with love, they *will* get it, and they'll learn to trust you.

As you learn to use this telepathic skill with the animal kingdom, you'll find your pets don't need a lot of words to know what you mean. They'll need only the right pictures and your loving energy.

The next few case studies are about pets who went through major changes in their lives without first understanding why. But each pet was able to adapt after being given the opportunity to express his or her feelings, and being sent pictures which explained why the changes had to take place. Like the situations in these stories, almost every problem can be resolved if we'll only listen to and talk with our pets, especially before something major is about to happen.

Our animals are excellent listeners and masters of reception who are living with a species of very active talkers. We just need to learn to speak to them in both our language using words, and in their language using pictures.

TWEEGS

The daughter-in-law of a veterinary associate came to see me regarding her four-year-old cat named Tweegs. She'd taken him to the vet for some blood tests because he started defecating around the house instead of using his litter box, but all the test results came back negative, giving no clues as to what was causing the cat's unusual behavior. The vet suggested Sandra call me.

Tweegs had been "pooping" right in the middle of the bed in the guest bedroom. Sandra told me this behavior was new and he'd never had any problems using his litter box before. She was desperate to find the reason why. She'd just found out she was pregnant and shouldn't be "cleaning up" after her cat. That meant her husband would need to do the "dirty work," and it concerned her that he might want to get rid of the cat if his bad behavior continued.

In my consultation with Tweegs, he told me they'd just recently moved into a new house and he was quick to confess he was the one making the mess. This struck me as funny because he was the family's only cat, so there *was* no one else to make a mess!

He also noted that, from his vantage point in the guest bedroom, he could see some small animals prowling about in his new yard, especially at night, and this frightened him. Tweegs wasn't allowed to go outside, so he couldn't investigate these intruders for himself. It was fear and worry that made him lose control of his bowels, leaving a surprise in the middle of the bed for Mom to find.

Then Tweegs complained that the family wasn't spending as much time with him as usual, and many of the items which were familiar to him weren't even here in this new environment. "Where's my stuff?" he asked.

Sandra confirmed they were just moving into their new house. The living room sofas hadn't been delivered yet, so they hadn't been having regular family time. She also hadn't had time to check the backyard for any strange critters, and it was very possible there were opossums in the backyard which were scaring her cat.

After listening to Tweegs, Sandra and I decided on a plan. First, she would add another litter box close to the sliding door in the spare bedroom. I told Tweegs if he needed to go when he was in that room, he should use that box. I also thanked him for letting us know there were animals in the backyard and told him Dad was going to take care of the intruders for him. And Sandra told him the sofas were going to be delivered that very same day, so family time would be "on" again. I also asked Sandra to talk to him out loud more often so he'd understand the new routines. This seemed to please him enormously.

A couple of weeks later, I found out from the vet himself that Tweegs never had any other mishaps and was back to being his happy self again. All he needed was for his family to listen to him and talk with him, with a little help from me. Beyond that, making a few simple changes were all it took to alleviate his anxiety.

After the new baby arrived, Tweegs was his constant companion. Whenever the baby started to cry, Tweegs would run to find Mom and meow until she followed him to the nursery. His only complaint, a year later, was that the baby cried a lot so he was a bit overworked, but he was now very happy with his family in their new home.

———————

Misunderstandings are common between humans and animals. We expect our animals to "mind" when they're in the house but our animals don't always understand exactly what we mean. The following is an example of such a misunderstanding, and a funny one at that. It shows how good communication with a pet can be all that's needed to resolve a difficult dilemma.

APRIL

Susan, a past client, who works at the Irvine Animal Shelter, in Irvine, California, asked if I'd be available to see one of the shelter's former residents. A couple had adopted a female dog several months prior, but the dog was having frequent accidents at home. They'd tried trainers, behaviorists, and doctors, all to no avail. The wife was at the end of her rope, and if the dog couldn't be re-trained, it would surely mean a trip back to the shelter.

Olan, the husband, called to set up an appointment for me to meet with April, an 18-month-old American Eskimo mix. He said he'd tried everything he could to make April understand where he wanted her to relieve herself. Yet, she continued to urinate and defecate all over the living room, refusing to go outside to do her business, except on rare occasions. Olan was desperate to find a solution to the problem.

I don't make empty promises, so I told him I couldn't necessarily change April's behavior but I could try to find out why she was doing her business inside the house instead of outside, and then communicate to her exactly what it was the family would like her to do. After our talk, she might then respond to some understanding and additional training on their part and finally begin to use the outdoors.

Olan had fallen in love with April during the five months she'd lived with them and was receptive to try anything that might work. Because his wife couldn't be present for the consultation, he brought along a tape recorder.

When I first established contact with April, she informed me that neither of the names she'd been given resonated with who she felt she was. She didn't care for either of them. During her time at the shelter, she was called Chaka but her new family had given her the name April.

Next she wanted to tell me where she originally came from. The pictures she sent me of her previous life told me she was raised in a large field from the time she was a pup. Although grassy at one time, the field had become dry and mostly dirt. There was a small area of green at the side of her first home where there was a flowerbed or a garden of some kind. This was a forbidden area for April (Chaka) and she would be scolded severely if she attempted to walk on it. I concluded she'd learned early on that grass was something to keep away from.

Olan was intrigued. He told me April never wanted to "go" on grass. She didn't even want to walk on grass. He'd often have to carry her over a grassy area to a place where there was cement or dirt. This was encouraging; we were getting somewhere.

Satisfied with the initial information, Olan now wanted me to ask April why she was using the living room as her personal potty. The first thing I did was to remind April her humans would like her to use the outside soil to do her "business." Hearing this, April responded that she didn't like having to go through the garage to get to the doggy door. Olan said he was aware of her discomfort and he tried to leave the lights on so it wouldn't be too dark for her.

Suddenly, April showed me that if I was standing by their front door, I'd see a long corridor that ended at a sliding door. She'd very much like to use that exit to go out to the backyard. Olan told me that when he's home, he does try to keep it open for her as much as possible. I suggested he might put a doggy door in that location and thus make the whole idea of using the backyard more acceptable.

"Come to think of it," he recalled, "in the past few days, April *has* been using the sliding door to go outside more often. She uses a dry spot of grass in the backyard and also the dry flower bed on the side of the house."

I asked April to explain. The pictures she sent me were a little confusing at first. I was seeing the living room on my left and the dry flower patch on my right, almost as if I was looking at two movies on a split screen. A question from April formed in my mind. She said, "What's the difference?"

I immediately asked Olan if the living room had light brown carpet and if it was similar to the color of the ground outside. Olan exclaimed with surprise, "Yes, it *is* light brown!"

There it was! That was the answer! April didn't know the difference between the patch of dirt *outside* and the living room carpet *inside*. It was only a misunderstanding. Now, I just needed to explain the difference to her so she could clearly understand Olan's request.

After she and I sent a few more pictures back and forth, Olan was able to leave, confident that April could be "cured" of her misunderstanding after he made just a few changes around their home.

Olan promised to do several things: he decided to experiment with changing her name to something she'd like better; he'd install a doggy door directly into the backyard at the sliding door; he'd keep the living room off limits to April for a while, and he'd make a dirt patch outside just for April to use. To help her lose her fear of grass, Olan also planned to take her to the park to socialize, all the while, talking to her and explaining that where she lives now, grass is a good thing.

April's problem wasn't that she couldn't be house-trained, but that she was confused about the color of the surface she was supposed to use for potty purposes. Animals are not color blind as most people believe. They see colors differently from how we see them, but they can recognize *the same* color in two different places as April had been doing. After our visit, she seemed to understand clearly where she was to do her business. It was a welcome change for everyone!

Next time you think your pet is doing something to upset you, think again and try to put yourself in his or her place. Talk with your pet about the situation or consult a professional animal communicator as Olan did. It would've been a shame in this instance to return an otherwise beloved animal to the shelter because of a misunderstanding which could easily be cleared up with a heart-to-heart talk.

This next case study is about a newspaper reporter and her cat. Diana first called to ask me to do an interview for a major metropolitan newspaper. They were writing weekly columns about unusual professions and she thought that since I was a full-time animal communicator, a story about my work would make an interesting article.

Diana told me she can interview someone and immediately have an intuitive feeling about whether the person is lying or telling the truth. She can feel it when someone she meets has a superiority complex, is delusional, or is "for real." She must have concluded that I was "for real" because, after our two hour interview, she decided to ask me, almost on second thought, if I'd go to her home and do a consultation with her cat, Kahuna. We made an appointment for the very next day.

KAHUNA

Kahuna is a male orange tabby cat about ten years old who lives with his parents in their family condo. Diana told me he was a little shy around people and was hiding under the bed. Though I don't have to be in the same room with an animal when the two of us are communicating, I asked her to bring him into the living room with us anyway.

When he arrived, he looked at me with curious and wary eyes, so to put him at ease quickly, I closed my eyes and introduced myself to him quietly in my mind. He then moved closer to me and sat down on the arm of the sofa watching me intently. Diana thought this was unusual, but didn't comment on it.

As you'd expect from a reporter, Diana had a list of prepared questions. She took special care to express them in a neutral manner, without emphasis, while sitting on the floor using minimal body language. I sat on the sofa with my eyes closed while receiving the corresponding pictures from Kahuna in response to Diana's questions. The session, which I recorded, went something like this:

Q: Does Kahuna have any friends?

A: I do, but I can only see them through the living room window.

Q: Can you tell me about the friends you had at the other house? (They'd recently moved.)

A: I had two feline friends. Both were female. One was my girlfriend and the other was just a friend.

Q: Can you describe them?

A: One has many colors; the other was part white, part black.

Q: What do you mean by part white, part black?

A: She was mostly white under her chin, but she also had patches of black.

Q: Do you like the music I leave on for you?

A: Yes, I like classical music, especially the piano.

Q: Why do you sometimes miss the litter box when you urinate?

A: There's always a reason, but I'll give you one example. I remember one time when Dad had been gone for a long time. I was very upset because I didn't know what was happening. No one explained anything to me. I was missing him so much. I was trying to show you I was upset.

Q: Do you want to spend more time with my husband?

A: Kahuna then sent me a picture of Diana's husband lying on the floor and another of him on the bed with Kahuna lying in the crook of his arm. He told me the two of them have a special relationship.

This session gave Diana much to think about. She then shared details with me about Kahuna's answers to her questions. They'd moved from another condo very recently and Kahuna was not allowed to be outside now, so he could only see his friends through the window.

At their other home, Kahuna had two female cat friends. One was a Calico (a mixture of patches of red, white and black fur) and the other, Diana's second cat, who'd recently passed away, looked just like the second cat Kahuna had described — white underneath the chin, with black and white patches here and there.

When it came to the music he liked, Diana commented that her brother used to play clarinet so she often played a CD with some clarinet solos. Kahuna's favorite, however, was *Claire de Lune* by Debussy, which was a piano solo.

Kahuna had told us he was upset about her husband not being there on one particular occasion. That final piece of information was so accurate that Diana was visibly shaken and no longer guarded when talking with me.

Her husband had actually been gone from home for nine months for a sabbatical and had only recently returned. She explained that he's an insomniac and often lies on the floor with Kahuna. Whenever he lies awake in bed, Kahuna cuddles in the crook of his arm. These vivid pictures, sent to me by Kahuna, gave Diana an even greater sense of confidence about what it is that I do.

I found it amusing when Diana later shared with me that her sister had told her to take down all of the pictures from the walls and be sure not to leave any books, notes, or personal items in plain sight which could possibly give me any clues.

Diana subsequently wrote an article for the leading newspaper in Orange County, which has a very large circulation in Southern California. In her final comments in this article, she stated:

"Critics tell me that I somehow gave Diedrich the answers to my cat questions. Or, she made several lucky guesses. Or, that somehow, she looked up information about my husband and me in the 24 hours between my initial interview

and meeting at my house. But she didn't know my husband's name or even that we have different last names. Truth is, she knew only that I had a cat and a skeptical spouse.

"Throughout the hour, Diedrich answered every question about Kahuna correctly. More importantly, she somehow determined that my husband had a strong bond with Kahuna, even though I often referred to the cat as mine. But Kahuna is his cat.

"My husband's response? He didn't say much – to me. But later that night, as he lay sprawled on the floor in front of the TV, arm crooked with Kahuna at his side, I heard him ask, 'Did it really upset you when I was gone for so long?'"

Even today, clients still call me from among those who've read this article. Diana's vocation is to listen carefully as she gathers information for the articles she writes. Now, with my help, she listened intently as she gathered information from her beloved cat. She understood how difficult it must have been for Kahuna to lose his friend (her other cat who'd passed away) and to endure the loss of another friend because of the move. What she'd underestimated, however, was the impact her husband's absence had had on Kahuna. Once she took the time to talk with her pet with my help, she now realized that even these seemingly small bits of information could have a positive and healing effect on the relationship they shared.

———

Elephants are not the only ones who have long memories. Dogs do, too. Just ask anyone who's ever rescued a dog from an abusive environment. Ah! But cats have an even longer memory, as you'll see in this next case study.

SOPHIE

A 15-year-old female tortoiseshell cat came to see me with her mom, Katherine. Mom wanted to know about Sophie's health and she also wanted to get answers to some other general questions.

Sophie told me she didn't appreciate the sudden change in plans that morning. She'd been contemplating spending the morning lounging in the sunlight, spread out on the ground. "With such a beautiful morning, it's the best thing to do," she said. Mom's jaw dropped. She told me that Sophie was already out on the patio that morning ready to lie down in the sun when she swiped her up and put her into her traveling cage.

Katherine then explained to me that Sophie always spent time in her bedroom up on the bed when they were at their former house, but in this house, Sophie wouldn't ever get up on the bed. Katherine wanted to know why.

Sophie said not getting up on the bed wasn't anything new. She was a little confused by Mom's question. So I asked Katherine how long ago she'd moved and was surprised when she said it'd been eight years! No wonder Sophie was confused.

Sophie continued, "At the time we moved into the new house, something changed and I wasn't allowed to go into the bedroom." In the mental picture she sent me, I saw a mattress and some white sheets flowing as if someone was making the bed. She said she thought she was forbidden to enter that room and simply believed she wasn't welcome on the bed any more in the new house!

I turned to Katherine and asked her if she remembered anything that happened which would account for Sophie's explanation. Mom knew *exactly* what she was talking about. Katherine then explained, "When I first moved into this house, we had another cat who was very rambunctious and untidy. Since my new bedroom was all white, I decided not to allow the cats to use that room at all. If I'd allowed only Sophie to come in, the other cat would've been very upset, so the bedroom was now off limits to both of them."

Mom couldn't believe Sophie's accurate description of events and told me, "I was just busted by my cat!"

"Yep," I said, "she told on you!"

Since the second cat hadn't been with them for quite a number of years, Katherine couldn't understand why Sophie still wouldn't get up on the bed. I explained to her that learned behaviors can't easily be changed unless both the pet and the owner understand the reason behind them. And, especially with cats, once a request from humans is learned, it's hard for them to change their minds. We have a "now you do it, now you don't" mentality which they do not. So it's important to talk to them and explain the reasons for any changes.

In a nutshell, you have to listen to your pets and talk to them using both words and pictures. You might be surprised by the answers your pet gives, but know that there is always an answer. Sometimes a clear explanation, or a small change, is all it takes to restore peace and harmony.

If there's some misunderstanding between you and your animal, find a translator. An animal communicator is not a miracle worker, but he or she can help you understand your pet's needs and wishes and help you learn to communicate with them.

CHAPTER 4

PHYSICAL HEALING –
UNCOMMON PETS

One day when I was in my 20s, I had a unique dream which affected me greatly at the time, and has remained vivid to me throughout the years. It seemed so real I almost felt as if I'd actually lived it. In the dream, I was a male doctor in a far away eastern country, high up in the mountains. Though I was an unusual kind of doctor, I didn't specialize in anything in particular. People sought me out for help when they had severe problems which other doctors couldn't diagnose. I could see only one or two patients each day. I was old and it was painful work, and my body couldn't take it much longer.

In the dream, I remember very clearly standing in a dimly lit room. I asked my first patient of the day to stand against a wall painted a scarlet red, the color of high energy. He asked me if he needed to disrobe and I replied, "No, you can remain fully dressed."

I then said, "Please describe for me what you feel and where the pain is located in your body."

He pointed to his stomach, but before he could even begin to describe it, I felt pain in my own body like the stab of a sharp knife at the same spot where he was pointing. He said, "I've had this pain for years, but just recently it's become unbearable."

As he spoke, I was doubling over in pain and wondered how much more agony this poor man could endure. Why had he waited so long to seek medical advice? Using sheer willpower, I somehow made the pain I was experiencing stop at once. I knew what the pain was from and gave the man some herbs and instructions on their preparation and dosage. He left me with a customary blessing and several polite head bows.

The next client in my dream was a woman, and I instructed her to stand in front of the scarlet wall as well. This time, because she was so timid, I didn't ask her to describe anything. Instead, I slowly allowed the pain to come into my own body. The pain was centered around her female organs, but I remember experiencing it as if it were my own, even though in the dream I was a man. I knew how difficult it had been for this woman to come to see me regarding something so personal and, in the minds of most women of her culture, so taboo.

Wanting to help her feel better, I immediately combined the necessary herbs and asked her to drink the mixture before I excused her. She did, and almost instantaneously her anguished expression disappeared. I'd been able to help her heal because I felt what she felt, because I knew where the pain was located and because I was very knowledgeable about the healing properties of herbs.

She kissed the hem of my robe and walked away bowing her head without speaking a word. There was no doubt in the dream that I was doing the work I was called to do, and I realized that so many people depended on me.

I woke up feeling refreshed and alert. I knew then, in real life, that I was gifted with empathic feelings and I'd have them with me forever and ever. It was as if my past had been revealed . . . and I'd seen a foreshadow of my future. Empathic healing, the ability to actually *feel or experience* another's pain in one's own body, was the way of the past, and in my mind, will become the healing way of the future.

Understanding and interpreting the complaint of the patient is one of the most difficult tasks for any medical practitioner. For example, when describing pain, one patient may call it dull while another may call the same pain sharp. Often that's because one person simply has a higher pain threshold than the other.

An empath, however, may be able to shed light more clearly on what the patient is trying to describe because the empath can actually feel the intensity of the pain. Medicine is an art form, not an exact science, and hopefully it will benefit soon from a partnership between empath and physician.

But my Life Assignment is to use my empathic gift to help animals heal. It's my heartfelt desire to bring comfort to them that keeps me in a perpetual state of learning and leads me into new experiences. Because I feel guided to share the specifics of what I've learned over many years of studying and practicing my craft, you'll be able to learn more about the art of healing in my next book which will give practical applications and how-to advice in easy to follow steps.

I'm always open to learning new things, so when there've been several occasions to work with animals not typically found as household pets, I've eagerly accepted those opportunities — even though I had no idea what I'd find! When I asked the pets in the following case studies about their pain, *this* was a whole new experience, yet not unlike what I'd seen in my dream. These communications often resulted in healing, but in one instance there was an unexpected outcome, one which even the pet knew was for the best.

ANNIE

At the prompting of my chiropractor colleague, I worked with my first patient at the clinic with whom I would have a long follow-up relationship. Her name was Annie and she was a light tan two-year-old wallaby (a small, kangaroo-like animal).

Annie had lost her appetite and she'd somehow become paralyzed from the waist down. She had no control of her bowel movements and was unable to stand to urinate because she had no muscle tone in her hind legs. Her legs bowed inwards from her knees down and she couldn't use her tail for stabilizing and balance, which is very important for a wallaby.

Dorothy, Annie's human, has her own business and holds one of the few wild animal licenses in the state of California. Established in 1990, her company, E & E Animals, performs educational shows to teach children about environmental awareness and wildlife conservation through a unique, up-close approach. She customizes each presentation and travels to schools throughout Southern California and the United States.

E & E Animals works with a unique array of creatures, among them, a hedgehog, a tortoise, a caracal (a large wild cat), a kookaburra (a small Australian bird), a cockatoo, a monkey, a kinkajou (a raccoon-like creature from South America), and Annie, the wallaby, among many other rare animals.

Dorothy said one day when she returned home from running some errands, she was horrified to find Annie lying paralyzed on her side in the backyard. It looked as if Annie had jumped off a balcony approximately 12 feet above the ground.

Dorothy rushed the injured wallaby to her veterinarian who took X-rays which revealed that some of Annie's vertebrae were displaced. She was immediately given pain medication as well as extra nutritional supplements and a special diet. Annie was also referred to a chiropractor who sedated her for an adjustment. Four months later, though, she was still unable to function normally, and her prognosis seemed very bleak.

It wasn't until this time that Annie was first brought to see my chiropractor friend, who then asked me to help her with this precious animal. She felt it was important for me to talk with her because even though Annie *had* been seeing another chiropractor for a while, she hadn't shown adequate signs of improvement. The chiropractor hoped I might be able to pinpoint the problem by making an empathic connection with her.

Dorothy came into the clinic holding Annie in her arms, a towel trailing along behind. Her pants and shirt had already been soiled by Annie's incontinence brought on by fear from the long road trip. We laid out several towels, but instead of lying down, Annie tried to crawl her way across the floor. She even began to growl and give a low bark, similar to a dog.

I introduced myself to Annie and waited for a response. Suddenly, I found I was apprehensive because this was my first wild animal reading and I didn't know what to expect. Would she be willing to talk? And if so, how would she communicate? What kind of pictures would I be getting from this wild creature?

I shouldn't have worried, though. Her pictures came through as clear as ever. In fact, they came in better than those of some domesticated animals.

Annie, who's allowed to spend time in the house and is only confined in the evenings, said she'd always been very careful when hopping around. She'd take little hops so she could manage her body in between the furniture and not knock anything out of place. She prided herself on being considerate and careful. She also mentioned how bad she felt that she couldn't use her hind legs now. "It's a disgrace," she said. After confirming with Dorothy what Annie had told me, it was time to discover exactly what happened on the day of her injury.

"What happened on the balcony?" I asked. "Why did you jump?"

Annie was offended by my assumption! "I did *not* jump," Annie said irritably. She went on to describe the balcony and how full of clutter it was, with piles of old newspapers and magazines, and things balancing on top of boxes stacked one on top of the other.

Annie said she hopped up on top of some boxes placed next to the railing, and when the pile started to wobble, she lost her balance and fell over the railing to the ground below.

Dorothy looked astonished, unable to believe that her wallaby was providing such an accurate description of her balcony. Without missing a beat, she started to ask Annie a multitude of questions beginning with, "Does it hurt very much?"

"Yes," Annie said without hesitation. "It hurts a lot, everywhere. I feel so useless. This isn't right. I'm supposed to be hopping around but I can't. It hurts every day, all the time."

"Can you tell us exactly where it hurts?" Dorothy continued.

"My neck and my lower back hurt and I have hardly any feelings below my hips, and my lower legs are beginning to turn inwards."

"Why aren't you eating?" continued Dorothy. "Would you like a change of diet?"

"My tummy aches and sometimes I'm nauseated."

Dorothy thought about what might cause the nausea and realized she'd been giving Annie enzymes which were probably upsetting the wallaby's delicate digestion. Dorothy then went through a list of items so that Annie could tell her which foods she preferred and, through me, Annie responded to each one.

When she was asked to describe her favorite food item, Annie responded with a very specific picture. I began with the disclaimer, "I don't know about plants and their names, but her picture is clear and it looks to me like a kind of berry or seed. It's red and at the end of a long stem. The plant's on the ground, and the branches are going in all different directions. The fruit is only at the very end of the stem. Annie keeps telling me it's delicious."

Dorothy knew exactly which plant Annie was talking about. This plant was growing on the back of her property and Annie used to go there daily and spend a great deal of time eating the delicacies. Dorothy said, "YES! I always knew that was her favorite."

Then I told Annie, "We need to give you some medicine to help you sleep while we do an adjustment on your back."

Annie replied, "No, not again!"

I laughed, but was puzzled, so I asked Mom, "Has Annie been sedated before?"

"Oh yes. Three times already," she replied.

I then explained to Annie, "Sedation is necessary to give your body an adjustment without hurting you. You'll feel a lot better when you wake up."

Half-reluctant and half-hopeful, she agreed to the procedure. She remained calm throughout the entire time because of the sedative. The adjustment went very well and Annie went home to sleep for the rest of the day.

When I saw her a week later, she was eating again and, for the first time in four months, she was able to stand on her hind legs. During a follow-up consultation, I spoke to Annie about building up her muscle tone by remaining standing for longer periods of time. A month later, she was already taking little hops, eating regularly, and looking forward to a healthier future.

One year later, I spoke with Dorothy again. Annie never regained full control of her hind legs but she now has about 70 percent control of both her legs and her tail. She's once again able to control her urination and bowel movements, and best of all, she's able to enjoy life. She's retired from working and loves her daily leg massage.

In Annie's case, the current adjustments now being done by my chiropractor colleague didn't bring about the complete results we wanted because we only saw Annie months after her original injury. My colleague says it's imperative to start working on an animal as soon as the injury occurs to achieve better results. But by the time we saw her, Annie had already lost muscle tone in both hind legs, which couldn't be reversed.

When my colleague works hands-on with a patient, she's unconsciously using her hands to "see" the injury. By touching the areas of pain, she's making a picture in her mind of how the spine looks, compared with how it should look in its perfect form. She then performs the adjustment, at the same time picturing a perfect outcome. She sends the healing through her hands almost automatically while doing her work.

I do my healing work strictly in my mind without touching the animal. I allow my body to sense and "feel" the pain, and then I can feel the healing when it begins to take place. Through teamwork and practice, we've found that when the two of us work together, we can provide the animals with a much more complete healing experience.

When I first met my next patient, I was still unaware of exactly *how* I was able to translate an animal's medical problems, and I remained apprehensive about my abilities. But there were many opportunities to refine my skills. As I continued my association with the chiropractor, I found myself in the middle of other cases which involved "not so common pets" whose "parents" needed some help.

CHLOE

I was intrigued one day when my chiropractor colleague called me into her office to see one of her clients. Her request was not unusual but the tone of her voice was, so I knew I was about to find something interesting.

As standard practice, she doesn't discuss specifics with me in private regarding a patient I'm about to see. She prefers to do it in front of her clients so they'll know I'm not being prepped with any answers beforehand. It also helps me not to form any preconceptions which might interfere with my listening to what the animal has to say.

When I entered her office, I was startled to see a white pigmy goat!

Chloe was lying down and someone had put both a towel and a diaper on the floor. She wasn't happy to see us and tried several times to move out of the way, but she couldn't get up on her own. She kept moving her body and baying, her eyes bulging out in fear. At one point, she had a bowel movement followed by quite a bit of urine.

I sat down cross-legged on the floor without touching her and mentally asked her to calm down. Sitting beside Chloe on the floor next to us was her "mom," Stacie. She told me, "Chloe's a Nigerian dwarf, almost two years old. She's more than a goat, she's my baby."

As I was explaining to Stacie how I communicate with a pet, Chloe was posturing her back and crying out in pain. So I asked her, "What are you feeling?"

She told me she was paralyzed and couldn't walk. Then she said, "I'm not sure I can trust her," referring to the chiropractor.

"Why not?" I asked.

"Because where she's sitting I can't see her. Tell her to move!" My chiropractor friend had been sitting immediately behind Chloe, near her tail.

I asked my colleague to please move next to me so that she'd be within Chloe's field of vision. This seemed to make Chloe very happy because she turned her head and looked the doctor directly in the eye, acknowledging that her demands were being met. Chloe relaxed at that moment as Mom stroked her head.

I said to Stacie, "She's sending me pictures of what happened. She was doing so well in the morning, but the next image shows her front legs bent backwards low in her body. I don't have a transition picture, just a well picture and then the injured picture. Now I can see another animal; she's showing me hooves. Do you have another bigger animal with hooves?"

"I have bigger goats," Stacie said nonchalantly, trying to say only what was absolutely necessary.

"That might have something to do with it." I continued. "I'm seeing a larger, hoofed animal engaging with her. He's very temperamental and was very angry with her. I'm surprised nothing was broken because there was a heated argument and an intense fight."

After we had a better idea of what had taken place, the chiropractor wanted to know how Chloe felt at the moment.

"I feel a little better," Chloe said. "But the pain is everywhere. I have different levels of pain. I don't understand why I don't have the strength I need to spring up on all four of my legs. I have to make a conscious effort to find them. I know they're there, but I can't feel them the same as I did before."

Through me, the doctor told Chloe, "I need to work on you a little more and do some traction on your neck to see if that will alleviate the pain in your legs. It won't hurt because you'll be sedated."

Chloe acknowledged what I was telling her and told me, "I want Mom here with me and I'll try to be on my best behavior." But then, Chloe insisted I give Mom another picture which she kept sending me.

I took a deep breath and said to Stacie, "Sorry, Stacie, but Chloe is adamant that I tell you not to grab her horns anymore. She doesn't like it and would rather you just pet her on top of her head, but not touch her horns because they're sensitive."

I was expecting a quizzical look on Stacie's face. Instead, she said with a chuckle, "I know she doesn't like me to touch her horns, but I'm only trying to protect myself. I have a bump on my forehead because she butted me with those horns."

I was relieved that Stacie didn't think I was crazy, so I told her that later I'd ask Chloe to be gentler with her, but for now I said, "Let's keep working on the problem since I have her attention."

Before sedating her, the chiropractor wanted to know exactly where Chloe's back was hurting. She said, "I'll touch Chloe and you ask her if that's the spot where it hurts the most. When I put my hand back here and press, does she have pain?"

Chloe responded, "I feel something different, but it's not in my spine. It's more toward my hips in this area right here. (To show the doctor, I pointed to the place Chloe was talking about.) It's almost like this strange pain is traveling."

When the chiropractor touched the place where the pain was the worst, Chloe started to shake violently. "Ah, so she's that sensitive when she's touched?" my colleague asked. Then she continued, "Something is pinching, but for me to release it, I'll have to touch her spine and work in that area with my hands. Will she let me pull her tail? That will help."

Chloe wasn't very pleased with the idea of tail-pulling. As she'd said before, she had a trust problem with someone doing anything from behind her. The chiropractor knew that Chloe would need an adjustment under tranquilizer. She said to Stacie, "I need to stretch the legs, move the pelvis and spine, and pull the tail. The traction will create space between the discs to allow time for the swelling to go down. In other words, she has the human equivalent of sciatica. Can you bring her back tomorrow?"

Stacie said, "I'll do anything for my Chloe girl."

But Chloe still had more to say to Mom. "Please don't get mad at the other animal. He really didn't mean it." Chloe's picture showed me the goat who'd kicked her. She didn't really want to give me any more information about the culprit. No matter how many different ways I tried, she wasn't about to tell.

A week after the adjustment under sedation, Chloe had a follow-up visit with the chiropractor and me. Imagine our surprise when we saw a happy goat standing on her own four legs!

Mom told us, "I tried to entice her to stand ever since her second adjustment. After a few days, I lifted her by placing a towel under her belly. Not only did she not move, it was obvious she didn't like it. Yesterday in frustration I removed the towel, and Chloe, defiantly as ever, took her first few steps. Today she walked into the office by herself, when only last week she had to be carried in."

I didn't waste any time telling Chloe, "We're all very proud of you."

Chloe, who has a sense of humor, said, "Well, I didn't know what I was supposed to do with that towel around my belly, so when Mom took it away, I just got mad and then walked off."

Stacie chuckled but then became serious. It was obvious she wanted to ask me something important but didn't know quite how to begin. After some thought, she said, "I want to know if *anything* else has happened to her lately?"

"What do you mean?" I asked. "Is it something else about her injuries?"

"Not necessarily," Stacie replied. "Just anything I should know."

I closed my eyes and asked Chloe if there was anything else she needed to tell me. She immediately sent me a picture. I said to Stacie, "I don't think this is related to her injury. She's talking about someone else, someone like her but smaller. I think she's really missing whoever it is. There's something I'll call a void here. Something or someone is missing and she feels really sad."

Moments later Stacie slowly said, "You'll have to pardon me for being so vague, but I was still a little skeptical. For you to sense anything like this is amazing. The truth is that Chloe was pregnant but she miscarried last Sunday so this really makes sense."

I was sorry for Chloe. She seemed to really miss the baby so I tried to explain to her that she could get pregnant again and have other babies. This seemed to satisfy her.

Stacie, who was now feeling more relaxed and trusting, explained, "Chloe got out two months ago and went to see Billy, her buck. Billy's a little aggressive when he mates and might have accidentally injured her in his excitement. Later, while playing with the other goat, she probably hurt herself again which compounded the injury and that's when she became paralyzed. I'm delighted that Chloe has such good motherly instincts and wants to have babies. Will you tell her I promise we'll make sure Billy is careful with her?"

The chiropractor next queried, "Can you ask her how her bowel movements are and about her ability to urinate now?"

Chloe responded that she had feeling whenever she was going. Her legs were no longer numb, though it was somewhat distressing to her that they trembled at times. The chiropractor then asked, "Would you ask Chloe to move her tail?"

I did, but my eyes were closed, so I didn't know what was going on until I heard the doctor say, "Thank you, Chloe, that was very good."

How much more responsive to our requests could this little goat be? If I'm ever tempted to take animal communication for granted, all I'll have to do is remember little Miss Chloe. And Chloe will no doubt remember us.

When we saw her again two weeks later, she was a happy little goat and still very special to her mom, Stacie. Chloe was now ready to take on the world again . . . including Billy!

———————

If a wallaby and a goat weren't enough to convince me that "unusual pets" have the same feelings as dogs and cats, this next little guy certainly could.

PEANUT

My colleague called me one Saturday and asked me to speak with Mary, who'd brought in her pot-bellied pig. She wanted me to prepare the pig to have an adjustment under sedation.

Mary grabbed the phone and in tears blurted out that Peanut, her pet pig, had injured himself by jumping off the bed and couldn't walk. When I tuned in to him, he told me, "I was learning something new." He then added very proudly, "I'm one of the boys now, but I still need to learn a few things."

When I told this to Mom, she explained, "I have dogs in the house and we were teaching Peanut to climb the stairs just like they do."

I then explained to Peanut that the doctor needed to adjust his back and pull gently on his tail. I assured him she'd give him medication to make him sleep so that he'd be relaxed and not feel any pain.

Peanut said, "I love my family, especially my daddy. If you have to give me something so I can sleep through the adjustment, then I want my daddy with me."

When I told this to Mom, she began to cry again and said, "Peanut was in bed with his dad and the dogs this morning when they were startled by a noise outside. The dogs jumped off the bed barking and Peanut tried to follow them. But when he jumped, he landed on his head and compressed his neck bones."

Peanut then added, "I'm in a lot of pain but it's all my fault. I don't want Mom blaming anybody else."

I'd felt that Peanut's request for his dad's presence was a bit unusual, but it all made sense when I found out later that Mom blamed Dad for not realizing Peanut was about to jump.

I told Mary I'd send remote healing to Peanut and would include him on my nightly healing list. To send healing remotely is just as important as doing it in person. What I do is visualize the Healing Light being directed to specific beings (persons or animals) as I say their names in my mind and heart.

I visualize this glowing light entering their bodies and filling them up from the inside, as you'd fill a glass of water. The light then overflows like a fountain, so it continuously surrounds the body and permeates it with its warmth and splendor.

Since the main purpose of this consultation had been to prepare Peanut for the adjustment under sedation, we then ended our conversation.

After the adjustment the next day, Peanut went home "fixed." In fact, he was feeling so good that, when the occasion arose, he decided to jump . . . again!

Two weeks later he was back in the clinic and this time I met him in person. He was lying on a towel in the waiting room resting on his side, his nose up in the air sniffing all the different aromas. I approached slowly with the intention of touching him lightly while saying hello, but as soon as I knelt beside him he started screaming. I spoke to him in a low voice but didn't touch him. He looked intently into my eyes while he pleaded, "Please don't touch me, it hurts too much!"

The chiropractor and I had to see another patient first. When we were finished, we cleared our agendas for the rest of the morning so that we could focus completely on Peanut. In the meantime, we could hear Peanut's squeals throughout the clinic. Hearing this wailing sound was very difficult for me because it sounded just like a baby's cry.

When his turn came, he cried and complained the whole time. When the chiropractor reached out to touch him, I asked her to wait. It took a few minutes to calm Peanut down. Then I sat in front of him and told him, "It's time to talk to us."

Immediately, he stopped crying and looked into my eyes. I closed mine. There was a poignant silence as we all waited for him to start talking. Finally he said to me, "I can't stand it any longer. I need help to be released from this excruciating pain. Please help me. This time it's more than I can handle. It hurts so much that even when you walk next to me, the vibration from the floor makes it unbearable. I want Mom and Dad to know how much I enjoyed being with them and how much I enjoyed being one of the boys, of course the smartest one. I've been a good pig but I've really messed up this time."

When the chiropractor asked him, "How can I help you?" his reply touched all of us very deeply. Peanut said, "You can't help me any more. The slightest touch of your finger is the worst pain I've ever felt. My neck is broken, and it's time for me to die."

Mary was distraught, but even in her agony she managed to ask Peanut to come back to them as another little pig in a new body. Her daughter then asked Peanut to forgive the family for trying to teach him to use the stairs. I, too, was having trouble with my own emotions, and we all shed lots of tears as we realized that euthanasia was the kindest thing we could do for Peanut.

This time there was to be no healing miracle. I opened my eyes to see Peanut relaxed with his eyes closed. He'd remained quiet and at peace for the 20 minutes of our communication, but within ten seconds of its end, he opened his eyes and started to cry again.

Mom knew in her heart that she had no time to spare because her little pig was in such distress, so she took him directly to their veterinary clinic. Peanut cried and complained all the way there but once in the doctor's office, he accepted the final injection with the same dignity as any of man's best friends. His suffering was finally over.

Did Peanut know he was being put down? Of course he did. Not only had he asked for it, he was relieved that his suffering would be over.

This brings us to a very important moral question. Is the pig, an animal we raise to consume as food, able to think, feel, and love?

Wild or unusual pets always inspire in me a sense of wonder and humility. How is it that a wild beast can communicate with a person when all they know in the wild is their kin? Do they, could they, have the same range of feelings and emotions as we and domesticated animals do? Do they know their purpose in life? Do they know that we've been given dominion over them?

I don't have the answers to these questions but I do know that animals of any species, who share our homes and have the capacity to feel pain, deserve consideration equal to their domestic counterparts.

My experiences prove, beyond a doubt, the existence of intelligence in many animals, as well as their emotional sensitivity, and their capacity for happiness and suffering alike. This has nothing to do with "sentimentality" toward animals, nor am I anthropomorphizing the human-animal relationship. It's based solely on what they're telling me and on the feelings they're transmitting to my body.

I began at a young age simply communicating with pets about everyday things, never dreaming there'd be something even more significant I'd be able to do beyond dealing with typical behavior problems. Every day, I'm amazed that I can communicate with other species, even about their health issues, and that their love for their humans is just as strong as that of a dog or a cat.

Many people seem to have lost respect for various animals as beings with needs and wants, with a place and a purpose. However, undeterred by what others think, happily there are those who always want to know more, do more, and help more.

My colleague and I could be stereo-typed as "two crazy ladies from Southern California," but I'm convinced there must be thousands of people out there who'd be willing to try to communicate with their beloved animals, of any species, in order to help them, if they only knew how.

CHAPTER 5

PHYSICAL HEALING –
MAN'S BEST FRIEND

L et me first explain what this chapter is *not* about. The physical healings in these case studies are not random miracles where the animal gets up and walks away after being "cured" of an illness or a physical disability in some unique way.

The healings for each of these pets required both the knowledge of a veterinarian and the able hands of a chiropractor. Even more important, they required a direct conversation between an animal communicator and the animal who needed healing.

In these case studies, the animals themselves identified the problems and sometimes even suggested what needed to be done to correct them. Without those conversations in which the pets gave us such vital information, healing most likely wouldn't have taken place.

You'll now meet three different dogs: Xanto, a German Shepherd, with both a medical and a behavioral problem; Vickie, a Dachshund, who was paralyzed for over four months until she was able to tell us how to help her; and Buddha, a Golden Retriever, who was paralyzed from the waist down after an unusual accident in his own backyard.

As you read about each case, you might want to ponder these three questions:

1) What would you have done if you were the responsible person in these experiences?

2) How would you have felt if your vet said your only choices were surgery, with no promise of a successful outcome, or euthanasia?

3) If you still thought there might be a spark of hope, even after all the options you tried had failed, and all your veterinary advisors recommended that you euthanize your pet, would you have thought about communicating directly with your pet in an effort to save him or her?

There was a happy ending to each of the following stories, but only after each pet was given a way to share important information with his or her caregivers.

XANTO

I was already at the chiropractic clinic when I was called in to see an emergency patient. A beautiful sable German Shepherd with a black face and large eyes was waiting for me in the front room with his mom, Glenda, beside him.

Glenda had acquired her dream dog directly from a breeder in Germany. Xanto, already named by the breeder, was eighteen months old by the time Glenda went to pick him up at the airport. He was trained to respond to commands in German from puppy-hood, so to avoid confusing him, Glenda continued his training using German instead of English. He did very well and was eager to please everyone. With his low-key personality, he became part of the family and was almost like a child to Glenda and her husband.

The day I first met them at the clinic several years later, Glenda's concerns were obvious as she related what had just happened. She told me, "Xanto is a three-year-old German Shepherd who's been trained in a special obedience class much like a police dog. In German, it's called *schund*. He competes against other people and their dogs in three skills — protection, tracking, and obedience — and must score at least 70 percent in each phase to pass the test. He can earn a maximum of 100 points in each category and I always encourage him to ace the tests and score all 300 points."

"When he's training for protection," Glenda continued, "he's supposed to jump up, grab the *very* well padded arm of the instructor and not let go until signaled to do so. Of course, all the while, the 'bad guy' desperately struggles to get the dog off by swinging his arm up and down, to and fro. Xanto has won many competitions but something's happened to him recently. He's been crying, he's limping when he walks, and his tail, which is usually up and wagging, has gone limp. I brought him in to the chiropractor's office for a series of adjustments on his back, and after a trial walk he seemed well enough to make it through to his next appointment.

"After the visit, he was just fine when we went out to the car," Glenda added, "but as I was positioning the ramp for him to walk up, he jumped into the truck by himself instead. As soon as he got into the truck, he started to whine and his tail went limp, so I brought him back in."

I tuned in to Xanto right away. First he told me he was frightened because of what had happened, and he was concerned because Mom was so upset with him. I sent him pictures to tell him she loved him and wanted to find out where it hurt.

He said, "Something's pinched in my spine. There's a very sharp pain and it hurts so much that I can't lift my tail. But that's not all. I also have a problem with the toes of my right hind foot. It's really bothering me and I can't seem to step on it without pain. I hurt it on a wooden ramp that has a groove in it."

When I relayed this to Glenda she looked puzzled. She told me the ramp that goes into the truck is carpeted. When I asked Xanto about it he said, "No, it's the ramp I practice on. It has a gap between the planks, and my toes got stuck in it."

Glenda's jaw dropped in disbelief. "Yes, I do have a wooden ramp at home that Xanto practices on, and, yes, it does have a gap between the two wooden planks."

As soon as I translated that, I had the urge to open my eyes and reach out to feel his foot so I could pinpoint the exact location. I usually don't do that, but his comment was so specific that I wanted to verify for myself what he said. He was already lying down on his side next to his mom so I could easily reach his hind leg without moving him. As I did so, he allowed me to touch him without even the slightest bit of apprehension, but when my hand reached for the pad of his foot, he pulled away fast and sat up looking at me.

"There," I said to the chiropractor, "that's where it hurts the most."

Xanto first needed to be examined by his vet before being adjusted again and the X-rays of his foot taken during that visit revealed there was a sliver of bone in his right rear paw which was out of place.

The next day, the chiropractor sedated Xanto and after adjusting the last bone in his spine, she also adjusted the bones in his foot. X-rays then showed that the sliver of bone was back in its proper place. Eventually it would correctly reattach itself and heal completely.

I wasn't there when Xanto returned for a follow-up visit, but my colleague told me his wagging tail was held high. He was in good spirits and walked without a limp. After that adjustment, the chiropractor discharged him.

As they were leaving the clinic and Glenda was readying the ramp, Xanto just couldn't wait. Again, he tried to jump into the back of the truck on his own, but he was too close to the tailgate. This time, he fell back on his spine, twisting as he did so. Glenda rushed him back inside the clinic, where it was evident that his tail was definitely limp again, and he was now having some trouble with his hind leg. The chiropractor did a light adjustment but wanted to wait for the swelling to go down before doing more. She also wanted to consult with me again, so she asked Glenda to come back in two days.

I couldn't believe Xanto was at the clinic again and was having so much difficulty. After they brought me up to speed, I asked Xanto to describe how he felt. He told me, "I can't even tell you how much it hurts. My body's at an angle when I walk, so it feels as if I'm walking sideways. Everything hurts all the way down my spine. It feels very sensitive, swollen and uncomfortable. Sitting and lying down are painful, so the best thing I can do is stand up and not move. And I'm concerned about her (the chiropractor) pulling on me."

I was amazed at the intensity of his pain which I was feeling empathically. It's very unusual for an animal (or anyone, for that matter) to endure intense pain and still be able to clearly communicate both pictures and sensations. His pain threshold was extremely high.

Glenda said, "I also want to address the fact that this is the second time he's gotten hurt by not waiting for me to set up the ramp. Will you please ask him why?"

Xanto responded, "She's too slow. I'm feeling better and I'm in a hurry to get going because there's something I need to do at home." He was talking about practicing for his upcoming police dog competition.

I communicated to him how important it was for him to always use the ramp and never jump into the back of the truck again on his own. I sent him a picture showing him he must remain seated on the ground while Mom was preparing the ramp. I also told him that every time he came to the clinic, we would all go out to the parking lot to see what a good dog he was. Since he likes audiences, he thought this was a great idea!

The chiropractor had to adjust him again under sedation because he couldn't relax enough for her to manipulate him without it. I saw Xanto again after a second adjustment when he was feeling much better. His toes no longer bothered him and his tail was up and wagging. Through me, he told the chiropractor, "You can go ahead and touch me now. It doesn't hurt anymore. Thank you for fixing me."

When Glenda asked him how he was feeling, he said, "I'm bored. It's no fun lying around all day. I miss my training. I want to do something again. I want my job back."

After that conversation, Xanto was taken back to the training grounds but steered clear of the instructor with the padded suit. He associated him with pain and refused to go anywhere near him. It took a lot of reassurance on my part to convince him to try again. I did let him know, however, that the decision was completely up to him. I told him the exercise could be fun, and Mom wouldn't get mad at him for not holding on tight. And I also suggested that he take it somewhat easy at first.

Very slowly and gently, Glenda introduced Xanto back into his full training routine. We knew he was feeling much better again the day he told me, "I don't want to do things half-heartedly." Generally before a big competition he has a "rough" practice and this was his way of saying he was ready.

Glenda asked me to continue consulting with Xanto, so I saw them periodically. In the fall of 2003, she came to see me about a different problem. Xanto had been practicing for the National Championship but she realized he was always making the same mistake. When tracking, he was supposed to track on a straight line by himself, while Glenda stood at the edge of the arena waiting for him to sit after he'd found his search target. His sitting position was her clue to move toward him. Instead, he'd look at Glenda half-way down the trail and want her to follow him the rest of the way.

I sent him a picture of exactly what he was expected to do and why. My mental picture took him through the trail with his nose pinned to the ground until he found the scent of the target item. Then, after he sat down, Glenda would come looking for him and praise him. I explained, "During the competition, you must do this flawlessly. A judge will watch Mom, and she must not move until you give the correct signal by sitting down at the target location. Everything depends on you and you alone, but your mom is very proud of you and she loves you whether you win or not."

A week later I saw Xanto and his proud mom, Glenda, who stepped into my office carrying a large trophy made of crystal. Not only did they make it to the finals at the National Competition in Denver, Colorado, but Xanto took third place when he aced the tracking test with a perfect 100 points!

Xanto had overcome his behavioral problems because he was willing to talk with me and listen to my suggestions. To resolve his medical problems, however, it took the cooperative efforts of Glenda, a veterinarian, a chiropractor, an animal communicator, and Xanto himself. Most of us were simply facilitators in his healing, but the real reason for his success was his ability to tell us about his problems and his own strong will and determination to get better.

The next case study is significant because Vicki, herself, directed her own healing. She knew exactly what needed to be done to enable her to walk again.

VICKI

Vicki's story started when my chiropractor colleague called me one day to tell me that she was sending me a client. She'd been working on a dog and was at her wit's end. She'd tried everything to get the dog to walk and yet, nothing seemed to work.

Dave, Vicki's dad, drove for over an hour to see me on a Saturday morning. When he arrived, he was obviously very concerned. In his arms, he cradled a tiny Dachshund who was trembling. I knew immediately she was scared being away from home, and probably also because of the long car ride. I tried to comfort both of them and allowed Dave to explain how he discovered her injury.

"A few months ago, I came home from work and saw Vicki outside in the backyard," he told me. "It was unusual for her not to come into the house to greet me, but because of her independent personality, I didn't think anything about it at the time. A couple of hours went by and she was still sitting in the same position on the grass so I went out to see her. That's when I realized she couldn't walk."

Dave went on, "I immediately did everything I could. We went to the vet, who took X-rays and prescribed some anti-inflammatory medication. The vet advised me to make sure that Vicki got lots of rest and was given plenty of time to heal. Well, time went by without any improvement, so I decided to change vets and then seek alternative help. That's what brought us to the chiropractor. She's been treating Vicki for six weeks now but Vicki still can't walk."

Although a little overweight for her tiny stature, there was no apparent medical reason why Vicki refused to stand up or make any effort at all to move about. Her spine had been adjusted and, to my colleague's experienced hands, Vicki's spine seemed aligned. Her joints were moving freely and she had good muscle tone in her legs. It was a mystery that needed to be solved . . . and now it was up to me.

Vicki explained to me that her accident happened while she was trying to jump off the bed. She sent me a picture of something positioned near the foot of the bed which had sharp edges. She apparently tripped on it, falling onto her back. Something was still out of place because her hind legs couldn't support her weight.

Dad told me it was difficult for her to jump up on his bed because it's very high so he'd designed some stairs made out of concrete blocks, which happened to have sharp edges. He immediately felt so guilty and wanted to know what else he could do to help Vicki walk again.

He also wanted to know how she ended up outside. Vicki explained to me, "I crawled out the doggy door that was only a few feet from where I fell. I hoped the pain wouldn't last long and I'd feel better soon. The effort of moving my body outside was all I could do and then I couldn't move any more. I rested there for most of the day until Dad came to pick me up. Now, I can't do my business on my own and I feel terrible that Dad has to constantly clean up after me."

In fact, as Dave was sitting holding Vicki in his arms, she wore a little diaper and was surrounded with a big towel.

I asked her, "Can you tell me how it feels and show me exactly where it hurts?"

She replied, "When the doctor pulls my tail straight out, the pressure goes away a little bit, but when she pulls my tail up it feels to me as if she should be pulling it down. One of the bones toward the end of my spine is actually pushing upward and pinching me constantly. I'm sure that once that bone is in place, the pain will stop."

Dave wanted to believe the treatment could be that simple but he couldn't bring himself to agree to the procedure right away, especially after a total of four months of various types of treatment with no improvement. He and I also discussed what the future might bring if Vicki couldn't walk any more.

Then we spent the rest of our visit finding ways to make her comfortable and meet some of her other needs. She readily responded to all of Dave's questions. When both of them left, I felt I'd done everything I could to put their various issues into perspective, but I still didn't know what the outcome would be when it came to her physical condition.

She was complaining about pain and I did wonder for a moment if this was partly an emotional issue. Did Vicki simply want to have Dave's undivided attention, and was this her way of getting it? However, I quickly concluded that she was much too independent for that.

I called the chiropractor to tell her about Vicki's assessment of her pain and the location of her injury. I also mentioned that she suggested the chiropractor pull her tail down rather than up. My colleague was very concerned, and said, "That's not a move I usually make. If I don't do it just right, she could remain paralyzed for the rest of her life! I'll have to think about that first." I could feel how carefully she was considering the pros and cons of the situation, and knew that the decision was in her capable hands.

Three days later she called me and was extremely excited. "You'll never guess who I saw today! Vicki . . . and she's walking again! She was right after all! I did the adjustment by pulling her tail down. It's a very dangerous move that I'd never do otherwise, but because of what Vicki was saying, I analyzed the X-rays again, thinking there might be something ever so subtle which just wasn't readily apparent in the beginning . . . and there was. What a thrill after the adjustment to see her push her little body up and be able to walk around!"

Soon after their chiropractic visit, I saw Dave and Vicki again. Dave was glowing as he said, "Look at Vicki walk! You can't even tell she was paralyzed for four months. Isn't this a great sight? I love her so much. Since our first talk, our relationship has improved a hundred percent and I feel as if I understand her ever so much better now."

When it came to her medical problem, it was the patient herself who directed her own treatment. Vicki knew exactly what was needed. When we listened to her and looked at things in light of the information she was providing, her healing could finally begin.

This next story was so remarkable that it was even featured on a TV show. Buddha's case study shows not only what we can do to help heal our animal friends but also how important it is to listen with care and attention to everything they're telling us. We need to understand their strength and determination when they're faced with paralysis, or even death.

The first part of this case study recounts events that happened before I ever met Buddha, but no one shared this information with me until *after* I eventually had my first visit with him.

BUDDHA

Kathy Stevens and her husband Steve are dog trainers. They have 20 dogs in kennels in their backyard, most of them Labrador Retrievers. Every morning someone, usually Steve, cleans the kennels, feeds the dogs and allows them some time to play.

One day as Steve was cleaning the kennels, he heard a very loud yelp. Looking to see who it was, he observed Buddha, a ten-month-old Golden Retriever, limping very slowly towards him. Since Buddha was still a pup, Steve thought nothing of it and figured he'd just been playing with the older dogs. *Somebody probably put him in his place again*, he thought as he helped him into his kennel.

When Steve and Kathy go out to train, it's necessary to rotate which dogs they take with them on any given day because they have so many dogs and only limited space. They use a specially designed vehicle, similar to the type used by shelters and animal control, with individual air conditioned compartments for each pet. This time, however, it was Buddha's turn to spend the day at home.

Kathy and Steve returned from their training session after dark. Kathy immediately went out to the kennel area to clean and exercise the dogs who had stayed behind. She found Buddha unable to move and drenched in his own urine. He struggled to go to her but seemed to have no control over his rear end. Kathy knew that something was seriously wrong with her beloved Buddha.

Spring had come early that year and the rattlesnakes were already active, so she quickly checked him for any telltale puncture wounds but found nothing. All the time, the frightened dog whimpered and tried desperately to stand up. What disturbed Kathy in particular was that Buddha had lost all bladder control. At the top of her voice, a distraught Kathy screamed for Steve, "Something's wrong with Buddha. I need help!"

Steve rushed out and scooped Buddha up, despite the fact that he weighed 70 pounds. He took him into the house and gently laid him in the bathtub. They gave Buddha a shower and continued to look for puncture wounds. They finally got him calmed down, laid him on the bed, and blow-dried his coat.

Gingerly, Kathy felt all over his body to see what was wrong but could find nothing. She became very concerned when she realized he couldn't stop urinating, so she and Steve laid several towels beneath him.

As she thought about who she might call for help, she looked at her watch. She realized it was after hours but remembered she had the chiropractor's home phone number.

"I'm going to call the chiropractor," Kathy said to Steve. "Maybe she can suggest something."

When the doctor picked up the phone, Kathy blurted out, "It's Buddha. He's not moving! He can't move! I don't know what happened. He's just a puppy. He was fine this morning."

After asking several questions to determine the extent of Buddha's injury and his current condition, the chiropractor reassured Kathy that he'd be all right during the night.

She then asked, "Can you bring him to the animal hospital first thing in the morning so that both his veterinarian and I can give him a thorough examination?"

Kathy agreed.

On her way to the veterinary clinic the next day, Kathy received a call on her cell phone with more bad news. Her son had been in an accident in which his car had gone over a 140-foot cliff! All she knew was that he was alive but he'd suffered many broken bones and internal injuries.

This could possibly be the worst day of our lives, Kathy thought. Steve was on his way to be with their son, while Kathy was on her way to get help for their puppy. She desperately needed to believe that something could be done for Buddha and she was willing to do anything to make him well again.

At the animal hospital, Kathy consulted with both the vet and the chiropractor. She wanted to know if euthanasia was inevitable, or if there was anything else that could reasonably be done. The chiropractor, who has a proactive rather than a dismissive attitude, talked about trying sedation and an adjustment first.

X-rays revealed that Buddha's pelvis was twisted, with each half going in the opposite direction. Worse yet, his hip was out of alignment and a disk was damaged in his lower back. The chiropractor said, "It looks as if Buddha somehow got his leg caught in something and struggled fiercely to get it out. But his struggling tore ligaments in the pelvis causing the left half of it to twist away from the right half. As he continued struggling, his leg was pulled from its socket, not completely but significantly. The bulging disc is due to an impact trauma and is pressing against the spinal cord, and this is causing the paralysis in his body."

Buddha was heavily sedated so the chiropractor worked to realign his spinal column. He was then admitted to the veterinary clinic's ICU where he was given fluids and medication.

Knowing she'd done everything possible for Buddha at the moment, Kathy rushed from the animal hospital to the people hospital to see her injured son.

When she returned to the animal hospital the next day, she was disturbed to see that Buddha still couldn't walk — two technicians carried him on a stretcher. The vet then explained, "Trauma to the spine results in swelling and causes all the tissues around the area to become inflamed. Because nerves don't stretch, the inflamed tissues pinch against them. This pinching blocks impulses the brain is trying to send to the muscles. The muscles don't move because they aren't receiving the messages that tell them to move. If the pinching on the nerves isn't relieved quickly, the nerves will die and no more messages will ever be sent to those muscles."

Allowing Kathy time to reflect on his explanation, the vet cautiously continued, "The time factor for the swelling to go down can be a few days to several weeks. I want you to continue Buddha's follow-up care with the chiropractor and bring him back to the animal hospital if the problem persists."

Privately, the vet was not holding out much hope that Buddha would ever walk again.

At Buddha's next appointment, the chiropractor again adjusted his legs, pelvis and spinal column, but sensed that something else was still wrong. She considered the fact that this was a ten-month-old puppy who should be young enough to heal quickly. But after two days, despite his valiant attempts to stand, Buddha's legs just couldn't bear his own weight.

Believing there still had to be something else wrong, my chiropractor colleague said to Kathy, "Let's ask Dr. Monica for her input. She's helped me before and I trust her."

Having run out of other options, Kathy welcomed my help and I met with her at the clinic the following day. My chiropractor colleague always gives every client private time to talk with me first, especially if it's our initial meeting, so she left us alone together until we were ready to discuss any information directly related to Buddha's injury or pain, or until we needed her help to interpret the physical aspects of what Buddha would be describing to me.

Kathy began our consultation by exclaiming, "I'm just devastated. I can't believe what's happening. One day he's my pride and joy, one of the best dogs I've ever trained, and the next he can't move. Even after a second adjustment yesterday, he still can't walk.

"I'm not ready to put him down. Is there anything you can tell me? I especially want to know what happened. He was in the backyard playing and there's nothing there that could have injured him. All the other dogs are fine. I thought he might have been attacked by a snake, but I can't find a bite."

Before beginning, I carefully explained to Kathy, "I'll only be able to tell you how the injury took place if Buddha is willing to tell me."

It's important to remember that, as I began to talk with him, all *I* knew about Buddha's case was that he couldn't walk, and Kathy wanted to know exactly what happened to hurt him while he was playing in the yard. She hadn't yet shared any of the medical information which either the veterinarian or the chiropractor had told her.

As soon as Kathy was ready to have me to talk directly with Buddha, we let my colleague know that it was time for her to join us again. When she came back into the room, I then closed my eyes and started to receive pictures from this beautiful puppy. I knew he was a bright young guy but I didn't expect him to be able to relate the events so clearly, considering his painful condition.

He began to share the following information with me. "My legs won't hold me up and I can't walk because of all the pain, and I don't have control over my bowels and bladder. But there's something else wrong with me, too. I can't focus my eyes, my tummy feels queasy all the time, and I feel too sick to even try to do anything. I think it's the medication they're giving me that's making me feel this awful."

I then looked up at the chiropractor and said, "I'm really feeling his nausea and intense pain." Telepathically, I received *her* thought which said, "Well, *do* something!"

At one point, I started swallowing hard and frequently so the chiropractor, worried that I might vomit, touched my shoulder to ask if I was OK. That momentary detachment from Buddha helped me re-center myself.

The chiropractor later told me she could see the pain on my face as I relayed Buddha's condition. This is not unusual because people often tell me they can see changes come over me as I spiritually meld with and "become" the animal at some level.

She asked me to tell Buddha that she'd have his medication changed right away. To me she said, "The vet uses steroids as part of our protocol to minimize the swelling but it sounds as if he's having a negative reaction to them."

After repositioning myself, I continued to communicate with Buddha. When I'd moved closer to him, I explained, "We want to do things to help heal your spine, so please try to be strong and let us help you."

Despite his pain and nausea, Buddha was trying to gather his strength to tell me what had happened to him. "I was walking around the yard, playing with the other dogs, when I looked up and saw a wooden building."

This puzzled Kathy when I told her and she responded, "I don't have any wooden buildings."

But Buddha continued to show me something that was definitely made out of wood. When I described it further, Kathy suddenly cried, "I know what it is! We're building a deck for the Jacuzzi and it's made out of wood!"

Next Buddha said, "Because I was so curious, I went to investigate and found a step-stool there. It was a white stool that I'd never seen before. My leg got caught in it, and I fell down on my back. Immediately my back started hurting."

Kathy cried out again, "Oh, my God! I just left that stool out there for the first time the day before yesterday. He wasn't used to seeing it there. That's why he stumbled over it. We'd emptied the Jacuzzi, cleaned it, and moved it into position, but we hadn't put any railings up on the deck yet. The contractor had taken away the temporary steps I'd been using, so I put the white stool next to the Jacuzzi the night before. I should have put it away, but I completely forgot about it and just went to bed. The deck is about three feet high and Buddha's mother likes to lie in the shade on the decking next to the Jacuzzi, so he probably wanted to go up there, too."

Buddha continued his explanation. "My brother, Seeker, was on top of the building (the covered Jacuzzi) and wanted me to come up and play. I knew I wasn't allowed up there but I started to sneak up anyway. I got nervous because a sound frightened me and because I thought I was doing something wrong. I turned a funny way and my leg got caught inside the white stool. When I tried to get it loose, I tumbled over backwards and hit the top of the deck really hard. Then my leg got free of the stool and I fell all the way onto the ground below and I yelped really loud. Dad saw me. I was very ashamed and scared because I knew I did something wrong. My back was hurting so much that I could hardly walk over to him, but somehow I managed to get back to my kennel with a little help from Dad."

All of this information, coming directly from Buddha, confirmed exactly what the chiropractor had explained to Kathy after seeing the X-rays. Now we all knew how the accident had happened.

Buddha, who was very weak, also complained that he felt overly tired and that something else was affecting his body. Kathy replied, "We're giving him sedatives as well as his other medications." I told her there still seemed to be too much pain. It was almost as if there was a broken bone somewhere in his spine. Concerned about this new piece of information she then asked me, "Will Buddha ever walk again?"

When I relayed the question to him, Buddha said, "I want to walk. I want to be well again and I'll do my very best to improve. I know I can walk again because something similar happened to me once before when I was a different kind of dog. I was smaller and my back was longer and my legs were short." I didn't understand exactly what he meant by this, though I did know he was probably talking about a past life, but neither Kathy nor I mentioned this again.

I saw Buddha the second time a couple of weeks later, but he was only able to walk a couple of steps before his legs would give way. Even though he was having regular adjustments, his progress was slower than expected, especially given his young age.

At first, Kathy had rigged a rope and towel around his middle to help him walk, but soon she bought a regular body harness for him which made things much easier.

As if there was a spark of faith from within, something inside Kathy kept saying, "It's going to be OK. Just keep going like this."

Buddha told me, "I'm feeling a little better, in fact, much better than I did shortly after it happened. I know I still have a long road ahead of me, but I don't mind the medicine now and I do feel pretty good." He added with puppy-like enthusiasm, "And I like all the attention I'm getting!"

When I asked Kathy how she was holding up, she said, "I'm really upset because I took Buddha to see a specialist who told me I should have had him put to sleep. But my love for Buddha wouldn't let me do that. Now that he's improving, I'm certain I made the right decision in spite of the vet's recommendation. I also feel really bad about being the one who left the stool out and not putting it away. I still can't get over the guilt."

Buddha told me, "I thought Mom was mad at me, and I was feeling bad that it was my fault."

So I had to help both Kathy and Buddha with each other's concerns. Kathy had a hard time letting go of the guilt, but was especially touched when Buddha told her he loved her and he didn't blame her for leaving the stool out there.

Kathy asked me to tell him, "I wasn't mad at you. I was only concerned because you were hurt."

There had been a specialist who, in fact, had strongly recommended that Buddha be put to sleep. Early on, when Buddha's progress was quite slow, I'd suggested to Kathy that perhaps there was something else wrong, so she made an appointment for an MRI. This is Kathy's account of what happened at that time:

I took Buddha in for his MRI and left him there for a day. The doctor called me to say, "I have a surgeon here who wants to speak to you."

The surgeon was angry that we'd been doing chiropractic adjustments on a dog in that condition. His attitude was one of "shame on you." He said, "This dog needs immediate surgery because his back is broken. There's no way he'll ever walk after what you've done with the chiropractic care. I can't believe you put him through far more pain than you had to."

The guilt trip he put me through was terrible. I called my own regular vet who advised me, "Don't do anything right now. Let me take the X-rays to a friend who's an orthopedic surgeon and then to another friend who's a neurosurgeon who specializes in these injuries."

Both specialists concurred and had the following comments: "I wouldn't do surgery. Is this dog walking?"

"Yes, he's walking," I told them.

"You mean he's actually standing up on all four legs?"

"Yes," I said. "He's a little wobbly but he's actually learning how to walk again."

"OK, if he's walking I wouldn't do surgery at all because surgery may well paralyze him for life. But if it was my dog, I'd put him down."

At that point, I became hysterical. Some surgeons were yelling at me to have surgery; others were telling me to put Buddha down.

Finally, I sat down and prayed with all my heart. Then something came to me and said, "You're doing the right thing. You're going right where you're supposed to be going. Don't worry about it."

Something inside me was speaking to me, saying, "Trust me, its OK, so go with it. It'll be OK; keep working at it. You're doing the right thing."

Although I felt good about what I was doing, apparently I was in the minority. My poor chiropractor was being yelled at, as was her veterinarian. All the specialists were calling my veterinarian and screaming and calling me names and saying I was insensitive to my dog, and I was caught in the middle. Everyone was getting yelled at even though we were all trying so hard to help Buddha. I was hysterical because it seemed that everyone wanted to put him down. On the other hand, my husband was saying, "Well, you know, he is starting to walk again. Whatever you're doing is working."

I remember Buddha telling Dr. Monica, "I can do this." I couldn't quite understand what he was leading up to, but now I know that he knew he would get better.

This whole thing has changed me greatly and I have a new respect for what animals are trying to say and can say to us. As a dog trainer, I had no idea just how much they retain, how much they try to communicate with us, and how much of a history they have.

And this is not their only life. Buddha once said through Dr. Monica, "I have the strength to do this because I had problems in a previous life. I was a Dachshund and had been injured because of my long body." I was amazed to remember this, but I did recall it when the vet who took the second set of X-rays and CAT scans said, "The oddest thing about this dog is that he has one extra vertebra, like a Dachshund has. It doesn't hurt him or cause him any problem, but it's really odd."

Buddha knew exactly how to deal with his healing and said, "Just let me work this out. I can do it if you help me. I can do this."

His strength, love and determination have actually changed me by teaching me not to give up and to have faith and hope. Rather than blindly put him to sleep, it was better to ask the animal what he wants and thinks. Animals have feelings and we must remember that. If they say they want to do something and can do it because they've done it before, we should honor that.

I've started Buddha on an acupuncture program to help him, so I'm doing my best for him. And with all the holistic healing available, there'll be no surgery under any circumstances.

When I saw Buddha for the third time, two months after his accident, he was walking fairly well. He was such a happy boy and it was a delight to see him almost well again. I had to remind him though, "You're not completely healed yet so you'll still have to take it easy for a little while longer."

After four months, Buddha was once again running, playing and swimming at his own pace. Kathy's goal is to have him become a therapy dog so he can help children who have the same problems he's overcome. If he can do it, they can do it, too. And she knows Buddha can give those children a lot of love. "It might take us a couple of years," she says, "but he'll do it."

Happily, Kathy's son also recovered from all of his injuries. The worst one he sustained was a bulging disc in his lower back that was pressing on his spinal cord. The fact that his injury was so similar to Buddha's didn't escape my attention, and I couldn't help but think about how close both of them had come to losing their battles.

Six months later a television crew for the James van Praagh show, *Beyond,* videotaped a segment on Buddha and his miraculous recovery. He was filmed happily chasing and retrieving a Frisbee, always with a wagging tail.

Kathy still can't believe the incredible recovery Buddha has made. His healing was part communication, part medical treatment, and part prayer. It made a living, breathing, jumping miracle out of her little Buddha.

Sometimes you know when it's time to release a sick or injured pet but other times you feel that spark of hope, that inner knowing, telling you to keep trying. When that happens, be sure to explore all of your possible options, and remember that even your pet may be able to share helpful information with you if you'll just ask him questions and listen to his answers.

CHAPTER 6

EMOTIONAL HEALING

S ometimes people feel a behavioral problem is their pet's way of punishing them for something they did or didn't do. "My pet must be angry with me about something!" is a phrase I hear from my clients all the time.

But I've found there's often an emotional component we need to consider. It's not at all unusual for pets to act in abnormal ways when they're confused, stressed, worried, sad or fearful about something. This often happens when there's a sudden change in their schedule or a disruption in their regular routines.

When animals don't understand why changes are taking place, they often react with visible signs of emotional distress. We usually think they're just behaving badly but, in fact, this is one of those times when they need our love and understanding in an extra special way because of what they're going through.

In order to feel more secure, our pets regularly need to be informed about many things — both common everyday things and unusual events. This, of course, will make *your* life a lot less stressful too! They need to know what's going on around them . . . for instance, when you're going on vacation, as in this first case study.

ZACH

Lisa and Kayce are roommates in Southern California. A couple of years ago, I went to see Lisa because her male cat was having a few behavioral problems. Zach, who's about two years old, is black with a little bit of white on his chest. He came to Lisa as a kitten. We took care of the problems in one afternoon and Lisa couldn't have been more pleased.

A year later, she called me again. "I need another consultation with Zach because I'm planning a trip to Hawaii. Usually when I go on vacation, he gets very upset. He'll run around and pick on Kayce's two female cats and get really grumpy with Kayce. He scratches her and bats at her with his claws out. One time he even bit her on the face!

"Then, when I get back, he won't talk to me for days. And he wakes me up really early in the morning just to get back at me. So while I'm looking forward to ten days in Hawaii, I'm not looking forward to the thought of upsetting him. Can you communicate this to Zach and see if you can make him feel better? And can you ask him to behave better toward my roommate?"

When I talked with Zach about Lisa's vacation, he was haughty and defiant right from the start. His first question was, "Who's going to feed me? Only Mom can prepare it just right. The amount must be exact — not too much because I can't eat it all, and not too little because I'll still be hungry."

Lisa laughed at this and then explained, "Zach gets really stressed whenever he feels there isn't plenty of food available. He was a really thin stray when I got him, so food is a big concern. Having the right amount seems to give him peace of mind. He likes his bowl to be filled to exactly a certain height."

I reassured Zach, "Kayce will take care of feeding you and she promises she'll do it just like Mom does."

Once we got that out of the way, he relaxed a little bit and told me, "I really love my mom and enjoy her company. She's a very special person."

Next, I asked Zach, "Is there anything else that will make you feel more at ease while your mom's away?"

When I closed my eyes, he showed me several pictures of Lisa's room. I saw him going up on the bed and sniffing around. He said, "Please ask Mom to put something on top of the bed that smells like her." He then sent me a mental picture of the exact item.

Turning to Lisa, I said, "It looks to me like he's talking about a blanket or shawl, something you use in winter which has your scent on it." Lisa understood his request and agreed to put the blanket on her bed while she was away.

Then Zach told me, "I'm very upset with the condition of the bed. Tell her to be sure to make it before she leaves!"

I relayed this to Lisa and added, "He wants to be sure I translate that thought to you, so he's repeating it over and over. It's like a videotape in my mind that keeps rewinding and playing itself over and over again!"

Lisa laughed and agreed with Zach that her bed is seldom made. She promised to make it for him before she left.

Zach continued, "There's a place by the window I like very much. I enjoy lying there so I can feel the sun coming in on me, but I can't get at that spot because there's something in front of it."

Lisa explained, "Yes, the computer desk is in front of the window, but right now I've got a lot of stuff on it so he hasn't been able to climb up and lie down as usual. Tell him I promise to clean it up and make some room for him before I go."

Zach then confided, "Mom's going on vacation with her boyfriend, and I'm a little worried that she might leave me behind and not come back home."

I reassured him, "Mom loves you and will always come back to you. Now Zach, I want you to be on vacation too. Try to get along with the two female cats and especially with Kayce since she'll be taking good care of you."

After the session, Lisa commented, "You know, Zach doesn't have the worried look on his face that he usually has when he knows I'm going away."

While Lisa was on vacation she called Kayce who reported that Zach was a totally different cat! She told Lisa, "He really is taking a vacation! He just lies around instead of chasing the other cats and tormenting them. He's even been friendly toward me and doesn't even look or act as if he wants to scratch me!"

When Lisa returned home, Zach was genuinely happy to see her and didn't "punish" her as he'd done in the past by waking her up at three o'clock in the morning. Lisa later told me, "Your communication with him took all the stress out of my trip for both of us. Even now when I spend a night away, he's still very calm. Just being reassured that I'll always come back to him has helped him feel much more secure. Thank you, Dr. Monica."

———

By now you may be thinking the changes in Zach's behavior were all just a coincidence. But there definitely is a connection between animal communication and emotional healing. Read on to see what happens next . . . in the same household.

ABBY

Six months later, I received an e-mail from Kayce, Lisa's roommate. This time *she* was going on vacation and wanted me to talk to one of her felines. Her e-mail read:

> Hi, Dr. Monica,
>
> I sent you Abby's picture. She's four years old and is some kind of mixed breed cat. I got her at the pound when she was two months old. She's always had too much energy and been very, very willful. She just gets so mad when I go away! She doesn't seem to accept changes very well. Lisa, my roommate, tries to be friendly, but Abby isn't accepting. She hides under the bed for the entire time I'm gone and doesn't come out at her regular feeding time. Last time she didn't eat for four days! I'm afraid to leave for ten days this time.

I'd like to have her relax more and not be so angry, and be more receptive to Lisa. There are two other kitties in the household, Ayres, a grandma cat and Zach, Lisa's cat.

Abby is a strange little kitty. I just want to know why she can't cooperate with Lisa for the short time I'll be gone and not be frightened that I won't return.

Thanks, Kayce

Because I'm able to communicate with my animal clients either in person or from a distance, people often send pictures of their pets to help me clearly visualize the animal I'll be talking with. In this instance, on the day of our consultation, I was speaking with Kayce by phone, while mentally and spiritually connecting with Abby whose picture was in front of me. This way I could immediately translate what I received from Abby back to Kayce.

Sometimes people wonder "technically" how I'm able to make the connection with their pet if I'm not in the same room with them. I need to have only a spiritual or heart connection with the animal. The phone line or the internet connection, in the instance of a phone or e-mail consultation, is used only to communicate with the person.

When I was "talking" with Abby before the session (something I always try to do so I can introduce myself to the pet ahead of time), she kept sending me a mental picture of fuzzy slippers. I saw the slippers just the way she'd see them from the vantage point of being under the bed. The same picture played in my mind again and again until I figured out what she was trying to say.

"Someone is calling me to come out from under the bed," Abby said. "As if I would!" she added with exasperation.

During our telephone call, I reported to Kayce, "Abby's very stubborn. When she gets something in her mind, it's very difficult to convince her to change. This has been going on for a long time. Abby knows when you're not around and she's not willing to budge. I'm telling her that ten days is a long time to be under the bed and that Lisa's nice and will do everything she can to be friends with her."

Abby then chimed in with, "I don't like her scent, and her routine is all wrong. Things are not the same when Mom's not home and I can't get used to it. Why can't I have water and food brought to me?"

"Well, that might be a possibility," I replied, "but in any case you need to come out of your hiding place at some point and be a part of the family. Everyone misses you and they'd feel better if you were acting normally. Then Mom wouldn't have to be so worried about you either."

Abby and I continued to talk about what would make her happy. First she showed me the bedroom and then she showed me another place — a rocking chair in the living room where she likes to curl up and snuggle for a nap. I told her, "If that makes you happy, then go there and I'll ask everybody not to disturb you."

I then explained to Abby how long ten days would be and I asked Kayce to talk with her, too. I reminded Kayce about what I'd told her roommate before, "Our animals receive information in pictures, and we automatically make pictures in our mind when we speak out loud, so you should express your feelings by talking out loud to Abby." Abby confirmed that Mom had not currently been doing this.

Next, I reassured Abby that Mom would be coming back. I then continued to explain to Kayce, "Abby can be self-centered, thinking the world revolves around her and what she wants, so when you're not around, everything crumbles. She never got used to Lisa and doesn't like her slippers or the scent of her perfume. I'm asking her to just relax, play, go anywhere she wants in the house and be happy. I've told her no one will disturb her and it will almost be like being on vacation herself."

Eleven days later I received this e-mail:

Dear Dr. Monica;

As you know, my little Abby is quite stubborn and self-centered. When I'd go away for four or five days, she'd hide under the bed and refuse to eat. She'd ignore or hiss at Lisa while I was away. This would last for the entire vacation time. It didn't make me happy to know this and that's why I called you when I was going to be away for ten days.

Well, Lisa said the first couple of days Abby avoided her but didn't stay under the bed. She stayed under the computer table instead and watched everything carefully. Lisa brought food to her and she looked as if she was ignoring it, but it was gone a couple of hours later. Then Lisa got the idea of sending Abby pictures (in her mind) that the food would be on her plate on the countertop at a certain time, just to see what would happen.

It worked! She came over to the counter and watched Lisa put the food out and when Lisa left, she jumped up and ate it all. Within a couple of days, she was up on the countertop waiting for Lisa at the specified time. Wow! The pictures worked!

She never went under the bed once but slept on top. Eventually she went downstairs and hung out in the living room sitting in her favorite rocking chair as was her usual pattern. She never hissed or ran away from Lisa the whole time. Lisa said she was just not the same cat. She played and wandered around the house normally and even went into Lisa's room twice to say "Hi."

Needless to say, I was thrilled that all went well. You did a marvelous job. Now that I'm back, she hasn't left my side and her attitude has been most pleasant, which is not her usual style. I hope this lasts. Thank you, Dr. Monica, for your wonderful support. You were most amazing and such a tremendous help to me to relax and not worry about my little spoiled kitty.

Sincerely,

Kayce

There you have it! Often, to relieve their emotional distress, all our animals need is a listening ear, some understanding and a little reassurance. The fact that we're having a "conversation" with them *does* make a difference. Communicating with our pets can affect how we perceive them. More importantly, it can also bring about changes in their behaviors and attitudes. It may even change how they perceive us and the rest of the world around them.

This brings me to my next story about a deaf Sheltie and how *he* felt his humans perceived him . . .

Troy

The first time I met Troy, a Shetland Sheepdog, he was 5½ months old. Nancy and Kay, who raise and train Shetlands, more commonly referred to as Shelties, had adopted him three months earlier. Troy, who had been bred by a Sheltie breeder, was the only one in the litter who was born all white and therefore deaf. From a breeder's point of view, this is a death sentence because dogs like this must not be allowed to pass on their "defective" gene. Although Nancy and her partner Kay were already devoted to their other two Shelties, they decided to adopt Troy to save him from being put down.

In addition to his white coat, pink nose and problem with deafness, Troy had one almost transparent crystal blue eye and one brown eye. This was another cause for concern because it'd been determined that not only was he already blind in the brown eye, but the blue one was also showing signs of problems. That he would be completely blind in the future was a grim reality.

Conversations with young animals are always difficult because they have such a short attention span. Talking with them is much like talking with a two-year-old child. Children will answer your questions, but in between they'll also talk about other subjects you haven't even asked them about, such as telling you what they like to eat or talking about their friends. I have the same communication issues with young animals because their pictures jump around and don't last for long. They shoot rapid images, all of which are usually unrelated, making my sentence construction more of a challenge, but it's just a matter of learning to understand their thought patterns

Troy was no exception, but I was still able to put everything together in coherent sentences. He explained, "Tell them that I'm very intelligent and I understand things, but I'm easily distracted. I need to have them understand the difference between being dumb and not paying attention. I'm not dumb! I'm very smart!"

This was an eye-opener for both Nancy and Kay. Later they admitted that, on more than one occasion, they'd wondered out loud if Troy was perhaps a bit slow because he didn't "get" some things as quickly as their other dogs did.

Kay and Nancy are active participants in agility training at both local and national levels. Agility training involves jumping, walking up and down A-frames, and running through long tunnels. Their other dogs are highly skilled and adept in this area but Troy seemed to be a little less so.

Kay then asked Troy if he enjoyed doing agility training. Turning to me she explained, "He's already done some jumps and also gone through some tunnels." Troy flashed me a picture right away telling me how good he is in the tunnel. It's his favorite thing and he has fun running through it.

He also showed me a picture of him being behind a fence and sent me a strong feeling of displeasure whenever this happened. "He doesn't want to be a spectator behind a fence," I told his moms. "He wants to be in the middle of it all."

Laughing, Kay said, "Whenever we put him behind the fence and go into the area with the agility training equipment, he gets really upset. Can you please tell him that we're always going to come back for him? We're not punishing him, but it's for his safety. While we train the other dogs, we need to keep him out of danger." I relayed this message to Troy.

Next, when I asked him about his vision, he sent me a picture of himself having to be very, very close to an object to be able to recognize what it was. Both Moms had noticed this before, so they'd already been trying to train him by using a flashlight and making hand signals close to his nose.

When I asked him about any pain or discomfort he had, Troy posed a question of his own. "Why can't I lift my tail up as high as the other dogs?"

Kay laughingly said, "Tell him that some Shelties can lift their tails high and some Shelties can't. That might be something he's able to do as he grows older. It's funny he should ask that because we were commenting just the other day about how Troy's tail doesn't come up as high as the others."

Kay asked, "Does he understand our signals when he's doing something? Like when we want him to stop, or when we want him to come to us."

Troy replied, "Some things I understand more than others."

"You have to remember," I told the Moms, "that just like any other puppy, you're not going to get him to do something if you only say it once. You need to repeat it quite often."

Troy decided to agree with me by adding, "I'm stubborn, but I'm not stupid."

One week later I saw Troy again. He came into my office brandishing a big, fluffy tail, held as high as it could go. He was happy to come in for another talk and started playing around with the light from a floor lamp.

He was quick to tell me that he was learning something new that he didn't like at all. Not sure of what he was talking about, I asked Nancy, "Is he learning to walk on a leash?"

"Yes, he's learning to walk on a leash with a harness and he hates it. He doesn't think he can move. As soon as we put it on, he just lies down and won't budge."

Troy said, "It's so much easier being picked up. Besides, the harness is too heavy and I don't like it."

I reassured Troy that all big boys have to walk on a leash, and that soon he'd be able to do it as well as his big brother Jake.

I saw Troy many times after that. He started to learn training commands with sign language and is walking on his leash with his tail proudly held high. He's become a great agility dog and makes his moms very happy and proud of him.

Once Troy's emotional fears of being thought of as slow, deaf, blind and inferior had been addressed, he was able to heal. He was also able to show Nancy and Kay that he was indeed a very intelligent being who, even though he had disabilities, was able to live a happy and full life just the same.

KODY

This story of emotional healing takes the form of a letter I received from a client, also named Kay. She writes:

> To anyone who's curious but skeptical about Dr. Monica's ability to communicate with animals and birds, even over a long distance, I've experienced firsthand the beneficial results of her remarkable gift.
>
> I'm a 56-year-old grandmother, who just completed the trip of a lifetime. I traveled alone with two cats, Chen Lee, a Siamese male, and Darby, a black male, and my nine-year-old Siberian Husky named Kody. I drove 9,000 miles roundtrip from Los Angeles, California to Coldfoot, Alaska, located 60 miles north of the Arctic Circle.
>
> Many people have driven the Alaskan Highway in the summer. But few, other than the rare Alaskan and long-distance truckers, drive it in the winter. About 260 miles of the trip was via a dirt road called the Haul Road, which runs parallel to the Alaskan pipeline. To get to this road, we drove through British Columbia on the Canadian Highway, and took the Alaskan Highway through the Yukon and Northwest Territories. We eventually arrived in Fairbanks, Alaska, having survived snowstorms and continuous ice-packed roads.
>
> My reasons for the journey were to see the Aurora Borealis (Northern Lights) and to take Kody to the snow country, the land of his ancestors. (Kody was born and raised in Southern California.)
>
> We'd had a consultation with Dr. Monica about three weeks prior to this trip and she'd asked him if he wanted to go. He replied that he was eager to go and that he loved the snow. However, he also showed Monica a picture of his head spinning round and round, which we took to mean he gets carsick. But he really wanted to go on the trip, so I took a supply of Acepromazine, a dog tranquilizer that also has anti-nausea properties.
>
> We left Los Angeles on February 28, 2003 and traveled north on I-5. We crossed into Canada on Sunday, March 9, and stayed in a small motel in Hope, BC. Kody was happy as long as he got his walks in all the strange towns we stayed in.

Kody had the whole back seat of the 4-wheel-drive SUV to himself, and was happy to jump the two feet to the back seat. But, as we left Hope, I noticed that he balked at jumping into the back seat. I knew he wasn't injured or stiff, and figured he was just being stubborn as only Huskies can be.

Up until now, we'd encountered no snow, but now we were driving on icy roads, and I wondered if he was recalling the time we once spun out on an icy I-80 in a blizzard on our way to Minnesota. Perhaps the snow and ice brought back the memory of the spinout. I suddenly realized that, although Kody loves snow, he doesn't like riding in the car in the snow.

To overcome his nervousness and to get him into the SUV, I'd open the rear door. Then he and I would run six to ten feet towards the vehicle so that his forward momentum would commit him to jumping in. (Of course, the problem with running on ice and snow is the risk of slipping, which I did more than once.) Even so, Kody would still balk and apply his "4-feet brakes" rather than jumping in. So I'd repeat the process of backing up and running at the car over and over and over, until he finally gave up and jumped in. Sometimes this took as long as 45 minutes and I think the only reason he eventually got in was that he was tired and thirsty.

In addition to this problem, he started to have anxiety attacks in which he would cry and pant, bite the door handles of the car, and try to lick his way out of the window. I thought about sedating him with the Acepromazine but the problem with that was he became aggressive when he was coming down from it and would chase and snap at my cats.

Driving from Seattle to Fairbanks, Alaska took eight long days, after which, I was at my wits end from having to deal with Kody. In desperation, I called Dr. Monica to ask her if she could help. From several thousand miles away, she told Kody he could make the rest of the trip easier on everyone if he would just jump into the car as I was asking him to do. She explained to him that it was necessary for him to get into the car without giving me such a hard time. Kody replied that he knows he's very stubborn but will try. In exchange, he asked to be allowed to play in the snow more.

Next, I asked Monica to tell him about a trip we'll be taking on a ferry and that it will last four nights. Kody told her he wasn't afraid of the ferry. In fact, he asked if he could walk around the deck to see and smell the water.

Dr. Monica told me that she'd continue to talk to Kody to help him get through the remainder of our trip.

I immediately saw an improvement in his behavior. I only had to make one run at the car with him and he jumped in. If he balked, which he did only a couple of times during the rest of the trip, I put his Velcro muzzle on and he jumped into the car on his own without the run. He still required sedation for his anxiety during the actual drive but he was more accepting of the situation.

On the ferry ride, the cats and dog had to stay in the car except for 15 minute potty breaks on the car deck, after which Kody hopped back into the truck without a second's hesitation.

You cannot imagine how difficult and stressful traveling with Kody was before Dr. Monica communicated with him. He improved 90 percent after their talk. He couldn't help his anxiety but after communicating with her even that improved. I cannot emphasize enough the value of her consultations. We assume we know our pets but we don't always understand what is behind their behaviors. They, in turn, don't always understand what we expect them to do.

Once your pet has had a chance to communicate with you through Dr. Monica, it feels like you really want to understand more about them and want to let them know how deeply you care for them.

You can see it immediately in their behavior. It takes your relationship to an even more intimate level.

Dr. Monica, our sincere thanks and blessings.

Chen Lee (Siamese cat)

Darby (black cat)

Kody (long distance Husky)

Kay (grateful client)

Emotional healing frequently changes a pet's behavior. We just need to care enough about communicating with them in order to better understand their worries and concerns. In extreme cases, an animal's fear may even manifest itself not just as a mild behavioral problem but as anger or full blown rage. To protect themselves, they may even bite. How can we avoid this outcome? In every case, serious or simple, we must find the emotional reason for their fears. Once we know where the problem lies, we can then take effective steps to correct it for the benefit of both human and pet.

CHAPTER 7

SPIRITUAL HEALING

S piritual healing requires only love and purity of intention. The intention springs from the heart, sometimes called the heart chakra or heart energy center. It melds with the Love of the Universe and is transmitted by a thought to the person or animal in need.

Spiritual healers focus on empathy, compassion and unconditional love in a profoundly deep way to bring about helpful changes at many levels. Typically, they use spiritual healing to balance energy patterns (sometimes called Ch'i) when an imbalance in those patterns has caused discomfort in body, mind or spirit.

When I work with an animal who needs physical, emotional, or spiritual healing, I repeat images of the animal's well being, and of love, over and over again in my mind, almost unconsciously. Happiness and love become all encompassing and I know the animal is receiving this energy by way of my thoughts.

It's easy to see how animals benefit from physical and emotional healing, but you may be wondering why they might also need spiritual healing. Some pets, particularly cats and dogs, are very advanced animal souls who come into this plane of experience to be of service. Their mission may be to "wake up" their human companions or to provide special support for them in difficult circumstances.

As I mentioned in the Introduction, occasionally pets may even take on health challenges to send their humans a message or attempt to relieve their suffering or discomfort. Once people have overcome their own health problems in these cases, the pets may then need confirmation that their work has now been completed. When they understand that this is so, they're often able to release the symptoms of illness they've taken on, though they may need spiritual healing for themselves in order to fully recover.

Most of the time, in addition to the healing and explanation I've given them, the animals will also require reassurance from the person they were trying to help. This enables them to better understand that what I said is true and that the animal's healing services are no longer required. This touching story of Thomas and Casey is a great example.

CASEY

My chiropractor colleague called me one Saturday morning. She'd been working with Casey, a five-year-old black male Cocker Spaniel, off and on for some time, but that day, Casey was not doing well at all, so she requested my help. She was very concerned that he might be having heart problems or some inexplicable kind of illness and wanted me to talk with his dad, Thomas. She added that Thomas was at home with Casey and asked me to call him there.

When I did, I learned that Casey was moping around the house, following his dad, with his head hanging so low his ears were dragging on the carpet. As Thomas was telling me how Casey was behaving, I began to receive the pictures Casey was sending and feel his symptoms in my own body. I then translated to Thomas what I was seeing and feeling. By this time, his wife was also on the phone.

I told them, "Casey has a lot of nausea and can't stand the smell of food. His mouth is constantly dry. It feels like every bone in his body is hurting and he doesn't have the stamina to walk or do much. He's tired all the time and feels depressed and upset. And his head is pounding from a horrible headache."

As soon as I finished my description, the wife exclaimed, "You just described exactly what Thomas has been complaining about. All of Casey's feelings mimic his."

I immediately understood Casey. He was only mirroring the same problems Thomas was having! He adored Dad and, in his mind, he was trying to relieve him of his pains, so he took it upon himself to absorb some of his ills in the hope that his dad would start feeling better. This may sound illogical to skeptics, but our animals sometimes do believe it's their "job" to try to make us feel better, and they may even try to achieve this by taking on the same symptoms we have.

I explained this to Thomas and his wife and added, "Casey needs spiritual healing. This is not a physical illness but a spiritual one, and we need to heal him at that level first. The body will align later."

I went on to suggest, "Try offering him some chicken soup so that he can get some food into his system. Then you, Dad, take Casey to where it's quiet and put him on your lap. Tell him you need him to be healthy, well, and happy. This way, you too will start to feel a lot better. But I stress that you should not only *think* about this but also *verbalize* it so Casey will understand how important it is to *you* that he feels better again. Tell him, 'If you feel better, I'll feel better. I need to have you be happy and make me laugh. I love to see you when you play and have a good time. Please get well for me.'"

When Thomas agreed, I added, "If you can do this for three days in a row, Casey will certainly begin to understand his role in your life a lot better. In the meantime, I'll also be doing remote healing on Casey to help him get well again. Please call me on Monday and let me know how he's doing."

As a side note, I actually do keep a list of clients, both animal *and* human, to whom I send healing energy every night until I receive a call or an e-mail telling me they're once again doing fine.

Monday came and went, and I didn't hear from Thomas or his wife. I meant to call them but my days were full with other commitments. In the meantime, I continued to send remote healing to Casey. Eight days later, Thomas left a message on my answering machine telling me, "Casey was completely cured by the third day and he has had no more episodes of pain, or any illness whatsoever. In fact, he's been his old self again, playing in the backyard and wrestling with his brother. I want to thank you deeply. I believe in your work and I'm delighted that you were able to do, in three days, what my veterinarian couldn't do in months. Oh, and is it possible for you to do remote healing on me as well?"

As I listened to Thomas's message on the answering machine, I chuckled to myself. How easy it would be to expand my work to also do remote healing, especially for all the people belonging to the many pets I work with! But my Life Assignment is to care for animals, so I'll leave the healing of the two legged species to others.

———————

A few months ago, I had the opportunity to meet two mixed-breed dogs who once again brought to light the complete selflessness and dedication animals have toward their "people." Both dogs wanted to tell me about their humans and how it was their deep desire to be of service to them.

MAX AND MISTY

This was an introductory reading (a session at a public place, where I spend a short amount of time with each animal so I'm able to see as many as possible in the time allotted). Because these readings only last about 15 minutes, we usually address just one or two subjects or questions.

First, I talked with Cheryl and her dog, Misty. Cheryl, who was around 17, was tall, heavyset, and had acute acne on her forehead and cheeks. She wasn't happy with herself, which was even apparent in her clothing preferences. Misty, was a small hound dog with long ears, short legs and warts on her nose and under her left eye. She was unable to walk easily and wobbled her way toward me. Misty first told me, "I'm trying to help Mom with her weight and thyroid problems."

Cheryl confirmed that she'd been to numerous doctors and was under treatment for a thyroid condition. But Misty, although tested, had no thyroid problems, nor was she on any medication. Misty ate a low calorie diet daily, but she continued to gain weight. Nothing seemed to help.

Misty went on, "I need to be overweight like my mommy. This is the only way I know how to help her. When she looks at me, she'll know that I understand how she feels. She'll see that I can still give and receive love, no matter how I look on the outside, and so can she."

I was staggered at the depth of love and insight Misty displayed. However, my thoughts were soon interrupted by the timer, which signaled that the 15 minutes were up. I didn't have much more time to think about Misty before Cheryl's brother, Kevin, stepped up with his dog, Max.

Kevin was a tall, lean boy of about 15. Max was a very friendly mixed breed, looking something like a tall, slender Cairn Terrier. Max began by telling me, "Kevin and I are meant to be with each other. I love my friend so much that I'm trying to fix him. I think I've been very successful."

Unaware of what he was talking about, I asked Kevin to explain what Max meant by "fixing him." Kevin explained, "For most of my life, I've suffered from seizures. They happen in the most unusual circumstances and sometimes more than once a day. After extensive medical testing, the doctors still have no idea what's causing them. They gave me medication that controlled their severity but not their frequency. Then one day, without explanation, my seizures stopped altogether and Max started having them. I'm now free of both medication and seizures, while Max's episodes are growing more severe each day."

Max then added, "Please ask Kevin to be with me and sit next to me when I have the seizures. He's the only one who knows how it feels. I'm so proud I was able to help him." I relayed Max's request to Kevin and he was more than willing to provide loving support to his little friend.

Unfortunately, the "parents" never made a follow-up appointment with me, so I don't know if Max stopped having seizures or if Misty got her weight under control. I'd like to have had more time to help both pets understand, at a spiritual level, how much their help was appreciated, and reassure them it was no longer necessary. I wish I could have been able to say to Max and Misty, "Job well done. Now it's time for you to heal."

I'm always gratified whenever someone requests a follow-up; however, it's usually not appropriate for me to initiate that kind of contact on my own. Ordinarily, as an animal communicator, my role is to translate *only* when asked to do so. Occasionally, though, I'll even receive unsolicited information from an animal for whom nobody's asked me to translate. It then becomes my responsibility to share that information with the animal's human companion so they may act on it if they choose to do so.

———

Sometimes there's not a clear distinction between spiritual and emotional problems, but often, when emotions are involved, it's actually the spirit that needs healing. This is true when an animal misunderstands information he or she has received, or has had to live in distressing circumstances.

Lucy

I received a call from an employee at a store called Omar's Exotic Birds. Terri and Cindi had heard of me and wanted to hire me to talk to some of their birds who were having very specific behavioral problems. When I arrived I told them, "I have limited experience with birds but I'll do my best to translate their pictures for you."

The first bird they showed me was an eight-month-old female African Grey Parrot named Lucy. Lucy was almost completely bald. She'd plucked out nearly every single feather except for those on her neck and head which she obviously couldn't reach. All that remained was some fuzz scattered over her little body. Terri told me, "Lucy was in perfect condition before recently being sold to a couple. They returned her two weeks ago in this sorry condition. I want to know what happened."

Right away, Lucy told me, "The people in the home where I went to live spoke to me in a language I didn't understand." Lucy mimicked to me the sounds of their voices, so I asked Terri, "Did the buyers speak Spanish?"

She replied, "Not in the store, but they had accents similar to Desi in the *I Love Lucy* show. I don't know what language they spoke at home."

Lucy then told me, "I hated that. It made me feel as if they had no respect for me. And the house was chaos. There were lots of children coming and going all the time, and loud noises, banging doors, screaming and loud barking."

I asked Terri, "Do you know if they have dogs?"

"Yes, they do!" she replied.

Lucy was emphatic. "I do *not* like dogs, and in particular I do *not* like barking dogs. They make me very nervous. I'm stressed out and it'll take me a long time to be the way I used to be. I also don't like it when those people come to the store to visit me. I'd rather they didn't come to see me anymore. I never want to go back to their house. I feel safer here for now and I need to grow some new feathers before anyone else would even want me. Can you ask if it would be possible for me to live in a quieter home, one with no dogs, and no loud children? I'd be happy there."

Terri confirmed, "Yes, the owner does come and visit with Lucy and talks to her in his "Desi Arnaz" voice. When he does, Lucy goes to the far back of her cage and just trembles continuously. She seems to have a particular dislike for this man.

When I asked Lucy about this, she replied, "The dogs are always near him." She then showed me a picture of him taking the dogs out for a walk and added, "I know if he's here, the dogs can't be far behind."

While we were talking, Terri was surprised to see that Lucy, who was perched on a branch, was staring into my eyes and wasn't shaking or trying to get away. Terri said, "This is as calm as Lucy has been in the entire two weeks since the couple returned her."

I mentioned to Terri and Cindi, "You know, animals need to know about their future and Lucy is terrified of going back to that home."

Terri said, "Well, you can tell her that she is definitely *not* going back to that house!" When I relayed that to Lucy, she became noticeably more relaxed.

A few months later, I revisited the store and was told that Lucy, now renamed Angel, had found a good home without dogs, and she was happily growing back all of her feathers. She'd recently been brought back to the store for a visit and her spirit, attitude, demeanor and plumage were all back in full swing. How little it took to make this bird happy! Because of the special care and concern shown by these two women, Lucy now has a happy and healthy future ahead of her.

―――――――

The next story is even more remarkable. It touched Terri and Cindi, but I think it touched me most of all. I was humbled at the candor of the exotic birds and glad to be able to provide some help for their future. These two pets were able to explain their life experiences and feelings in pictures, something I won't soon forget. It's also very important to note that spiritual healing can happen solely by taking the time to listen to what our animals have to say. This is a perfect example.

TERRY AND RHETT

This time when I visited the pet store, Terri and Cindi brought out Terry, another African Grey Parrot. This one was a male, about four years old. They knew where Terry had previously lived and were concerned with the bird's emotional well-being. Since they didn't want me to have any preconceived ideas, they didn't fill me in on his past. Instead, Cindi asked a few general questions. She said, "We want to know if Terry can talk about his home and whether he feels his previous owner was a happy man."

Terry told me, "In the last days, all I can remember is neglect. My food dish was usually full, but only with the shells of seeds I'd already eaten. My water was muddy, and the bottom of my cage was dirty. Something was very wrong in our home. It felt like sadness combined with illness."

I didn't understand this last statement very well, and sensing his sorrow, I didn't pursue the subject. Terry went on, "I've been so sad thinking about the last few days." He then physically turned and faced away from me while perched on his stand and said dejectedly, "I don't feel good talking about it anymore."

When I explained to Cindi what Terry had said, she was visibly shaken. She then went to look for Rhett, a beautiful red and blue Macaw, who'd come from the same home. He didn't want to perch, so Cindi held him on her arm. She told me that both birds belonged to the same household and that since Terry no longer wanted to talk, maybe Rhett, the Macaw, would. Rhett told me, "I didn't see it happen but I know about it."

When I asked Rhett what he was talking about, I heard Terry say, "My dad's gone. He committed suicide."

Too afraid of being wrong, I didn't convey that to Cindi yet. Instead, I allowed her to ask Rhett a question. "I'd like to know if they want to go back home."

Both birds answered at the same time. "Where are we supposed to go? There *is* no more home for us to go back to!"

I translated this exactly as it came, and then to verify what they were saying, I told Cindi, "I heard from Terry that his dad committed suicide and they both know they can't go back."

Cindi started to cry. She didn't tell me, but I had the feeling she knew the man well. Rhett took the opportunity to ask Cindi, "Will you take me home with you?"

Rhett had become really attached to Cindi and talked as if she were already his mom. Terry said, "I'll consider a new family too, but I'm concerned because it'll take me a long time to adjust to that change. I really loved my dad." I let both birds know they would soon have new homes. They told me their preferences and I was able to translate this important information to Cindi.

When I left the pet store, both Terri and Cindi were visibly shaken and in tears. They told me the bird's previous owner was a friend of theirs who had, indeed, committed suicide. They were very curious about what the birds did or didn't know. That was why they called me but intentionally didn't share any information with me before the session.

Because they were so astonished at the accurate information the birds were able to provide, Cindi and Terri later decided they wanted to find out more about animal communication, and attended one of my workshops.

When I went back to visit with them at the store, I learned that Terry, the African Grey, had been placed right away with a nice man who fell in love with him the moment he saw Terry. They were doing very well together. Rhett, being a little more selective, was placed with a woman who adored him, and he was able to reciprocate the feeling. Both birds were happy to have homes and families again!

This one-time session was a magnificent healer for these exotic birds. Their spirits were uplifted once they knew there were loving people who cared about them and with whom they could share their lives again.

Remote / Absent Healing

The first story about Tom and Casey touched on the idea of remote or absent healing. This is a form of healing you may also find particularly helpful to use yourself, especially when there are no other options, or you're too far away from a person or pet to help in other ways.

Sending absent healing is a way to be active, to be aware, and to be doing something instead of waiting on the sidelines, crying or feeling helpless. The healing energy the Universe sends through you will always benefit the other person or pet to whom you send it. The benefits will help in whatever way is for their highest good, whether you actually see a healing or not. For another example of remote healing, refer to Peanut's story in Chapter 4. An entire chapter on remote and absent healing will also be included in my next book, *For Pet's Sake, DO SOMETHING!*

CHAPTER 8

PETS WITH UNIQUE CONDITIONS

W hat if something seems "just not quite right" with your pet but you can't identify exactly what it is? You've taken him or her to the vet regularly for checkups, and your pet seems to be essentially in good health. You've provided basic training in obedience, and maybe even advanced training such as good citizenship or agility classes. You've even hired a pet behavior specialist or home trainer, and yet your pet still seems to have difficulty adapting to daily living or worse yet, acts in curiously strange ways.

A lot of people simply say, "My dog is stupid," or "He can't be trained," or "I give up."

But my experience tells me that we sometimes have to look beyond the usually accepted reasons, and when we do, we may discover that some of our pets are dealing with some very uncommon problems.

Since I can freely move into animal bodies to "see" and "feel" what they're experiencing, I'm able to understand some physical irregularities and mental frustrations that you as an owner, or even an accomplished veterinarian, might not be able to detect.

This chapter includes several very unique cases where the pets needed either the help of a professional or a special kind of empathy. In the first case, the pet decided to resolve his problems in a manner of his own choosing, while in each of the other cases, my conversations with the pets confirmed either their need for advanced professional care or simply a need for continued love and understanding.

GWYNNE

It was such a treat to hear Marilee's voice on the phone again, but the consultation was not to be a joyful one. We'd consulted before about her cat and her other three dogs, but this time she needed to talk about her one-year-old dog named Gwynne, who'd been hit by a truck and subsequently died under unusual circumstances.

Since I'm able to receive information from pets who are now in the spiritual realm, Marilee wanted to know what Gwynne had to say.

Gwynne was a very free spirit who only wanted to have fun no matter what the consequences, much like a child who only wants to play and constantly ignores his school work.

He told me his purpose was to show his family that each animal is unique, and as much as pets love to do things that make us happy, they aren't always going to do what their "parents" expect of them. They have distinct personalities which their humans need to accept and respect.

He also said to tell his mom that she hadn't made a mistake by bringing him from Wales to the United States, though he did miss the open fields and the smell of his original home.

For the first time in my career, I hardly knew how to express what was coming into my mind. I remember stumbling over my words and saying something like, "Marilee, you're not going to believe me when I say this, but Gwynne wanted to go. He couldn't take it any longer. Actually, there's only one word that comes to mind now." Then we both said it at the same time, "Suicide!"

"Yes, Marilee, suicide," I repeated.

Marilee couldn't continue to talk that day. She was so crushed that I'd translated the answer which she already felt in her heart, but hoped wasn't true. Consequently, I didn't know the whole story until a few months later when she recounted it for me during an in-person visit.

Marilee and Steve had gone on their dream vacation to Wales. They'd been riding horses as a tourist pastime when they noticed the owners of the farm had Border Collie puppies for sale. Out of a large litter there were only two left. Marilee always loved the way a Border Collie worked on a farm and how intelligent they were about communicating with other animals, always showing them what they should be doing.

She instantly fell in love with one of the puppies and pleaded with Steve to let her bring him home. After all, Marilee herself was of Welsh descent and the puppy seemed the logical companion for her and her daughter, Nora. Reluctantly, Steve gave in to her request and the puppy was flown to Massachusetts.

Almost immediately, they noticed that Gwynne wasn't happy. He was a recluse; preferring solitude to the company of the family's other three dogs. Soon, he even started eating separately from the rest of the group. He often slept by himself and wasn't involved in any games or pack activities. He seemed to be lonely, unhappy and possibly homesick.

Dad took him hiking, hunting, to the beach, and for long walks, but nothing helped lift him out of his sadness. He was always wandering off by himself acting as if he wanted to be an only dog. His nickname became Billy No-mates.

By the time he was a year old, he began to escape from an enclosed patio. Steve tried to remedy the situation by installing chicken wire, but Gwynne promptly chewed through that. Then Steve made a chain link fence around the patio but that didn't deter him either. They often found him sitting by the front door after a long day of being by himself on the extensive grounds surrounding the home. Finally they enclosed the patio, but Gwynne always fought, chewed and scratched his way out.

He'd gone through regular obedience classes and knew all the commands, but he chose to ignore them so often that at one time they thought he might be deaf.

The family decided that Gwynne, who'd been born of working farm parents and raised in the green belts of the countryside, needed some kind of work to do, so they signed him up for agility classes.

While attending class, he'd do everything possible to ignore the commands. He'd turn around and give his back to the other dogs who were already performing in the ring and he completely ignored basic commands which he knew. On one occasion he was being led to jump through a hole in a tire. As soon as he got close to the tire he veered to the left. Nora, the daughter who was training him, decided to have him try it again and this time he veered to the right. The third time he ran all the way up to the tire and then promptly lifted his leg and peed all over it.

Needless to say, it created chaos with all the other dogs who were training that day because none of them would jump the tire after that show of rebellion. It didn't come as any surprise to Marilee and Nora that Gwynne was kicked out of class for the remainder of the day and asked not to come back.

Marilee and Steve were at the end of their rope. They didn't know what to do, but they knew their dog was very unhappy. One fine spring day, Steve took all the dogs out to a 20-acre pasture surrounding his land for a good exercise run. Everything seemed to be just fine, when all of a sudden Gwynne started to run as if he knew where to go. No calls, whistles or demands from Steve would make him turn around.

It was over in less than a minute. A huge truck hit him head-on and Gwynne lay still on the road. Fortunately, the man driving worked as a technician for a local veterinarian, so he rushed Gwynne and Steve to the hospital. The technician's wife went to get Marilee at home and rode to the hospital with her and Nora.

In the waiting room, Marilee and Nora, who were both trained in remote healing, were sending Gwynne healing light, telling him that he'd be well again and be able to live a happy life. In a short while, after the vet had had enough time to completely check Gwynne's condition, she came to talk with the family.

She told them Gwynne appeared to be fine and only had a bruised shoulder. She'd clean him up and he'd be ready to go home immediately. She'd barely spoken the words when an assistant came into the office and asked the vet to come out. Minutes later when she returned, she had to tell the family that Gwynne had suffered a massive heart attack and died.

Marilee knew right then and there that the minute she stopped sending him the healing white light, he disconnected enough from her to make a swift exit, almost as if he was saying, "No, thank you, Mom, I'd rather not stay. I'm not happy."

Sometimes our pets don't want any special help from us and they choose to resolve their problems in their own way. Marilee knew in her heart, as most intuitives do, that this had not been an accident, but that Gwynne had made his choice. She had only come to me to receive validation of what she, herself, had already felt. Although her heart will always grieve for her Gwynne, what I was able to tell her was exactly the information she needed in order to have her own intuitive feelings confirmed.

B.O.B.

Sarah assists the Golden Retriever Rescue Association by caring for foster dogs until the association can find permanent homes for them. She called me about a year ago for help with one of her rescue dogs who had trouble being placed in any home because of his unusual behavior.

B.O.B actually stands for Big Old Boy, but we'll just call him Bob. When I first met him, he was a ten-year-old male Golden Retriever, with a sweet face and a beautiful coat of soft golden fur. He'd been found walking the streets of Southern California and after a short stay at an animal shelter, the Golden Retriever Rescue Association found a new home for him. But it didn't last long. Each time they tried another home, Bob had problems adapting to his new surroundings and would have panic attacks any time, day and night.

When these attacks occurred, Bob was usually sleeping or lying down. He'd be startled by them and start to bark, pant and basically ignore all commands or attempts to settle him down. When he had continuous panic attacks during the night, no one was able to sleep and someone would have to spend most of the night awake with him until the episodes subsided. Even though he'd been returned more than once, the rescue group was still willing to try to find a way to help him, and each time Sarah took him back as a foster dog. A friend of Sarah's, who was already one of my clients, suggested she bring him to see me.

When Bob visited with me, he was eager to explain everything he could from his point of view. He told me in a matter of fact way that he heard "voices" in his sleep. He'd usually wake up from horrible night-mares (acting anxious as Sarah put it) and continue to "hear" the voices. He tried to get away from them (by pacing around) while getting more upset at the fact he couldn't get the voices to subside (observed as pant-ing). At one point in our conversation, Bob told me he could even see things flying at him, trying to hit him. When I translated this piece of information, Sarah told me that often Bob would act as if whoever was next to him didn't even exist. It was as if he was in another world.

When I asked Bob if he could show me how it looked in his mind's eye, he sent me a disturbing picture. I can only describe it as looking some-thing like what I've seen on television when addicts go through withdrawal symptoms when they stop using drugs. But Bob wasn't being medicated at that time. My only conclusion was to tell Sarah that it "felt" as if Bob was schizophrenic. I recommended he be seen by a vet right away. Possibly some anti-anxiety medication would help him, but in any event, he needed a professional evaluation in light of this new information.

Sarah, with the help of the rescue group, did much more than that. She made multiple trips with Bob to a veterinarian, an hour's drive away, who specialized in behavioral problems. He put Bob on three drugs: Amitriptyline (an anti-depressant), Buspirone (to reduce anxiety) and Diazepam (to relieve symptoms of anxiety, agitation and hallucinations). He prescribed Ambien (a sleep aid) to help with sleep if the other medi-cations weren't sufficient.

In addition, he also started Bob on a special training program designed to help him better respond to the person who was with him whenever he had an attack. Sarah was to use a Gentle Leader harness which helped to turn Bob's face toward her so that he could pay better attention to commands. She faithfully practiced leadership exercises with him to show him that she was the leader and must *always* be first, and he was subordinate and was *always* to follow. She went through the door first, ate first, and gave a command for Bob to follow first before he received a reward.

Under Sarah's guidance, Bob also practiced directed relaxation exercises where he learned to remain on a sit, stay, or down for progressively longer periods of time until he was released. And at all times, the nothing-is-free rule applied. This meant that Bob *always* had to respond to a command before receiving any of his meals or treats. All of these exercises were essential to be able to help Bob get out of his "red zone" when the attacks set in.

Bob did very well with only a few relapses. When I saw him a year later for a follow up visit, he told me he no longer had night "visitors." He might still be startled if someone came up to him while he was sleeping; however, now he *was* able to recognize that he'd just awakened, and he understood that this was a real person he was seeing, not someone in his dreams.

Sarah confirmed that he only woke up occasionally at night but went back to sleep once she put his Gentle Leader harness on him.

About a year after that visit, he subsequently ate a non-food item which needed to be surgically removed. It wasn't anything that came from within his home and no one knows how he found it, unless possibly it had been tossed over the fence into the yard.

He came through the operation successfully, though his vet made it clear the next few days might be touch-and-go. Sarah had the opportunity to spend a little time with him after surgery and she also enjoyed a loving visit with him the following day. But sadly, Bob made his transition that night after everyone from the veterinary clinic had gone home.

Thanks to Sarah, who'd taken him permanently into her own home, and was willing to go many extra miles for him, even literally, he'd been enjoying the happiest time in his life since his recovery from his earlier difficulties. She'd worked very diligently with him every day to re-condition him by keeping the rules simple and consistent. Once he received the help he needed, he became an even more loving and wonderful companion — one who will be deeply missed.

The next time you think a dog is beyond help, remember Bob's experience. Know that with the right kind of communication, followed by proper training and treatment, heartwarming results *can* be achieved.

JESSICA

When a friend visited her home and saw first hand how Nancy's dog, Jessica, was acting, her friend referred her to me. Nancy sent me a hand written letter requesting a consultation and she included a picture of her pet. Even though Jessica, part Labrador and part German Shepherd, was already 11 years old, Nancy still wanted to understand her better.

The picture was interesting and I thought for a minute that Jessica was smiling because her mouth was a little parted, but something in her facial expression made me doubt that it was indeed a smile.

Nancy wanted to find out why Jessica was mad at her. This, of course, didn't strike me as strange in the least. All of us who live with animals know that, at one time or another, they'll express their feelings about something "we must've done." They may simply ignore us or they may leave us some unwelcome gifts around the house, whether that be a mess, or our new socks or shoes chewed to pieces. Whatever the case, I know that sometimes our animals do get angry.

Nancy's other questions were about the time before Jessica came to live with her. Like many other clients who've adopted an older pet, she wanted to find out if anything had happened to Jessica when she was living with her previous owners. Had she been abused or lacked food or shelter? None of these concerns raised any flags for me because they're very common among all "parents" of adopted animals.

On the day of our appointment, I sat down to connect with Jessica. As I always do first, once I felt she was ready to receive my pictures, I asked her if there was anything she wanted to talk about before I began asking questions.

It was a strange situation because Jessica didn't want to engage with me at all. She just listened to me, but I knew and felt that she wasn't even trying to send me any pictures or information. I tried for several minutes, and when nothing happened, I started to send her the questions Nancy wrote for me, one at a time. Still nothing. This was most unusual. "I always get something," I thought. I then decided to just move into her body and almost "become" her to see what, if anything, I could gather.

What I found was so new to me that I wrote my notes so that they were speaking directly from me to Nancy, instead of from Jessica to Nancy. I had to speak for Jessica because she couldn't communicate the way other animals did. This is what I wrote:

"Nancy, you've done a remarkable job with Jessica. I doubt there would have been many people who had the love and dedication to make it work. It's because of your love that Jessica is able to cope with the world around her at all.

"I'm not a vet and can't give you a diagnosis, but it feels as if Jessica is suffering from a kind of neurological disorder that affects the functioning of her brain. If she were a human, I'd venture to call this autism because she seems to manifest many of the same problems: difficulty communicating, not able to interact socially, and not able to engage well in play activities.

"It's hard for her to listen and respond in a calm manner. She's constantly on edge and responds in the only way she knows how, by having a fit or a temper tantrum. In her case, she starts to bark and growl for no apparent reason as if the world is against her. Any change in routine is enough to cause her to be stressed out to the max. Most of the time, when she's around people, no matter how familiar they are to her, it's enough to put her in the "red zone." It's very hard for Jessica to be touched, and even harder for her to accept the touch of a stranger.

"Please don't think your love is not enough for her. In fact, it's the only thing that's kept her going all these years."

I read the above to Nancy at our scheduled time. She said what I expressed made so much sense that now everything just fell into place. Nancy had the opportunity to be around autistic children and immediately she could see the similarity. She mentioned that Jessica looks angry all the time, that she can't touch her for very long at a time, or even give her a hug without receiving a growl in return.

Nancy also said that whenever she has company, Jessica constantly barks and growls, to such an extent that not one of her friends will come over to the house any more. Also, if Jessica has to be taken to the vet for any kind of procedure, she has to be sedated because otherwise she goes absolutely crazy. The vet told her that Jessica was schizophrenic.

This was such a validation for me because I was only working from a photograph and didn't have the animal in front of me. It made me realize that mental diseases also plague the animal kingdom, though very often, we're not even aware of them.

Nancy was relieved to know that she hadn't done anything wrong. In fact, she said she knows that anybody else would have given up on Jessica a long time ago. It was through her patience and determination that Jessica had grown old in a home where she felt safe and loved.

TINY

About twice a year I attend a fair at a local adult school in my area called The Learning Light Foundation where I'm their resident animal communicator. I also hold frequent classes for people who're interested in communicating with their animals.

Pat was one of my students who was in her late 60s. She'd been a breeder of miniature Maltese dogs for as long as she could remember. A couple of years ago, she had three females left at home and no more males. She decided to buy a breeding stud from another breeder friend to do what she called "her last breeding batch before retiring." She had two very good friends who wanted dogs from her line. They're much sought after since they're tiny, weighing in at less than five pounds at maturity.

Pat was excited to know I was going to be having an all day consultation at the Learning Light Foundation and decided to make the two hour trip from the mountains of Big Bear to the valley of Anaheim just to bring her dogs in to "talk" with me about their issues.

I spoke with the girls first and they all seemed well-adjusted with very few complaints. They were all eager to talk and to ask for their special wishes, like more treats, a different bed or a new toy.

Tiny, the four-year-old male, came to see me last. I had to ask Pat twice if indeed this was a male because he kept insisting that he loved to have his hair pulled up in a knot to look more "beautiful." He sent me mental pictures of how picky he was at dinner time, but it had nothing to do with his choice of food. He wanted me to see his manners and the way he was eating. Not picky I thought, more like prissy.

I was a bit confused because it looked and felt as if I were talking with a girl not a boy. Finally he said, "I know Mom got me to make babies, but I can't, I just can't. I don't like the girls, especially when they're in heat. They look for me all over the house and I try to hide from them. I don't want to be next to them. Please tell Mom I feel like another girl!"

Pat's jaw couldn't have dropped any lower. "*That's* why he's never interested in the girls," she said out loud. "He always hides under the bed or under the sofa when one of them is in season and I couldn't figure out why. We've been trying for the past three years to get any of these girls pregnant, but he just didn't perform. The poor dear, please tell him I understand and will never put him in that situation again. I'd given up on him ever fathering a litter anyway, but it's so great to have a validation. Thank you."

Yes, there are gay and transgender animals in this world! Animals are open-minded about sexual expression and, although most animals mate male-female, there are those who prefer same sex relationships or friendships.

Homosexual behavior occurs in more than 450 different animal species worldwide, and is found in every major geographical region and every major animal group, according to biologist Bruce Bagemihl. His book, *Biological Exuberance: Animal Homosexuality and Natural Diversity,* provides a detailed account of homosexual behavior in a wide variety of species. And there's more to this than the odd fling. Some birds and mammals appear to form lifelong gay relationships. Gay parenting has also been observed.

In 1992, the Rotterdam Zoo in the Netherlands reported that two male flamingos came together and bred a flamingo chick. Apparently, the two had been trying to steal eggs from females to hatch for themselves, so zoo officials finally provided them with a fertilized egg of their own and they've faithfully raised the youngster as any good parents would.

I'm not surprised by this. Animals are true to themselves. While humans worry about the social impact and acceptability of homosexuality, animals simply exhibit behaviors that come naturally to them. Our animals know and trust themselves!

––––––––––

The little dog in this next story encountered her own unique problem that required a special kind of understanding when she gave birth to her first litter of puppies.

DUNG-GU

I received an e-mail from a TV producer in Korea who wanted me to do a consultation for one of their television programs. She sent me some information about a two-year-old female Shih-Tzu named Dung-Gu who'd just given birth to two puppies but wouldn't nurse them.

"The owners don't know what to do," wrote the producer. "Dung-Gu not only doesn't love her babies, she seems to hate them. If they put them next to her, she tries to bite them. She has a little bit of milk but isn't allowing them to feed from her so the family has been bottle feeding the puppies for two weeks."

When I started my conversation with Dung-Gu, she was very forthcoming. She told me, "These puppies just don't smell right. Surely they aren't mine." I asked her if she knew she was pregnant and she said, "Of course I knew!" But then she added, "All I know is that I'm not pregnant anymore." This response surprised me because I hadn't been given any other details before I started to talk with her.

When I asked her mom about this, she told me Dung-Gu had not been able to deliver the puppies normally. Because she was so tiny, the vet had suggested a cesarean delivery. I told her right away that Dung-Gu said the puppies didn't smell right and suggested that maybe the vet had cleaned the babies too well before allowing her to smell them and do some of the cleaning herself.

Because Dung-Gu wasn't able to deliver her babies naturally, she didn't experience seeing and smelling them so that she could know, by instinct, that they belonged to her. In effect, she went to sleep pregnant and woke up as a mother with cleaned up puppies whom she didn't recognize as being hers. It wasn't a smooth transition for her.

The hormonal, audio, visual and scent stimulation, all of which occur prior to, during and after birth, were not there to *bond* the mother dog to her puppies. Perhaps if someone had taken the towels from the delivery room which were used to rub and stimulate them after they were removed from her uterus, and then placed the mother and her puppies on these same towels, she would have had some stimuli. But because she didn't, their characteristics had not been imprinted on her. They were "too clean" and therefore she wasn't able to recognize their scent.

There were two other problems that also needed to be addressed. Dung-Gu knew that she'd been pregnant and therefore should have puppies to take care of. To remedy this, she began to treat her stuffed toys as if *they* were her babies. When her toys were taken away from her, she acted exactly as a distressed mother would, as if her actual babies had been taken away.

And while Dung-Gu felt that the new puppies were not really "hers," to make matters worse, she was beginning to associate them with pain. When I asked her why, she sent me a picture of a man's hand holding and stretching her. She was already curled up in pain, and when he tried to stretch her out, it made it even worse. She was blaming this person for making her hurt more and wouldn't be able to forgive or forget very soon.

Dung-Gu's mom validated this when she told me that her husband had tried to encourage Dung-Gu to feed her babies by uncurling her and holding her in place.

I gave Dung-Gu an explanation telling her that her puppies really needed her and her humans wouldn't cause her any more pain. She was reluctant to listen to me and said she needed some time and patience from her humans.

Now, the interesting thing about this consultation is that it was being done over the Internet, with a Webcam, while at the same time it was being filmed for Korean TV. I knew I'd be talking to Dung-Gu's mom, but what I didn't know was that the producers had all of Dung-Gu's family as well as her attending veterinarian in the studio also.

It was only near the end of the consultation that the producers told me there was someone else who wanted to speak to me. It was the veterinarian who'd attended Dung-Gu. At first, I was concerned that he might have taken my comment about the puppies being too clean in the wrong way, but he was only concerned about helping the dog and felt her predicament was partly his responsibility. He told me how stressed out she was and asked my opinion about giving her some mild tranquilizers until she was reassured the babies didn't pose a threat to her well being. As it turned out, Dung-Gu had been so traumatized that a mild anti-anxiety medication in very low doses proved to be very effective.

A few weeks later, I received a call telling me that Dung-Gu had finally accepted her puppies and was now nursing them. She also seemed to have forgiven her humans and had begun to accept petting and treats from them.

Bonding of mothers and children is just as important in the animal world as it is for human mothers and their babies. Neither the vet nor her "parents" would have guessed that a little female dog could suffer so much from not realizing that these new puppies were *her* offspring. Fortunately, with just a little talk, I was able to help her understand the situation so that she could accept her babies, and know that her toys were just toys and not real.

————

There is now an increased interest in the treatment of behavioral problems in pets, and it's becoming one of the hottest new topics in veterinary medicine. Veterinary schools are developing courses in animal behavior and providing similar continuing education courses for practicing veterinarians.

If you're experiencing problems with your pet, seek the help of a regular veterinarian first, and if necessary, ask for a referral to a veterinarian who specializes in behavioral problems. Don't be afraid to pursue several avenues of treatment. Your job is to keep track of every detail so that you can explain everything to the specialist, even your talk with a pet communicator if you've consulted one first.

If you're thinking about putting your dog or cat to sleep because of a behavioral problem, consider especially the case studies about Bob and Jessica. Remember that they were able to share a home with the people they love because those people loved them enough to find ways to make their lives easier, even if it meant finding the right kind of professional help.

Who knows, maybe it's *your* Life Assignment to provide a home for a pet who needs extra medical care, or some very special love and understanding.

CHAPTER 9

HELPING OTHER INTUITIVES

E ven as a professional in this field, I know it's not always easy to communicate with a pet, especially if it's your own. That's why I sometimes find myself helping other animal communicators, or intuitives, with their animals. It's not because they're unable to communicate. Instead, they simply may be too close to the situation to be objective.

Often, they realize their own conscious thoughts may be getting in the way of a clear communication with their pet because they think they already know what the answer will be. That's when they reach out to me as someone who can listen objectively, or because they want me to validate the information they themselves are getting. I may also ask questions they're unable or unwilling to ask, and their animals may speak more readily with me, much like children will sometimes say things to another grown-up, but not to their own parents.

The case studies in this chapter are about a professional intuitive, an animal communicator, and someone who experienced her intuitive gift for the first time later in life. Although it is a gift, these stories will demonstrate that it is not always an easy one to receive!

In the first case study, the client felt he already knew his pet's problem but just didn't know how to solve it. He discovered that there was much more to it than that.

AGAPE

For the better part of five years I'd been communicating with a beautiful Persian cat named Agape, who was now about 15 years old. His human companion, Shaun (the name has been changed to protect his privacy), is a professional intuitive who asked for my help with his beloved pet so that he could get a more objective and professional view.

Initially, Shaun contacted me because Agape was eating very little and had started urinating on the rug in his absence. His housemate at the time, Cindy, had moved in six months before with her tiny dog, Marlana. Shaun thought that Agape was upset because there was a dog on his turf, but during our talk, Agape communicated that he couldn't care less about an insignificant dog (Agape was larger than Marlana).

He was mainly upset that Shaun had gone away for three weeks without properly saying goodbye and explaining when he'd return. Agape thought Shaun was abandoning him. Of course, when I translated that, Shaun felt terrible since, indeed, he had rushed out the door when leaving for New York because he was running late. Shaun had tried to make amends, but nothing was working.

This is an excellent example of how even professional communicators can miss the point an animal wants to convey if they've already decided what the logical reason is for their pet's behavior.

Since Agape was always such a finicky eater, Shaun decided to ask me if I could translate any of Agape's food preferences during our first in-person meeting. To my question, Agape responded, "Well . . . I've been hearing a lot about cottage cheese lately, and I think I'd like to try it." Of course Shaun offered that to him immediately, but as usual, he took one good sniff, turned his back and walked away. Why, then, had he been so interested in trying cottage cheese?

Shaun told me that because of a medical condition, Cindy's dog, Marlana, had to take pills, and Cindy was constantly challenged to find ways to disguise them in appetizing food. She'd cover the white pills with cottage cheese, and stand in the kitchen reciting the mantra, "Oooh! Cottage cheese. You love cottage cheese! Mmm mmm."

Agape would stand by watching, no doubt wondering what treat he was being denied. But when he finally had the opportunity to try some, he discovered it was something he didn't even like.

This first consultation was very important because it was an indication of how Agape's personality would display itself in many of our future conversations. He was curious and always had a list of wants and complaints. He was also a stubborn cat who thought the world revolved around him.

Shaun had a good relationship with Agape, except when Agape got mad and expressed it by not using his litter box, preferring instead to use Shaun's bed or the bed belonging to a guest or housemate. That's when things got tricky.

After one such incident, when Shaun now had a different housemate, I received an e-mail from him expressing the thoughts, comments, and concerns which he wanted me to convey to his beloved friend.

This was Shaun's message to Agape:

> I totally love you and will never abandon you. I'd really appreciate it if, when you want more attention, you'd come to me and touch me so that I'll know. When you pee and poop on my beds, it really hurts and upsets me, and there are better, more constructive ways of getting my attention.
>
> I'd also appreciate it if you'd keep the earlier agreement you made through Monica that if you need to throw up, you do so only on the tile floors. I know you prefer a soft, warm surface, and the tile is cold and hard, but I'd really appreciate it, and you did promise.
>
> What can I give you that's healthy and good for you that you'd like to eat, and will actually eat if I serve it to you? Why do you throw up

so much? Do you have any health problems I should know about? How are you feeling in general?

I know that where your litter box is now isn't great for you because it's in a cramped area. I really appreciate your willingness to be flexible and use it there, since it upsets the others in the house to have it in the main bathroom. Is there anything you need to tell me about your box?

When I sleep out on the terrace, I have the windows open and sometimes a bird flies in. Since you've killed a couple of them, I don't allow you to be out there with me. I'm not rejecting you, only making sure that if a bird happens to fly in, it will be safe.

When I sleep in my bedroom, you're welcome to be with me, but I must close the door so that I don't bother my roommate and so that he doesn't wake me in the morning. I do open the door for you in the middle of the night in case you need to go out to use your litter box. Does this work for you?

Sometimes I need to go away on a trip. I'll always tell you in advance that I'm going and for how long. Please understand that I'm not abandoning you, that I love you and will always come back. I know it's hard for you to be without me during those times, and I miss you, too. Unfortunately, our neighbor who used to visit you has moved away.

Is there anything else that you like or dislike that you want me to know about?

During my early morning consultation with Agape, I discovered that he had many things he wanted to say. This was Agape's reply to Shaun:

My Dear, Dear Soul,

I have no doubt in my mind that your love for me is complete, as mine is for you. We have, in fact, gone through a lot together and we still have time to share more.

I hope you still feel, now more than ever, that I inspire you sometimes to say just the right thing to your clients and friends. (In fact, Shaun told me that Agape lies next to him when he's working.)

Love is such a grand feeling. And the fact that you "get it" makes me feel important, like I've been a catalyst for it.

But now let's talk about us and about other people.

There's no question that I'd be happier if only you and I shared our lives together. I've endured many other people, some good, some not so good. I hope my defiant sign last week is a turning point in our lives. To you it was a warning, to him it was a statement. (Agape was referring to the fact that he had soiled the beds. He was making a statement about the new housemate because he didn't like him.)

There have been what I consider small but determined efforts to undermine my superiority in this house. It all started when my litter box was moved to a much less desirable place. This made it much less pleasant to take care of one of my most essential needs. Then during the night, I, the master of this house, have been confined to one room. It's preposterous. I need to be able to go anywhere in the house at night. Who else is there but me to converse with your guides and spirit visitors? Do you think you're the only one who talks to them?

I was at the end of my rope and I sincerely apologize for having to do such a dirty deed. I felt left out and my feelings had been hurt. In your search for companionship, you tend to dismiss others who already love you, including me. I'm told it's a very human trait. Nevertheless, I can't cope that well with some of the changes, no matter how important you feel they are, or how determined others are to change your way of doing things.

How can I convince you that I need better access to the litter box? I need more room, more light, and pleasant smelling sand. I'm getting older, heavier, and yes, maybe crankier, but I don't think this is too much to ask.

Let's talk about food now. As you know, I'm very demanding and sometimes a little finicky about my food. I always like fresh food. I like to see the bowl full, and have the aroma flowing throughout the whole house. I also crave some wonderfully tasty morsels, but you consider them junk food. Granted they might not be the best of the food chain, but I LOVE THEM. At my age, it's my choice and my only delight. Is it too difficult for you to understand that I, too, have free choice? I'm not asking you to JUST feed me junk food, but a few times a day wouldn't be so bad.

Lately my stomach is giving me more trouble than usual. My digestion is very slow. Even when I take a nap after a big meal, I wake up still feeling stuffed. Occasionally I have soft stools depending on what I eat. Other than that I feel fine. I'm still pretty strong and able to jump up to my favorite places.

Now let's talk about the terrace. We've talked about this before and I've mentioned how much I love to be out there in the sunshine. But you've always given me excuses for not letting me be out there. First, it's because you want to leave the windows open and you're afraid I'll jump out. Now, you're worried about the birds! I guess after living together for this long I understand you, but do I like it? NO.

I'm sorry to hear that our neighbor lady has moved away. She was extremely nice and understanding. When you're gone, I feel empty. The hours don't go by as quickly as you said they would. When your roommate comes home, he's so tired he usually goes to his own room. He's not much company.

You do a great job communicating with me about when you're coming back from your trips. I understand the pictures you're sending me, and I can "hear" you when you aren't home. Do continue talking to me while you're away. I like to receive messages from you.

I'll be with you always, now and on the other side. Don't forget that real love is forever!

I told Shaun that Agape seemed a little frustrated that day. But I also said, "One thing's for sure, he's a great soul, one who loves you beyond the physical realm, and one who's made a covenant with you eons ago to always be together."

Although we had some additional consultations in between times, a year and some months later I received another e-mail from a worried Shaun. Agape was again messing up in the wrong places and Shaun asked me to remind him once again that he'd promised not to do that anymore.

Agape was also upset and this is what he said to me:

Let's talk about promises. Shaun promised me that he'd move my litter box back to the bathroom once the last roommate (who was allergic to cat litter) was out of the house. I distinctly remember him making that promise, but he hasn't kept it. Why then, would he expect me to keep mine?

Whoever comes into this house from now on should do so with the understanding that I was here first, that this was my home before it was theirs. The only thing I ask is to have a place to call my own for my litter box, where I can use it comfortably to do my business.

Shaun, who travels extensively, came home another time after a few days away to find Agape had had accidents all over the house, including vomiting in a few places. He wrote me again wanting to find out why. This was my answer to him after I'd consulted with Agape: "Agape is not very happy that you still don't get it. He says that he hasn't been feeling that good lately. Something on the inside is wrong and it has *nothing* to do with fur balls. He was upset that you were gone and it wasn't his intention to punish your roommate. Instead he wanted to send you this message: 'You're leaving me again? You're going away *now* when I don't feel good and need you the most?'"

I then added a message to Shaun from me: "I really feel you need to take him in to see his doctor. The vet might be able to find something. At least then you'll know what's going on and you can look at your available options."

I want to emphasize that Agape had made routine visits to the veterinary clinic *several* times both before and after our other conversations. The results were always normal and there was no reason to suspect any medical problems. That's why, even though I'd just suggested a trip to the veterinarian, I was surprised to find this e-mail from Shaun several days later.

Dear Friends,

Most of you know my cat, Agape. I just took him to the vet for an exam and learned that he's in the early stages of kidney failure. The doctor thought he has maybe six months to a year to live, in part because he's quite thin.

In my communications with him, he says he feels fine, and isn't planning to die yet. He's been receiving a great deal of healing energy, including every time I do a session, so maybe that changes the prognosis. We also recently had three sessions with a wonderful animal communicator/healer, and he's never been so open and clear.

Agape was 15 in April, and has been with me since he was seven months old. He's been part of my work, always at my side when I do sessions. He's said that he filters out energies coming at me so I can do my work more freely. I'm grateful for his gifts.

Please send him your loving energy.

Love,

Shaun

Shaun e-mailed me a couple of months later. In his heart, he knew that the time had come, and he was prepared to ease Agape's pain, but first, he wanted to let Agape talk with me to tell me about *his* feelings. For the first time, he asked me to find out what Agape had to say, rather than giving me a list of questions to ask him. This is what Agape wanted to convey to Shaun:

"We've been through a lot together and it's helped both of our spirits grow, learn and mature. If I've been 'difficult,' it was only because we had an agreement. I was the one who was always supposed to put your feet back on the ground, so to speak, and show you the other side of yourself. It's been a great journey.

"But I'm tired and the time has come to be very explicit with you, my friend. You need to let me go. I'm not able to continue on any longer. I love you friend!"

Satisfied with the information he'd received, Shaun took Agape to his vet who agreed the time had come to release him from his suffering. Holding him in his arms, Shaun said his last goodbye for now, knowing they'd meet again under new circumstances.

It seemed to me that Shaun and Agape had a very interesting relationship. I suppose it was their interaction and their individual understanding of what they were both in the physical realm together to learn that made their relationship so loving and difficult at the same time. Granted, Agape was a little bit stubborn, but it seemed that Shaun would often listen to him without following through. Shaun seemed to have an argument for almost everything Agape asked of him, and I pointed that out to him several times.

It's my hope that they've both realized that the lessons they were learning could have been made much easier if each one of them could have better understood things from the other's point of view.

I always tell my clients that, in order to change a behavior, they not only need to listen to what their animals are telling them, but they also need to meet them half way, or at least allow some changes to occur so their pets will know that they're indeed listening.

The next case study is about an animal communicator who sought my help when she was frustrated with the difficulty of communicating with her own pets.

Lucy

I received a letter from Auriella, accompanied by pictures of her animals. We set up a phone consultation for the following week.

When she called, she said we'd met before when she used to live close by. Auriella reminded me now that I'd visited her home on a Saturday a couple of years ago to talk to her female dog, Kelli, an Australian Shepherd. Since it's impossible for me to immediately remember all of the clients I speak with, at that moment the information didn't ring a bell. Auriella then refreshed my memory by sharing the specifics with me.

Her dog, Kelli, used to wake her every morning by jumping up on the bed and resting her body — all 60 pounds — on top of her. Auriella wanted me to tell Kelli that the pressure of her weight made it difficult for Mom to breathe. I'd suggested to Kelli that she lie beside her mom instead.

That Sunday morning, Kelli jumped up on the bed as usual, and for the first time she laid down *beside* her mom instead of on top of her. Auriella told me that in the two years that have elapsed since I made that suggestion, Kellie has always remembered exactly what she should do whenever she jumps up on the bed in the morning.

Auriella, herself, was now working as an animal communicator and using her gift to do healing energy work. She'd moved away from Southern California and had also welcomed Lucy, a Labrador Kelpie mix, into her home.

The family now lived in a somewhat rural area on a half acre. In the winter when Auriella originally brought Lucy home, few people walked by the house. Therefore, it didn't give her the opportunity to acclimate Lucy to people and animals going by.

When spring came, people started walking and bicycling past the property, with and without their dogs. Lucy would sprint down to the road and run circles around them, barking the whole time. On occasion, she'd even cross the road which, of course, was a very dangerous thing to do.

Since the beginning of spring, Auriella had been trying to communicate to Lucy, who was now a year old, that this was not acceptable behavior. Lucy, however, was not responding to the message. Remembering my previous success with Kelli, Auriella called to ask for my help.

When I tuned in to Lucy, she said, "I'm a little bored sometimes. I need a job that keeps me busy and moving around. I get excited when I see a stranger."

I could sense that, because Lucy had a lot of Kelpie in her, she was far too work-oriented and energetic for a house pet. Her instinct was to herd people, animals, bicycles, and anything else that was moving. However, she was easy to train like a Lab and had a heart of gold.

"Lucy doesn't understand the perimeters of your home very well," I told Auriella.

"Although I'm trying to tell her not to go out of her yard, it's a little bit difficult for me because I don't have a clear picture of your property's boundaries. I need to have you walk her on a leash all around your property telling her that this is her home and she's not supposed to go beyond an imaginary line. You need to speak out loud and talk to her as if she understands every word you say.

"She also talks about the neighbors having lots of interesting smells in their yard. Do they have children? She keeps sending me a smell almost like plastic, as if she gets plastic items from the neighbors. I can smell what she has in her mouth.

"And she's showing me a pair of boots on someone who comes to play with her. She follows those boots around with great delight. In general, Lucy's a very happy girl who loves her home and family life. She's at ease inside the house and can be at rest when she needs to."

As we were winding down our talk, Auriella gave me some validations. She confirmed that when she visits a friend who has cows, Lucy runs out in the open field and takes on the job of herding the cows in a circle. "She does the same thing to people," Auriella continued. "I do have a neighbor who has children and she's fascinated by their sneakers and brings them into our yard daily. The boots belong to the boy next door who comes in and plays with Lucy all the time. She loves it when he comes to visit."

The next day I received this e-mail:

Dr. Monica,

Thank you for the notes and wonderful communications with Lucy.

I took her for a walk around the perimeter of the property about an hour after our phone conversation. When we'd gone around one time, she sent me a picture of what she felt was the boundary of our home and she was correct.

Upon further reflection, I feel that the plastic smell that Lucy was sending to you was from things she was bringing home. The retrieving part of her Lab blood is strong and she has, since puppyhood, brought home objects that she finds. Most of the time it's some sort of plastic bottle or container.

Thank you again for everything and I'll keep you posted.

Warmly, Auriella

This particular case shows that even if you're an animal communicator like Auriella, you may be missing a piece of the puzzle when it comes to sending information to your own pet. Lucy needed to clearly be shown the boundaries of her home and understand that she must stay within them. Once she grasped that concept, she was then able to understand the message that she must stay in her own yard even when she sees people and other animals. We also concluded that Lucy needed a job and, soon afterwards, she was sent to a herding school for dogs so she could participate in an activity which she dearly loves.

After an article about my work was published in a major Southern California newspaper, I received a call from Michelle Lorne-McClure. She lived too far away to visit in person, so she asked for a phone consultation instead.

FAITH AND A HORSE

I remember our conversation very well. At first, Michelle wanted to ask me about a dog she'd rescued named Faith. Faith had been badly abused and couldn't trust anybody. After our session with Faith, Michelle then seemed to feel that she could safely talk to me about a confusing and disquieting event she had recently experienced.

She began slowly, trying to open up to someone she didn't know on the other end of the phone line. She'd never talked about this unique experience to anyone else before, and she was concerned about what I might think of her.

She told me she'd been fond of animals her entire life, but now in her 50s, she found that at times she could "almost" read their minds. She'd never paid much attention to this "knowing" before because it had always involved her own pets.

But a few weeks ago, in the stables at a horse show with a friend, she "heard" a horse complaining as clear as day. The horse, while being prepared for show, had become very agitated and reared back in his stall. Michelle mentally sent the horse the idea that if he did what the trainers were asking him to do, they'd stop giving him pain and he'd be OK.

As clear as a bell, she heard the horse respond, "I can't do it. I'm too afraid." She continued to send him a mental answer saying, "Yes, you can. You can do it. Calm down."

This "conversation" continued for a couple of minutes, but it wasn't until it was all over that Michelle realized that she was actually receiving information from an animal and communicating information back to him. This jolted her so much that she became uneasy and thought she might be going crazy. She didn't want to tell anybody — not her friend, not the trainer, not even her family.

We talked for a long time and I helped her understand that she has a gift, and this gift has consequences. She must act on the information she receives. Otherwise, the gift has no purpose. I explained that her mission is to tell the person who's caring for the animal what she believes to be true, and then let it go. She was not required to do anything else other than to give the information away freely in a spirit of love and service to others.

Our conversation was an eye-opening experience for Michelle, and shortly afterwards, she even ventured to say something about it to her grown daughter. Her daughter put her fears to rest by accepting what Michelle was telling her, while at the same time reassuring her that she wasn't crazy, but rather "enlightened" about the animals.

DENVER

Not long after our phone conversation about Faith and the horse, I set up a group consultation in her area and we had the opportunity to meet in person. That was also when I first met Denver, her four-year-old Chihuahua. Because Denver's story is so special, I'll let Michelle tell it in her own words. Here's what she wrote.

It isn't easy to put into words what I'm now attempting to do. Some things in my life are so cherished, that it's difficult for me to feel that anyone else could possibly feel the depth of what I've experienced. However, I've always loved the feeling when someone else's story has touched my heart — so I hope this will touch yours and not leave you where it found you.

I'll never be the same because of my experience with one tiny little guy. When I was going through an extremely difficult time in my life, a very close friend of mine invited me to go see a litter of Chihuahua puppies. My quick response was NO!

I already had four wonderful large dogs, and although dogs were the love of my life, I truly had no interest in a little Chihuahua. Big dogs were my protectors, my comforters, my companions, the best friends I'd ever experienced, but for some reason, the little ones had never won my heart.

I did end up going that evening, although I wasn't sure why. Yet, from the start of that experience there was nothing but joy. The breeder was a delightful person, the mama dog was a bundle of love, and then came the puppies. As we sat on the floor, the five-week-old babies were put in the middle of us. They just wagged their tails and wobbled around, quite oblivious to what was going on — except for one.

A long haired puppy, marked just like my Rottweiler, looked at me from about two feet away. He was actually headed in the other direction but he backed up all the way until he touched me and then never moved. He just leaned against me and looked up at me. Yes, I purchased that little boy that evening, all the time wondering what in the world I was doing. I came to realize very quickly, though, that the evening didn't happen by chance! A much higher Source knew exactly what I needed in my life and was supplying it.

No bigger than a "Beanie Baby," this little man's name became "Denver" and we became inseparable. I never went anywhere without him. I became known all over as "Denver's mom." I had no name of my own. Without realizing it at the time, he was always there for me and knew exactly how to lift my spirits.

He never took away the love I had for my big dogs. He was just bringing something to my life that I'd never experienced, that I never knew existed. I came to understand that he knew my every thought and knew just how to reach me.

Later our lives took on quite a change. Denver now had a Daddy in his life, and because Denver had the biggest heart in the entire world, he happily accepted this man. I believe it was a tremendous adjustment for my husband, marrying a woman with five dogs.

However, one of his first comments was that he'd always wanted a "whole bunch" of dogs. He'd also always longed for a dog of his own who'd be very close to him, one who'd lie on his legs whenever he'd sit down. Shortly after my husband made this statement, there was Denver, snuggled right down on his legs whenever he was sitting or lying down. It warmed my heart to see this!

Now Denver still went everywhere with me, or us, but gradually I began to see a change. Denver went with me when I picked him up and carried him out, but if I called him to go, he'd run and lean against my husband, as he'd done to me at our first meeting. Again, I was glad to see the love expressed to my husband, but honestly, I was beginning to wonder.

It became more and more frequent until one day, before I left the house, I told Denver that we'd never been without each other for five years and I wondered what was going on.

I spoke to him, but I didn't listen. I just left by myself, quite sad. I then began to think, to pray, to listen, to reach out for an answer.

The next time I asked Denver, I listened, and he answered . . . "Because he needs me now." I said, "Denver, I need you too," and he said, "You're OK now, you're strong, but he needs me." He looked at me with such sadness, feeling my sadness, I'm sure.

Two things took place then. First, I did realize that my husband had been struggling with some difficult situations. He was working through them, but it wasn't easy, and Denver knew this.

Second, not only did Denver know this, but he knew what to do about it, just as he did with me, and when I listened, he was able to tell me this. Although I felt strongly that I'd heard him, I began to doubt myself. Maybe that was just my own thoughts I was hearing.

I'd spoken with Dr. Monica shortly before this took place about a rescue dog we'd saved and now I decided to bring Denver to meet with her because Dr. Monica impressed me so very much, not just because of her ability, but because of her love, her insight — a very special gift that was deep within.

I didn't share with her what I felt Denver had said to me. I simply explained the situation and asked for her help. After meeting this four pound little man, she just said, with such love in her eyes, "Oh, he has the biggest heart!" Then she asked him why he didn't want to go out with me anymore.

Dr. Monica looked at me and said, "Denver says, because _he_ needs me now." The exact words Denver had already spoken to me. I _had_ heard him. As I remember, Dr. Monica's words were, "You heard him because your love reached out to him — don't doubt yourself." She made me realize we speak with our hearts — the language of love.

The ending to this story — the very best part — I went back to Denver and held him close and told him it was OK, even though there were tears. I understood and I was actually happy. He'd taught me a kind of love I'd never seen the likes of before. Denver instantly became happy himself — no more sad look. He was doing his job! When he knew that he had my support in what he was doing, he was the _happiest_ I've ever seen him. What a gift!

As you can see from Denver's story, he knew that his job was to give love and comfort to the person who needed him most at the time; to be a friend, confidant, and partner; to give hope and to be a reason to move forward.

This particular case study serves well to illustrate a number of things.

1) There's often a reason we're brought together with an animal, even when adopting one is the furthest from our minds. We may not understand why at the moment, but the Universe is always taking care of us, and Its reasons will usually become very clear to us in time.

2) We must allow our animals to do the work which is *their* Life Assignment, even though it may mean letting the animal spend more time with another person and less time with us.

3) Emotional healing can happen for both the human and the animal. Michelle no longer felt sadness because she now understood that when Denver wanted to stay home with his dad, he hadn't stopped loving her. She was touched and comforted by the fact that he wanted to serve a higher purpose. And Denver could now go happily about his work once he knew that Mom was no longer sad because she understood the importance of his mission.

4) We can all communicate with our animals if we will quietly listen with our hearts.

5) And finally, one of the most important lessons our animals are here to teach us is the lesson of unconditional love.

FAITH – A LATER CONVERSATION

Some time after the group consultation when I'd met Michelle and Denver in person, Michelle had another experience which confirmed for her that she did indeed have a gift for communicating with animals.

She sat down to have a heart-to-heart conversation with Faith as I'd taught her to do. She asked Faith why she couldn't be happy in a home where everybody loved her so much. Unexpectedly, Michelle "heard" Faith say, "Because you're people."

This startled her, not only because she knew she'd heard it, but because it wasn't an expression Michelle, herself, would use, and she didn't know what it meant. Undaunted, Michelle asked, "What do you mean?" Faith replied, "Because PEOPLE did this to me (*the abuse*). I can't trust people."

That was the day Michelle knew with certainty that she *was* speaking to, and receiving information from, animals. She's still learning today. Michelle took the first step in her Life Assignment by telling her family what she's able to do and by sharing her experiences with others who are willing to listen. She's living proof that even later in life a person can experience that special moment of "knowing" which gives them a new mission for the rest of their lives.

———————

While those who are discovering their gift for the first time benefit greatly by working with an experienced intuitive, the stories in this chapter have shown that there are times when even a professional intuitive or an accomplished animal communicator needs the help of another intuitive.

Sometimes our animals are more willing to "talk" about different things to different people, much the same way we choose which friend we're going to talk to about events in our lives. This is because some friends either listen differently or they understand things at different levels.

Just as you often consult with your doctor even if you think you know what's wrong, it's sometimes important to seek out the skills of another intuitive in order to help you resolve an issue, or to confirm the information you feel you've already received. Doing so helps you know that you're on the right track, and it's often the step that's needed to discover what your animals most want or need from you.

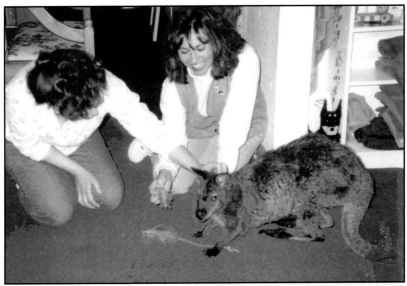

Above: Annie, the wallaby, able to stand on her own two legs following her final treatment by me and my chiropractor colleague. Right: Annie resting in her Mom's lap (see Chapter 4).

Golden Retriever Buddha and I talk about him getting tangled up in the white stool near the Jacuzzi (see Chapter 5).

Chloe, the goat, receives lots of TLC from her Mom, my chiropractor colleague and me, after her treatment (see Chapter 4).

Terry, the African Grey, and Rhett, the Macaw, in the pet store after their human committed suicide. They both went on to find loving, new homes (see Chapter 7).

Kody, the Siberian Husky,, who refused to jump into the car and just laid down in the snow on the trip to Alaska (see Chapter 6).

Zach, who demanded that his home and meals be "just so" (see Chapter 6).

Jessica, the 9-year-old Lab/Shepherd mix, who showed symptoms of "canine autism" (see Chapter 8).

Denver, the 4-year-old Chihuahua, who became his Daddy's favorite because "He needs me right now" (see Chapter 9).

Wolfie, the 15-year-old Golden Retriever, who was sad when his Mom died, and went to live with his "Granny" (see Chapter 13).

*Dachshunds Fritz and his sister Puggy (top row and lower left).
After crossing over, Puggy told Mom that she would soon
reincarnate along with a new friend (lower right) (see Chapter 14.)*

*Sarahorsie, the magnificent 16-hand mahogany bay and Pamela,
who discovered that they're soul mates (see Chapter15).*

Cyndi and her German Shepherd Gunner, who lived each day for her ... until the pain became too great (see Chapter 2).

Gwynne, the Welsh Border Collie, who missed his homeland so much that he became very depressed (see Chapter 8).

Left: Chance, the blind kitty; right: Froda, the new arrival in the home, about whom Chance complained. Froda was anemic and her body emitted an ammonia-like smell, which made Chance pull his fur out (see Chapter 12).

Troy, the deaf and almost blind Sheltie whose tail always drooped. Once he knew his humans saw him as an intelligent dog with disabilities, he improved and held his tail high (see Chapter 6).

Rosco, the 2-year-old miniature Dachshund and observant pet detective. Left: the wood chip pile where his friend Dakota sleeps; right: catching some well-deserved sleep (see Chapter 11).

Casey, who taught his mom so much about life, especially in his last few months, loved his afternoon "walks" in his stroller (see Chapter 18).

Cover photograph of me with my canine family (left to right) Chop-chop, a 14-year-old Shih-Tzu; Princess, a 12½-year-old Shih-Tzu and the love of his life; and my two 6-month-old Cocker Spaniel grandpuppies, Clyde and Bonnie.

CHAPTER 10

LOST PETS

O nly in rare instances do I become involved with lost pets, because, as an empathic being, it puts an enormous amount of pressure on me, both physically and emotionally. However, I feel deep compassion for people who've lost their animals and call me, hoping I can help locate them.

When I do accept this type of case, it helps if I'm called immediately after the disappearance, because the pets' descriptions are usually better when the change in their surroundings is still clear to them. But on occasion, I've been asked to help find pets who've been missing for weeks or even months.

It's very important for people to understand that it's impossible for me to pinpoint an exact location where an animal can be found. When pets are lost in the city, for instance, they can't tell me what street they're on. If pets are lost in the country, it's even more difficult for me to explain their whereabouts. What they *can* see and describe in pictures in these circumstances may be too general for my senses to interpret clearly. Also, when an animal is in distress, the communication often takes longer.

Nevertheless, I try to be very specific whenever the animal is offering clear information. After that, it's up to the "parents" to follow the clues their pet has provided. Sometimes there's a happy ending to the story, though not always. These are some of my case studies about lost pets.

FELIX

I've already mentioned that I prefer *not* to work with missing animals. There's so much sadness involved and it's hard to have to give unpleasant information to people about their pets. Often what I see, hear, or sense is not the same thing they're hoping to hear.

However, when Pam and Pat came to see me in person about their lost cat, I couldn't refuse. Pam works for a veterinarian I know and Pam's mom, Pat, is wheelchair-bound. The family's three cats are Pat's joy and responsibility.

Pam's cat, Annie, a consummate alley cat, has lived with Pam for years and was very used to her outdoor surroundings. Pat's two cats had been indoor pets most of their adult lives. It wasn't until Pat moved in with her daughter, Pam that the younger of her two cats, Felix, started venturing out into the back yard under the watchful eye of Annie.

The two of them would venture over into the neighbor's yard now and then, but would always come back home for their evening meal. That is, until the evening of July 7, when Felix didn't come home. By the time they came to see me, it was July 24 and they'd been out looking for him every single night.

At this visit, they were both visibly upset, but even though they lived in a semi-rural environment, they weren't yet ready to consider the thought that Felix might possibly have been injured or killed by a wild animal.

I reminded them that I have to rely heavily on what the lost pet is willing to share with me and what he or she is describing. In addition, this information is all from the animal's point of view, and that in itself can prove challenging.

When I connected with Felix, I found he was very shy. At first, I had a hard time communicating with him and trying to get him to trust me. When he did talk to me, the first thing he told me was that he'd been startled by some firecrackers or loud noises that came from the corner house. The sound he sent me was very clear and I told Pat it reminded me of those small explosives that look like tiny white pebbles which go off the moment they hit the ground. Pat told me there were two little boys next door and they, too, heard those noises because it had just been the 4th of July weekend.

Felix told me that when they were startled, Annie ran back over the fence to the house, but he got all turned around and went the other way. He was hiding where there was a lot of vegetation and he was down in a ditch where he couldn't be seen. For many days he stayed in hiding until his hunger got the better of him. He said he visits the home of an elderly woman who's been nice to him and puts food out for him when he comes into her backyard. Sometimes he stays and sleeps on her lawn chairs where it's very comfortable.

Pam and Pat left with renewed hope and a pledge to continue looking for Felix. But to everyone's disappointment, including mine, they returned the following week, this time with Andrew, Pat's son-in-law. He came in armed with paper and pencil, and started drawing the location of his home, the ditch around the area, the location of the highway, electrical wires and vegetation. He wanted me to specify where Felix could be found!

I almost panicked because although I've been asked to try to be more specific before, I'd never been given a map and asked to pinpoint a location. I worried that they didn't understand it's rare to be able to know *exactly* where the lost animal is located, based only on what I'm seeing from pictures the animal provides.

But again, I couldn't refuse Pat who was sitting in her wheelchair looking intently at me and keeping her hands folded in prayer. I felt the love this woman had for her companion and I felt the pain and emptiness in her heart. Yet, the chance of pinpointing the whereabouts of a lost or disoriented animal is difficult to say the least.

We started slowly zeroing in on this makeshift map. As Andrew was describing the area, my mind and heart were reaching for information coming in from Felix. Andrew asked, "Did he cross the ditch?"

Felix gave me the response of, "No, I didn't cross the ditch. I went to hide in a small tunnel."

"Where is he now?" Andrew asked.

Felix showed me what kind of plants or bushes he could see and I tried to describe them accurately, even though I didn't know much about horticulture. Then Felix talked about the patio and the elderly woman again. He said he could see the light at night, and I translated this data without knowing its significance.

Andrew stopped for a moment and looked at me. Trying to manage his surprise, he exclaimed, "I go out every night and shine a lantern up in the air. As I do this, I tell him to look at the light because this is where home is. You mean to tell me, he's actually hearing me and seeing the light?"

"Yes, Andrew," I replied, "he is, but he's too afraid to move. There's a huge empty field between the light and where he is. He's too afraid to leave the place where he feels somewhat safe."

Suddenly Andrew understood that Felix must be on the *other* side of the empty field and not directly behind their home. He put the map into his shirt pocket, sat back in his chair and told me they'd keep looking.

Pat and Pam then set out on a house-to-house search around the area Felix had helped me pinpoint on the map. The two women searched slowly by car on the other side of the big empty field, all the while calling out Felix's name. Andrew canvassed the street on foot.

He came to a home directly behind theirs (across the empty field) and knocked on the door. A woman in her 80s opened the door and smiled at him. He couldn't find the right words at first, but then he said slowly, "Hi, my name is Andrew and this might sound silly to you, ma'am, but have you seen a gray cat around here lately?"

"Yes, I have," she said. "Is he, by any chance, gray with green eyes, very skittish and wearing a blue collar?"

Andrew nodded, unable to utter a sound.

"He's been around for a couple of weeks now. He comes out in the evening to eat and sometimes I see him sleeping on the cushion on top of the patio chair. However, I haven't seen him recently, maybe for a couple of days," the friendly neighbor continued.

Andrew's mouth fell open. For a few seconds he still couldn't speak. Then he asked her if she'd mind repeating this information to his wife and mother-in-law. When she agreed, he ran out to the car to get them.

He showed the woman a picture of Felix and she immediately recognized him as her recent visitor. They all called and searched in vain, but Felix was nowhere to be found. They did, however, spend several hours talking about cats, about how intelligent they are, and about animal communication. The woman promised to call any time of the day or night if Felix returned.

Sadly, they never did find him. The next time they came to see me, Felix didn't send any more pictures. When pets are no longer sending pictures about being scared, in pain, or preoccupied with their whereabouts, then it's usually a good sign they've made their transition out of earthly experience and are free from any discomfort.

But it was hard not to keep wondering about him. Had he given up? Were we too late? Was he caught by a predator, causing him to make his transition before his family could locate him? There weren't any answers to those questions.

You may be wondering if possibly I can still find the answers to questions like those even after a pet is gone. It may or may not be possible. It all depends on what the pet wants to share.

After pets have passed on, it's best to wait a while until they've adjusted to their new spiritual surroundings before trying to communicate with them again. And once they've made their transition, they're often no longer interested in talking about their earthly experiences and instead want to talk only about their feelings of happiness, calmness, and the beauty around them.

Even though the family never saw Felix again, and it was probably too soon to communicate with him in spirit, finding his last known whereabouts was, in itself, their little miracle. They were at least comforted by the reassuring fact that they'd done all they possibly could to try to bring him home.

BABY LAWFORD

Debra e-mailed me with her request and a picture because she was feeling so desperate. Her rare and beautiful cat was missing and she was almost sure he'd been stolen. A Scottish Fold is indeed rare. The ears fold forward and down, showcasing the eyes and giving the face a well rounded look. In the picture she sent, I could see his thick white angora coat which made him look particularly regal. His bright blue eyes were looking straight into the camera.

"He's so beautiful," she assured me, "I just know anybody who saw him couldn't resist the temptation to take him home. You must find him for me. He never goes out. He doesn't know how to survive outside my home. I had people visiting last night and they must have left the door open. What's worse, I didn't even realize he was missing until this morning! I feel so ashamed for not paying better attention. Please tell me anything you can! I can't live with the uncertainty and I can't concentrate on work. Please, please tell me anything you can!"

Because I felt the intensity of her pain, I couldn't refuse. I knew I had to at least try to communicate with him to see what was happening and I had no problem finding and talking to Baby Lawford. He said, "I didn't think Mom cared about me anymore because she didn't seem to have time to take care of me. So I decided I needed to go out and have an adventure for a while. I thought she'd call me, but she didn't."

He then continued, "I heard the dogs barking and I got scared and ran across the street. I'm in front of a house, hiding under the bushes. I'm afraid to go back."

Debra confirmed that there were two dogs next door but couldn't believe Baby Lawford would actually cross the street. She agreed to go out looking for him and said she'd call me back. A day later, on Friday morning, she called saying he still hadn't come in, and she'd searched most of the night.

When I tuned in to talk with Baby Lawford, he told me he needed to stay in hiding because someone almost picked him up and he didn't want to go with her. "I can see Mom walking with a can in her hand," he said.

Debra agreed, "Yes, that's me. That's what I've been doing. I shake a can of his favorite treats."

I told Baby Lawford that he'd have to be the one to make the first attempt to go home. Mom would leave the door open for him first thing in the morning and he could come right in without being seen by the neighbor's dogs or by any people. I also told him she promised to play with him more, never ignore him when he wanted to be hugged, buy him special food, and be more attentive.

I emphasized that Mom was very, very sorry for not paying enough attention to him before he left, and reassured him this wouldn't happen again. I told him she was exhausted from looking for him and was begging him to come home so she could make amends. He seemed receptive and said he'd try.

The weekend came and went. I didn't hear from Debra until Tuesday's mail when I received a check along with a lovely note. It said:

> Baby Lawford came home Saturday morning at 6:00 A.M. when I opened the door to go look for him. He was very dirty and walked with a little limp, but today he's feeling much better. Thank you so much.
> Debra

Often when I receive calls to find lost cats, they're not actually lost but have simply decided to leave home on their own. Just as Baby Lawford did, they usually feel that their people are ignoring them or not responding to their needs. And many will *not* come back as he did. In this case, it was only after he left that Debra realized she hadn't been paying enough attention to her beloved cat and resolved to do better. Baby Lawford forgave Mom, but I'm sure he kept an eye on her for a while to be certain she fulfilled her promises!

T-Bird

My friend Betty, who breeds Manchester Terriers, called me about finding a lost dog for her friend Debbie. Debbie also breeds Manchester
Terriers and Betty had known her for a long time.

Debbie was going to be showing some of her other dogs, so for a
few days, she left an 18-month-old female puppy named T-Bird with a
dog sitter about 25 minutes from her home. T-Bird jumped the fence at
the dog sitter's house and hadn't been back since. Everyone thought she'd
probably try to find her way back to her own home, but they were very
concerned about the distance she'd have to travel to get there, and the
fact that she was in such unfamiliar territory.

It became apparent that this communication might be a lot more
difficult when Betty told me the dog had been missing for *three weeks!*
That's when I said I wasn't sure I could help. Betty pleaded with me to try
to communicate with the dog, just to see if she was still alive. She said it
would mean the world to her friend Debbie just to be able to know that
much. Wouldn't I *please* try to speak to T-Bird? Again, I couldn't refuse.

Debbie, herself, called me the next morning. Although she didn't
have a picture of T-Bird, I knew what a Manchester Terrier looked like,
so identifying with the dog was not a problem. She told me she lived in
Texas and gave me the name of the city. Again she mentioned that T-Bird
was lost in a city that was farther north. Once more, I was careful
to explain what she could, and couldn't, expect from me, but at that
moment it was obvious that any information was better than none.

It didn't take me long to locate T-Bird. She was very scared and didn't
want to approach other animals or people. She was completely lost, but
not far from the pet sitter's house. I told Debbie my feeling was that she
was no more than four blocks away.

T-Bird continued by giving me an image of a white picket fence that
looked worn and had some greenery around it. I told Debbie, "I can see
about five or six white sticks. Then a vine, or something green, is cover-

ing the rest of it. The houses aren't very close together. She can also smell horses a little ways away. She's hiding and comes out at night. Someone's feeding her."

I also told Debbie that T-Bird had been very emotionally distressed by this event and was not the same little girl she was before becoming lost. I suggested that even if she found her, Debbie shouldn't expect to be able to "show" T-Bird for quite a while — if ever again. This experience had been much too traumatizing.

After giving Debbie this information, she confirmed that T-Bird was indeed seen by a woman who puts out food for stray dogs, and this woman said she'd seen T-Bird coming in for supper. Debbie had put up posters all over the city and she began to receive calls from people who'd seen her dog, but every time she got there, T-Bird was gone, sometimes by only 15 minutes. Other times, when calls came in from well-intentioned people, they turned out to be false alarms.

"How can I find her, Dr. Monica?" asked Debbie, her voice breaking up with emotion.

Thinking fast, I suggested "How about if I ask T-Bird to go back to eat at the home of the woman who puts food out for strays? I could tell her to stay around the corner until she sees you. Would that work?"

"Yes, yes that would work. I can go up there tonight!" responded Debbie.

She was to park her car and walk the neighborhood while being especially attentive to any movement where there were bushes. I also asked her to call T-Bird's name in her usual sweet upbeat voice. In addition, I suggested that she bring T-Bird's mother along, a female named Tara, so she could urinate and mark territory. This would help T-Bird understand that she was on familiar ground. Debbie agreed to try everything.

Four days went by before she called me to say that she, her husband, and Tara had all gone back to the spot a couple of days in a row, spending the night in her car. Knowing her little girl was alive, she wouldn't stop until T-Bird was safely brought home.

It really bothered me to know that this wonderful couple was spending their nights sleeping in the car because of the suggestion I'd made. I could only hope that a happy outcome would make up for their temporary discomfort. So, every night before going to sleep, I would send the same picture to T-Bird and ask her to go back to the house where she was fed. I assured her that her family would be there.

After five more days of not hearing from Debbie, I checked my e-mail at day's end on September 29. I was thrilled to find this message:

> Dear Dr. Monica,
>
> I just wanted to let you know we brought T-Bird home last night and it was one of the happiest reunions! It's been an answer to our prayers. It's so good to have her home again.
>
> I also want to thank you for your kindness which helped me through a very difficult time. We appreciate our friend Betty for putting us in touch with you. I'll send you an update on T-Bird. We have all the time in the world to let her adjust from her trauma. We can tell she's so happy to be home, but not happier than we are!!!!
>
> Thank You, Debbie & Charles Williams :))

Debbie called me to complete the details of how T-Bird had been found. She'd received a phone call from *another* woman who'd *also* been feeding T-Bird. The dog had gotten close enough to her so that she could make out the phone number on her tag.

Debbie again took Tara with her to this other woman's house and, sure enough, when feeding time came, T-Bird showed up for supper. It took her a little while to realize that this was her mom, but as soon as she did, she came leaping into Debbie's arms.

Though I didn't know there were *two* women who were feeding strays, T-Bird was probably following my instructions all along, by going to at least one of the two homes where she'd been fed. If she understood my message, she was no doubt wondering where her mom was!

Yes, Debbie, you were right not to lose hope. There are miracles all around us!

MARISSA

Cindi called me to ask if I could help. As always, I said, "I don't usually accept this type of a case because it's very difficult for all of us. If I *can* communicate with lost animals at all, their pictures may not be clear since they're often frightened and confused." Yet, something in her voice told me I had to at least listen to what she had to say.

This situation was a little different. It wasn't *her* lost pet. It was the pet of her boyfriend, David, who was in Ohio. He was there to liquidate his mother's estate and to bring back his two cats who'd been keeping her company during the last months of her illness.

On a previous visit to Ohio, David had visited his mother and stayed there several months. During that time, he befriended a little wild, grey tabby. He named her Wildy because she was *so* wild that, at first, she wouldn't come close to anyone except him. When David went back to California, he felt that Wildy would be better off staying in a familiar environment, so she became one of his mom's two companions.

Both David and Cindi were very spiritual people and they weren't asking for miracles. They just wanted to know how she got out of the house and wondered if I could tell them whether or not she was still alive.

I felt comfortable trying to get that information for them, so I set up a consultation by phone with David in Ohio. I was floored when he told me the cat left home *six months ago*, and he'd learned that *at least three months* had gone by since anyone last saw her.

If finding a recently lost animal is difficult, how much more would it be to find one who'd been gone for such a long time? But David's persistence, and his understanding of how the Universe works, compelled me to at least try.

Sometime, well before she disappeared, she'd been renamed Marissa because David felt the original name no longer fit her. Marissa was able to send me some pictures, but I couldn't tell whether they were recent or from the past. I was able to see (as if from her perspective) that her collar was lying on the ground, close to where there was a little bit of water. She said the water was dirty but she had to drink it anyway.

When I asked her if she was afraid of wild animals, she told me she was used to them and outsmarted them every time. All these pictures were from a very rural country area and I told David that Marissa kept showing me cats with pointed ears who were bigger than she was.

David confirmed there were lots of cougars in the area and he was distressed thinking that one of them might get her. I assured him Marissa was a bright girl and wouldn't let that happen.

But he still pressed hard to know with more certainty whether I thought she was alive or dead. Because of the information I was receiving from Marissa, I felt she was still alive, but I couldn't be certain. I didn't want to mislead David in any way and I didn't want him to worry, so instead, I kept him focused on the clues I'd received. I directed him to go to his neighbor on the left and look for a place Marissa had specified low on the ground. I asked him to see if he could find anything there.

David went out that afternoon but was unable to locate her. He couldn't stop thinking about Marissa, but at the prompting of some friends he agreed to go out to dinner. As they were coming back to the house, David and one of his friends saw the shadow of something running from the house to the fence. Thinking that it was probably a wild animal, David dismissed the episode and went to bed.

The next evening, after a long day of errands, he came home to find the same shadowy figure running out from under the house. This time, he paid attention and said a small prayer. He decided to find out what kind of animal was out there.

He called out Marissa's name, hopefully, and went to open both the front and back doors. In the kitchen, he opened two cans of food — one to put in the back yard and one to carry with him. In a flash, he saw a cat running toward the back door. It then zoomed into the house. As he ran ahead to close the front door, he couldn't believe his luck. Was it really Marissa? Was she back? David held her close, and upon further inspection, he was sure that this scared, skinny and wild little cat was his one and only Marissa.

David called me right away with the good news. "Six months is a long time," he said. "What made Marissa come back now?"

I'd like to believe that my communication helped her better understand the situation. Knowing her best friend was back in the house and looking for her meant that he hadn't given up — so neither did she!

When David was finished with his work in Ohio, he brought both cats back to California with him. Although she had to adapt to life in the city and leave her wild days behind her, Marissa is now happy and content just being with her best friend.

CHAPTER 11

PET DETECTIVES

If you've ever had any doubt that animals are highly aware of what goes on around them, or that they can remember specific details for a long time, these next stories should help to dispel some of those misgivings.

Over the years, I couldn't possibly have known, or even guessed at, some of the incredible things that animals were going to say. And their families have often been quite astonished, as well, by some of the precise information their pets have provided, which they themselves have definitely been able to confirm.

Our animals are acutely aware of a great many details about things going on around them. Sometimes they even try very hard to give specific information to help us solve problems, or maybe bring closure to a particular episode in our lives, as they do in the following case studies.

Something else I find most significant is that even though we haven't asked about it, our animals may take the opportunity, in the course of our conversation, to talk about a completely unrelated topic. This happened at the end of the first story. Even though it wasn't something his mom originally wanted to know, Rosco felt it was important for him to bring up two other points while he had my attention. But first he responded to his mom's questions.

Rosco

The first case study finds my little pal Rosco, a two-year-old male miniature Dachshund, at home in the state of Washington. His mom wanted him to tell me about one very extraordinary day in his life.

I'd first met Rosco when he was very young during a much earlier e-mail consultation. His story appears in my first book, *What Your Animals Tell Me*. His human mom, Jan, wrote to me nearly two years later with this request.

> Hi Dr. Monica!
>
> A couple of weeks ago our house was burglarized while Rosco was home. Fortunately, he wasn't hurt physically. I think Rosco knows quite a bit about this and wondered if dogs can actually describe physical characteristics of people.
>
> Do you think you can help?
>
> Jan

I only knew Rosco from his pictures but, based on our previous "talks," I also knew he was one of the more intelligent dogs I had ever spoken with. I eagerly set out to determine what, if anything, he could remember. It would be a difficult task, but as always, I put my trust in the Universe and settled down to meditate first and then communicate with this little guy by picture telepathy. This is what he transmitted in pictures:

"There was a big guy who must have come in through the back door because when I saw him he was already in the hall. He was big, bigger than my daddy. His pants were dark and kind of baggy and his shirt was all the way down to his thighs, but his black jacket was only to his waist. He looked to be in his 20s. The other guy was very skinny and looked to be in his teens. He stayed mostly outside or at the edge of the house. I was a good dog because I barked and barked. The big guy tried to kick me but I was faster than he was and I hid between the sofa and the wall, but I still barked."

I knew that Jan would also want to know where Dakota was during all this. Dakota is a large male Labrador mix who's supposed to guard the grounds.

Rosco replied:

"Dakota and I were taking our mid-morning nap. Dakota always goes to his favorite spot where he makes a hole in the ground and sleeps without being interrupted. It's in the big back yard where there're bushes and trees. He feels secure and he likes it there. He couldn't hear them at first. But he almost got them this time (making some kind of reference to the fact that he might have known them from before). They didn't stay that long. Tell Mom they were looking for something inside the can in the kitchen and they were messing around with the cables. They left in a hurry and climbed out the side of the house."

I also heard the name "Alex" three times in my mind. I made notes about all of this and waited for Jan to call me back at the appointed time. (When I receive an e-mail request to do a consultation, I usually ask the person to call me back in a day or so to be able to discuss my interpretation of their pet's pictures).

But just before I was ready to thank Rosco for the pictures he'd sent me and finish the session, he interrupted my thoughts with more pictures. These were things *he* wanted to discuss which Mom hadn't even asked about. "Please tell Mom that when I go to the vet to get my shot, I get a headache. I'd like her to ask the vet if I'm getting the right dose. And my food doesn't always taste really good. It feels as if it needs more flavor."

When Jan called me, I recounted the entire conversation. She was so amazed at all the things her little guy had said that she couldn't tell me her thoughts on the phone because it was too much information for her to process all at once. Instead, she wrote me an e-mail later giving me her interpretation of the events based on what Rosco had told me. Here's what Jan wrote:

Dr. Monica,
Here's my interpretation:
Rosco sleeps on the couch in the living room. The short hallway is between the living room and kitchen where the back door is. He hid

between the couch and the wood stove which is where his bed used to be and it's a safe place.

When Rosco said: The big guy went into the kitchen to look for something . . .

To me this is what happened: There was a jar of change missing from the kitchen, as was the laptop that was sitting on the counter, and they opened a large plastic carrying case that had barbeque tools in it.

The guy that came in must have been a big guy indeed since the wood stove in the living room was moved out of place, as if someone had fallen into it, tripping over the hearth. I've done this before and not moved the stove. It's such a heavy stove that only someone big could've moved it, like Rosco described.

Dakota's sleeping place, as Rosco described it, is 100 percent accurate. We have a big back yard and Dakota goes to the shavings building at the back of the yard and digs a hole in the corner to lie down.

They left in a hurry . . . we received a telephone call around 10 A.M. on our answering machine which had the volume turned way up. It was a friend of mine, who thinking I was home, left a message saying he was coming over.

The cables referred to by Rosco belong to the sub woofer that was taken. The climbing is the gate they had to climb over to get in and to leave.

About his headache Jan said:

Rosco has a shot every 28 days for Addison's Disease (adrenal insufficiency) and after he has his shot he wants to stay on his bed and burrow under his blankets, sometimes up to a day or two. I knew something was wrong but thought only that he didn't like the trip to the vet. I never thought that animals could get headaches! I'll be trying aspirin before his next shot and address this with his vet too. Rosco likes his food better if I put some canned green beans in it. I'll continue to do that.

One thing Rosco didn't mention was the CD's or the Antique Milk Can. And finally, I don't know of anybody named Alex.

I replied by return e-mail:

> Oh, but he did, Jan. He did talk about the can. When Rosco told me about the can it was *my* interpretation that it must have been in the kitchen. Actually the picture he sent me was that of a *large tin can* and how they *opened it*. He was of course referring to the Antique Milk Can. I'm sure he feels that it was important to you because his picture was very clear. He didn't say anything about the CD's though.

Jan answered:

> The milk can was in the hallway and was full of newspapers we use for starting the wood stove. The robber dumped the newspapers on the floor and I believe he filled the can with CD's. And YES, the can was important to me because it was given to me for Christmas by my parents a few years ago. The CD's, well, they weren't nearly as important to me as they were to my husband.
>
> Thank you for sending Rosco your love and healing. We both appreciate it!
>
> Jan from WA

Rosco is an amazing dog and the perfect pet detective. He was able to tell me about the events of that awful experience with his highly detailed pictures. Now if we could only convince the police to go looking for these burglars based on his eyewitness account . . . that would *really* be something! But even better still would be finding out if one of the culprits was named Alex.

You might think that dogs pay more attention to detail than other types of pets, but what about a cat? The following is my favorite story about a cat detective. For me, the most amazing thing about this next case study is that the information came from the owner's much beloved cat who'd died about a year ago.

Yes, like people, our animals' lives also continue on when they pass from this earthly experience. They no longer need the physical body they used while they were here, but their love is everlasting, and if we reach out to them in spirit, they, too, can communicate with us in pictures. After all, true communication with any other being is *always* taking place at the spiritual level, even when we're in the body. We don't communicate body to body, but rather spirit to spirit, even in our daily lives.

HARRY, BUTCH, LUCAS, AND DENNIS

Early each morning, you'll find me in front of my computer. I receive all kinds of e-mails, and this particular morning was no exception. One of them read:

> Hi, a friend of mine met with you at Wild Oats in Long Beach last weekend. I was all excited to come see you tomorrow, but I just called there and was told you weren't scheduled again yet. I'd love to have you come over to my house to see my boys (cats). I have Butch, Harry and Lucas. I just got Lucas at the Seal Beach shelter because I lost my buddy Dennis last year.
>
> Can we set up a time when you could come over to see us?
>
> Thanks, Kevin

It wasn't an unusual e-mail. In fact, most of my e-mail requests pretty much resemble this one — a large family of animals and their special person wanting to know something about each one of them.

We coordinated a time to meet on a Monday afternoon. I arrived at a large white Spanish style house in the older part of Long Beach, California, where I found very little parking and lots of cars. I went up to the door thinking I was going to meet with Kevin and the three cats. Imagine my surprise when I was met, not only by Kevin, but also by Vicki, Jeff and Frank, all of whom were roommates and part of one big family. As I was introduced to everyone, I thought this was unusual, but nice. After they were each seated on the living room sofa, I was then introduced to the other three residents of the house — the three male cats.

There was 10-year-old Harry, who was mostly white with a few tan and black patches; 13-year-old Butch, who was a very light tan tiger male, and Lucas, an orange tabby, who was just a little over a year old.

I should also mention that a little marble box containing Dennis' ashes was placed in front of me, along with his framed picture, so that I could get to know the other orange tabby who'd been such a special part of the family until last year.

Harry talked with me first. He was a character, but an easy going kind of guy. Harry told me, "I think I'm going blind, because I need to see things up very close. Sometimes my nose is even touching them. My whiskers help me to sense things and my sense of smell is still working very well."

When asked how he felt about Butch (the older cat), he said, "I need to be on my toes when it comes to Butch because he has a short fuse and if I so much as look at him the wrong way, he'll get me." Everyone was laughing out loud at this very true and honest answer.

"How do you feel about Lucas?" Vicki asked.

"Lucas is a scaredy cat. I can't even play with him because he gets all spooked. What's wrong with him? Tell him to chill out. I don't want to hurt him. I just want to play a little!"

Everyone was laughing hysterically at this point, knowing full well that every word Harry was saying was completely accurate.

Harry also volunteered, "I took over Dennis' job of sleeping next to Dad because Dennis asked me to."

Suddenly the laughter turned into tears. Dennis had been Kevin's favorite and throughout his life he'd been sleeping right next to him on the pillow. Dennis' request had propelled Harry into a position of dominance and trust within the group. Dad couldn't account for the change and had wanted to find out why. Now he knew, thanks to the information coming directly from Harry.

Vicki broke the somber mood by asking Harry a question. "What do you think about Andy (a former roommate; not his real name)?"

Harry said, "I don't trust him. There's something very wrong with him."

Everyone looked at each other as if they knew exactly what Harry was talking about. When I asked what Harry meant, they told me they'd rather not say anything just yet, so we kept on going.

Next, I talked with Butch, the 13-year-old light tan tabby. He was very underweight and his fur was dull and lackluster, but that wasn't too unusual for someone who was almost 91 years old as we count human years. He didn't want to stick around, so I caught only a brief glimpse of him before he chose to go back to his safe hiding place. However, that didn't mean I couldn't talk with him.

It's a common misconception that an animal and I must be together while we talk, or that I must be holding or touching the animal, but this is not the case. If an animal has been able to pick up my scent by being with me for a few minutes, it may help him recognize who's talking to him, but this isn't a requirement.

A spiritual connection can be made whether the animal is present or not, and distance does not make any difference either. Telepathic information can travel around the world and back in an instant. So although I don't need to see or meet my clients in person to be able to talk with them, it does give me a special feeling of closeness when we can be together in person and it also gives them an opportunity to become familiar with my scent.

Now back to Butch's story. Butch is very introverted. He doesn't like others. It doesn't matter to him whether they're people or animals. He just wants to be a little hermit.

He said, "Dad (Kevin) is the only one who's allowed to pick me up. I won't allow anyone else to do it. I love my patio and I love to sunbathe. Even though I know I'm aging fast, I still want to be number one. I have to remind everyone I'm still the boss and I take every opportunity I can to slap someone when I go by, just to let them know I'm coming through. I know my seizures are getting worse and I know that the time for me to die is drawing nearer. Still I'm not quite ready to leave yet."

As an afterthought he said, "I have this great ability to look someone in the eye with a mean look and make them be scared of me. I love that I can do that."

Vicki laughed and said this is exactly what he used to do to her when they first met. Even now, after she's grown to know and love him, he'll still sometimes look at her with an intense stare and she just knows there's something he doesn't like. She felt this piece of information was made clear just for her.

Now Vicki changed gears and asked Butch about Andy. (Andy, again, I thought!)

Butch said, "I didn't like Andy at all. He seemed nice enough on the outside but I could see his aura and he wasn't a nice person."

I was beginning to think the same thing myself, even though I still didn't really know anything about him. I mentioned to everyone that something about the way each pet described Andy was very disconcerting. I couldn't put it into words yet. All I could say was that something about him made me feel very uncomfortable. Again, no one said anything, so I thanked Butch and moved on.

Lucas was just a year old and had been part of the family for only a couple of months at the time of my visit. He mentioned that this home was very different from his last one where he'd been an only cat. He said it was taking him a long time to learn to socialize with the other cats in the family and he wasn't very open yet to spending time on anybody's lap. Consequently, he spent most of his time hiding away from everyone. Rick asked me to tell Lucas that he was welcome in this house and would always be treated as a respected member of the family for the rest of his life. Lucas listened, but didn't want to send me very many pictures.

It was time to talk to Dennis now. It had been about a year since his unexpected death at the age of nine. I closed my eyes and listened for him. It didn't take long at all. Dennis had been listening all the time! He started by making fun of Dad saying, "Ha, he went out to get Lucas to replace me, yet Lucas is the very opposite of me. Sorry, Dad!"

Next, the group of roommates wanted to know how Dennis felt when he died. I thought that was a strange way to word the question. It was vague. It wasn't "*Were you in pain, how did it happen, or why?*" It was "*How did you feel?*" Since I learned long ago not to question any comments or requests from either the people or the animals I'm communicating with, I just went along with their question and didn't change it.

Dennis responded, "It was very, very hard for me to breathe. I was panting heavily and my heart was beating very fast. Even having my mouth wide open I couldn't seem to get enough air coming in and I couldn't swallow."

"Ask him *how* he died." (Here we go again, another "how" question, I thought.)

Dennis showed me that he was lying on the ground in their backyard. He was on his side with foam coming out of his mouth. I waited for the next picture to give me something indicating either action or more information. Instead I saw a word materialize in front of me with a light color background and huge black letters. I became very uncomfortable.

I knew better than to question any information coming through during a consultation, but this was really different. I wondered if I should say the word or just move on. I had to concentrate on the fact that I train people all the time how to communicate with their animals, and one of the first things I tell them is, "Do *not* change ANY of the information you get." I tell them not to think about it, or intellectualize it — just say it!

I took a deep breath and opened my eyes. "You may think I'm crazy, maybe even more so than you already think right now, but this is what I saw in front of me. Dennis clearly showed me a word, and that word is: *poison*. I think he was poisoned!"

Vicki gasped, and with her mouth still agape, looked at her other roommates. Frank silently mouthed the phrase, "I can't believe it!" Jeff just sat staring wide-eyed and unblinking. Kevin pulled his hair back with both hands, slouched down on the sofa, and could only shake his head.

Vicki was the first to recover her composure and she asked, "Can you ask Dennis who did it?"

When the next pictures came through from Dennis, I said, "This has to do with someone Dennis knew!" A cold shudder hit my body more strongly than I've felt in a long time. I mentioned this out loud and Vickie said she'd just experienced a cold shudder as well.

Dennis clearly showed me that a man had been there when he lay dying. He also said he felt this person was somehow involved. It's very interesting that Dennis never mentioned that the person who was with him was concerned or frantic, or gave him any love or care during his distress, as most people would do in that situation. And animals usually acknowledge any kindness a person has shown to them when they're dying.

Vicki mentioned that ever since Dennis had died, she had the feeling that something was wrong. She couldn't bring herself to actually blame their former roommate, who'd been living in the household at the time, but her heart and intuitive feelings told her not to trust him. She'd mentioned this to Kevin before. So not only did all the animals in the home feel that he was untrustworthy, the rest of the family had their concerns, too.

After this consultation, they all felt sure the case had now been solved. The cause of Dennis' untimely death had been revealed by Dennis himself, a whole year after he died. And he also provided a possible clue to indicate who may have been responsible.

In the accounts described in this chapter, we've looked at two animals who played an integral part in solving, or shedding light on, a situation that was a mystery to their families. Rosco and Dennis were two amazing animal detectives who provided important information which, in turn, helped their humans unravel the details behind two very unusual events. Their help was a clear sign of the unconditional love which binds us to our animal friends, not only during our time on earth together, but also after they've gone before us into spirit.

CHAPTER 12

PETS AS DOCTORS

Sometimes when I visit with animals, they're a little uncomfortable if I seem to be pointing a finger at them by asking something like: Who peed on the carpet last Monday when Mom wasn't home? Yet, other times, because certain things are apparently top priorities on *their* list, they're so open and talkative they'll tell me things I didn't even ask about. Occasionally, I'm even surprised by the depth of their wisdom, especially when they can describe their ailments and what's necessary to fix them.

As an empath, or medical intuitive, I begin by feeling what they feel. There are times when this works very well because I'm then able to pinpoint exactly *where* something hurts through actually experiencing it. At other times, experiencing their pain or nausea has been almost overwhelming and I've found it difficult to continue. But ordinarily, my experiences lead to some very interesting and helpful information.

The following case study is an example of a pet who knew himself quite well, where my empathic feelings could be put to good use.

CHUBBS

I'd met Chubbs a couple of times and knew him well. He was a beautiful Dalmatian, about nine years old, who went to work every day with his mom, the owner of a day care facility for dogs. For privacy purposes, I'll refer to her as Sylvia.

Sylvia spends her time caring for other people's pets because she believes that other dog owners appreciate having someone provide specialized services which she herself had been unable to find.

On their way to work in the morning, people drop off their dogs at her huge facility, and later pick them up on their way home. (Yes, I know, doggy day care, and these days, not only in California!) This arrangement seems to work wonders for pets. It allows them to play and be around others, while diminishing the chances of hurting themselves or destroying property at home because of separation anxiety. If the family needs to go on vacation, Sylvia also has accommodations with kennels prepared for long term stays.

Another wonderful service she provides, is pet-sitting 24/7 with a caregiver available at all times. This is especially important for senior citizen pets who need medications on a 24-hour schedule.

Her business, which she named in honor of her companion, grew out of her love and devotion to her own pet, Chubbs, and her logo was designed as an image of her beloved Dalmatian.

Sylvia was so attached to Chubbs that she thought of him more as a companion angel and confidant rather than as a dog. But Chubbs hadn't been his normal self for the past week, so she'd taken him to the vet. Sylvia also wanted to consult with me to find out if Chubbs could provide any information. He could. What he said was simple and direct.

Chubbs relayed to me that not only was he feeling bad, but he knew he was dying. I had no idea what the vet had said to Sylvia, but based on how Chubbs was describing his feelings and how I was empathically receiving the information, I ventured to say that his liver was not functioning correctly and that something was pushing on his stomach. He didn't want to eat, he didn't feel thirsty, he was extremely tired and didn't feel like moving at all. He didn't even want to go in the car anymore — something that was completely out of character for him.

Chubbs tried to tell Sylvia that he'd trust her judgment when the time came for him to release his body, but asked to be helped when she could see he couldn't take the pain anymore. Sylvia listened to what I had to say but told me she would *never* be able to put him down. I understood the depth of her feeling.

A few days later I received this e-mail:

Dr. Monica,

You were right. I had X-rays done the following day. The vet felt it could be a brain tumor, so I scheduled an MRI the following Wednesday. But by Friday morning I wanted more testing right away.

They didn't want to perform the MRI on Friday based on some information I gave them about Chubb's condition, so they did a blood panel and found it indicated his liver wasn't functioning very well. They next did a liver function test and then had proof that his liver is REALLY not functioning well. He had a liver biopsy on Monday.

I'm so nervous. I'm praying it isn't cancer.

(I had to stop writing for two days because it was just too difficult. I wanted to finish telling you what happened now.)

To make a long story short . . . thank you. It is his liver that's pushing on his stomach. When my usual vet kept telling me that it could be a brain tumor, your voice was there in my head, telling me that something was pushing on his stomach. That led me to agree to alternate testing.

Thanks for everything!

Sylvia

Chubbs was declining very rapidly until finally he couldn't move his body any longer. Sylvia was able to take a few days off from her busy job and spend every possible moment with him. When the time arrived, she had to muster all of her strength to provide the very last act of kindness she could for her beloved pet. She called her veterinarian and asked him to come to their home to administer the blue liquid that would send Chubbs home again over the Rainbow Bridge. In spite of her own sense of pain and loss, she'd found the inner strength to honor his special request.

Do all animals have the ability to describe their feelings? I think so, but I wasn't really prepared to hear as much information as I received from a long-haired guinea pig named Dotje. This case study was done by e-mail and I'd received some pictures of the guinea pig by regular mail.

DOTJE (A DUTCH NAME PRONOUNCED DOTTIE)

Mom wrote to me because she was hoping to find some answers her vet couldn't give her. Dotje was continually having health problems, from ear mites, to eye infections to diarrhea. Mom wanted to find out if there was anything physically wrong with her that she could help to correct.

Dotje told me: "It all started with the vitamin C deficiency. All of a sudden my tummy got bombarded with a lot of new things. I think I couldn't take so many different things all at once — new food, new taste in the water, new medicine. New, new, new (huff)."

"I hate changes," she said, reminding me of how a cat talks. "I used to be a very active and happy girl. Lately I feel like an old lady. I don't have the stamina to run or play around as I used to. I feel old and tired. When my sister wants to play, I have to get mad at her and tell her to stop. I don't want to play anymore. I want to rest and sleep.

"When Mommy goes away, I'm lonely. Not that I need to always be on her lap but I like it when she's home. There's a warm atmosphere and it smells good." (Mom later told me that she travels for work and that when she's home, she often bakes cookies.)

"My health is weak and I'm having problems fighting my own battles. I feel like my immune system stopped working well and I find myself with a new ache almost daily. On top of that I'm stressed out when Mom's not around. I like it when she talks to me and tells me how pretty I am. I love it when she treats me with such respect, like a little princess.

"We also need to talk about the location of my cage and what's right beside it. I find it a little irritating because it hums." (Mom told me she had the cage next to the big screen TV with the speakers on the sides.)

"And when she has to go away, she needs to tell me in advance. She shouldn't just leave without saying a word. It leaves me with an empty feeling."

Dotje also mentioned two more things, without any prompting from me: "I love bananas but I shouldn't have any because they give me diarrhea. I also need something salty in my diet." And finally, Dotje made a comment about Mommy singing and how very much she enjoys it.

Mom was delighted that Dotje recognized she was being treated like a little princess. She was also surprised to receive so much helpful information from her long haired guinea pig who'd been constantly sick with different ailments. She promptly changed the location of her cage, decreased the amount of vitamin C, consulted with an expert on specialized feeding, and set up a nurturing and loving schedule to satisfy all of Dotje's needs. The result is a happy and well-adjusted little pet who no longer suffers with bouts of diarrhea or various infections.

Sometimes our pets' analysis of their own health is vital to their well-being. At other times, as in the following case study, their comments, while somewhat "Oh, by the way" in nature, are still very important.

CHIP

Tanya came to see me with several of her animals. Tinkerbell and Little Bell were her two precious Pomeranians. She also brought along one of her big dogs, Chip, a four-year-old black Labrador mix whom she'd rescued. During our conversation Tanya told me that she operates a rescue and adoption center. She rescues animals from shelters on the last day before they're scheduled to be euthanized. She cares for them, trains them and sees that they get veterinary services before finally putting them up for adoption. Few people know pets as well as those who do rescue work, and Tanya was no exception.

She and I had a nice talk with Chip about his expectations in life and how he was dealing with the two little dogs who occupied much of Tanya's time and attention. He was a good dog and was frank and direct.

As I finished the consultation, I gave the animals one last chance to say anything which might be a concern to them before saying our good byes. Chip spoke up and said, "Would you please tell Mom that I have a growth on my gums that's bothering me? It rubs against my cheek when I eat. I'd like to have it taken care of!"

Tanya was a little confused at first and I could see her face changing as if she was trying to remember. Then she said, a little exasperated, as if I was blaming her for some neglect on her part, "I clean his teeth at least once a week, every week, and I haven't seen anything there that requires attention."

"Nevertheless," I said "let's just have a look, shall we?"

"Well I'll be d——," Tanya said when she found exactly what Chip was talking about. Protruding out of his upper left gum was a medium-sized growth, something like a mole. "I'm taking you to the vet right now to have that thing removed," she said, still not able to believe her eyes. And then reassuring me, she emphasized, "I'll take care of it right away, Dr. Monica."

Although he only brought it up as sort of an afterthought, I'm sure he was happy he mentioned it and that his mom took such quick action.

———

I do many consultations for animal rescue and non-profit associations. To complete the adoption picture, I'm often able to bring to light some information that will help humans understand the past trials and tribulations their new pet may have undergone.

Sometimes the organization needs to know if and how the pet was abused. Other times, they'd like to get a clear understanding of whether an animal would be more comfortable around a male or female human. Important also are details such as knowing if they've been around other dogs or if they were kept in the house or in a backyard. All of these questions are crucial to understanding their behavior and they're also very useful to help foster parents assimilate them into a home environment.

OREO

Needless to say, Tanya was convinced that communication works, and it wasn't long before I had another visit from her. She'd recently rescued several Pomeranians from a breeder who could no longer keep the dogs. Most of them were placed in homes, but one of them, a four-month-old little male named Oreo (because of his black and white markings), remained with her.

Tanya was worried because Oreo had been coughing for the last couple of weeks. It started shortly after he was rescued and brought to her home. "He's such a sweet little guy. He's full of energy and loves to play with the female dogs, but he can't, because as soon as he gets excited he'll start coughing and then he can't stop for a few minutes. I'm afraid he'll choke.

"We thought he had pneumonia, like one of the older females who was rescued at the same time, so he's been taking antibiotics, cough syrup and cough medicine. Three days ago, I also started him on a plant-based whole food nutritional supplement, but nothing seems to work. He starts coughing and can't stop, and he'll do that several times a day."

Tanya was looking for some answers, but I was wondering if little Oreo would be able to provide them. Generally speaking, young animals don't have the ability to give me exact pictures.

Never the shy one, though, I went ahead and began to ask Oreo some questions.

"Where is the pain located?" I asked.

"In my throat," he responded immediately.

"Show me," I said.

He showed me a picture of the inside of his throat. He said the air passage was impeded as if it was out of alignment or pinched.

"How does it feel?" I continued.

"I can't get enough air going through when I get excited and try to breathe more."

He repeated that something was wrong, and he was certain it was in his throat and not in his lungs. "Is the medicine helping?" I asked. He assured me that the medicine he was taking was doing absolutely nothing to comfort him or make him feel better. In fact, the way his description went, it seemed to me that the medicine might be making him worse over time.

Fortunately, Tanya works for a veterinarian and wasted no time taking Oreo in to see him. He listened to Tanya's explanation of our conversation, and without hesitation, he took some X-rays of Oreo's neck. Dr. Sig has worked with me before, and is one of those rare veterinarians who's open to other forms of healing. He never closes a door when it's in the best interest of an animal to seek all possible avenues of recovery.

"I found it," he said. "He has a collapsed trachea! I know exactly what to do next."

Imagine that! A little four-month-old guy being able to tell the doctors how he felt. He gave us all the information we needed to solve his problem.

SHANNON

Shannon, a 13-year-old female Golden Retriever, came to see me on one of my consultation days. She arrived followed by her two moms. They were sisters who lived together and had grown to love their golden girl, now a senior citizen.

Shannon sat comfortably at my feet and the consultation was soon under way. She had a great sense of humor and immediately began to talk. "I'm very stubborn, but I fit perfectly into my family since both my moms are just as stubborn as I am." They laughed and agreed wholeheartedly.

Then Shannon said, "I have aches and pains all over but what I really want to know is, when are they going to take off the hurt from inside my mouth?"

One of the sisters opened her own mouth wide and, with an astonished expression, asked the other one, "Did you tell her?"

"No," the other said. "I didn't."

"It hurts me when I chew on my food," Shannon continued. "Sometimes I even bite it and it bleeds."

I didn't know, until they explained, that a growth had been found two weeks prior and it was growing daily. A consultation with the vet gave the dreaded results — cancer — untreatable.

Shannon said, "It's been there for awhile. It's on my lower neck and has grown around my jaw on the outside. Now it's growing inside my gums and cheek and is really bothering me, especially when I'm eating kibble." She politely requested (again!) that she wanted to have it taken out.

Then she added, "I've enjoyed our time together and I'll continue to have fun for as long as I can. I'd like to stick around until my tail no longer wags with delight but I know I'll need to leave before long. In the meantime, let's laugh and enjoy each other's company."

With that she rolled on her side on top of my feet and offered her tummy for a few pats.

Contrary to their vet's recommendation, the two moms decided to go ahead and have the growth removed from Shannon's mouth. A year later they called me on an unrelated matter, and told me that Shannon was still around, and as loving as ever. "If it wasn't for what you translated," they told me, "we would've put her down last year. Having a conversation with you was the best thing we ever did. Thank you!"

ICHIBAN

Hazel didn't know exactly why she'd made an appointment to see me, but in her heart she knew she had to. She came in with Ichiban, a six-year-old female Lhasa Apso.

Ichiban had been having seizures for the last couple of years. She was on medication and although the seizures were short in duration, they occurred frequently.

I reminded Hazel, as I often do with my clients, that I'm not a Doctor of Veterinary Medicine and my job is not to cure the animals, but to give the owner a better understanding about the pet's feelings and needs. She understood my comments and told me she wasn't expecting a miracle.

Ichiban, a pampered pet who was treated like a permanent puppy, had a lot to say to her mom.

She began with, "I want Mom to understand me. Sometimes I get these terrible headaches that push on the right side of my head. They're just above the right eye and they travel down to the middle of my neck. I can feel a spot behind my neck throbbing with a dull pain. These headaches are so strong that I find them hard to cope with. That's why I don't pay attention to her when she calls me. I just need to stay in a quiet place."

Hazel had observed time and time again how Ichiban would cower in a corner of the living room and put one of her paws up covering her eye, as if the light was bothering her.

She knew exactly what Ichiban was talking about. For years, she'd suffered from migraine headaches herself, and in her heart, she just knew that Ichiban was having them, too. But no one had ever told her that dogs also get headaches. Now, what Ichiban was telling her made perfect sense and gave Hazel a feeling of knowing and understanding.

She said, "I knew there was a reason why I had to come to see you today. My husband said I was crazy, but I needed to know. And now I do. Thank you! This makes all the difference in the world for me."

It took just a little understanding and validation to make both of them feel better!

TARA

Just recently I received an e-mail request for a long distance communication with a little Shih-Tzu female who's nine years old. Her mom, Debby, was frantic. She'd been caressing her dog, Tara, when she noticed she had a big bump next to one of her nipples. She'd taken Tara to the vet who said she might have mammary cancer and would need to be operated on immediately. Debby decided to call me first. She wanted to find out how Tara was feeling before she made a decision to do anything.

Tara said, "I'm not particularly feeling pain, but it bothers me a lot when I lie down on my tummy." (I questioned this answer because Debby told me the bump was only about the size of a quarter, maybe an inch wide). Then Tara continued, "I think it has to be a lot bigger than it looks because it feels as if it's pushing inward."

"It sounds as if you're only seeing the tip of an iceberg," I ventured to say to Debby.

She wasted no time taking Tara in for a biopsy and then wrote to me:

> Dear Dr. Monica
>
> I was worried about some mammary lumps that the doctor was suspicious of. Tara went in for the biopsy and I heard back from the doctor tonight that the cysts were benign. I just wanted to thank you for your help with Tara. I was very worried about her and it made things a little more bearable to have her communication from you. By the way, just as you said, only the tip of the cyst was visible. It was actually a very large lump protruding into her stomach. Your reading was accurate. Thank you and God Bless.
>
> Deb

———————

In the stories above, each of the animals told us what was causing its distress, and in some cases, what could fix the problem. What's sometimes even more surprising is listening to one animal describe the symptoms that another animal is experiencing, and then having that "diagnosis" confirmed by a veterinarian, as happened in the second of two consultations with Chance.

CHANCE

Tina was one of my early appointments at the clinic where I was spending all day Saturday doing consultations. I was surprised to see a video camera set up in front of me with someone taking aim. They asked me if it was OK to tape the session and, as always, I agreed.

"Who do we have here?" I said in a cheerful voice.

"This is Chance," Tina replied. "He's my kitty. He's about three years old and he's blind. He's been pulling his hair out for a while now and I can't make him stop. He's such a good kitty. I feel so bad for him."

I could see round patches of missing hair in his otherwise sleek black coat. I let him smell my finger and asked Mom if it was OK for him to be out of his carrier. She put him next to us and he seemed to enjoy our company because he remained seated beside us throughout the 15-minute consultation.

The reading started out very slowly. Although I was focused on him, I couldn't make a connection with this cat as I was used to doing. Something's wrong, I thought, because I wasn't getting any *pictures* as I always do. I started to worry. Was it because the cat didn't want to talk to me? Did I temporarily lose my gift? It took me a few moments to put the pieces of the puzzle together.

This was the first time I'd ever consulted with a blind kitty. Blinded since birth, the cat had never seen the world through his own eyes. Unfortunately this lack of vision didn't allow him to store or send images. Consequently, I was forced to tap into his other senses and hoped to gather enough information this way to create my own pictures. I closed my eyes and used my inner hearing and my senses of touch and smell to communicate with Chance. As it turned out, once I understood how to communicate with him, Chance had a lot to say.

I slowly began the journey through the mind of this kitty as I "became" him. I felt my way as I walked through the darkness of his home and was led to a place that seemed comfortable to be in. It was a common area in Tina's home. My walk through this very recognizable room was suddenly hindered when my foot caught on something. Chance couldn't identify it and wanted to know what it was. I asked Tina if she'd changed anything in the living room. Tina said she'd acquired a parrot, but his cage had been in the living room for over a year now. Nevertheless, Chance wanted to know about it.

After this exchange, Mom couldn't contain her eagerness to learn about why he was pulling his hair. The first thing I heard was a loud noise and I tried to imitate it for Mom. It sounded like a long baaah, baaah, baaah, possibly like the sound a Cockatoo would make, though maybe not so loud. She said that her parrot didn't scream, but talked. I kept hearing the same sound and knew it was frightening Chance. We needed to find out where it was coming from. I also mentioned that I noticed a foul smell coming into the room from somewhere.

Suddenly, Mom realized that the mimicking sound I was making was similar to that of a baby's cry. She told me she'd had a new baby over a year ago and coincidentally, or not, it was around that time when Chance started pulling out his hair. Now we were on to something.

I proceeded to explain to Chance where the new sound he was hearing was coming from. He said the sound sometimes moves around and he gets scared and runs away. "Yes," Mom said, "the baby is growing up and is now walking around."

I told Chance that this was a human baby and part of his family, and although it couldn't talk yet, it did yell or cry at times. I also reassured him he didn't have to be afraid of it. Mom was going to make absolutely certain he was protected from this toddler and that no harm would come to him.

He loved his mom so much that he believed me immediately and knew she would indeed take good care of him. We continued to talk about other matters and the time was up very soon.

Many times I don't get to talk to my clients for a follow-up appointment and don't really know in what way the consultations helped. That's why I was so happy to see Tina briefly two months later. She was radiant when she said to me that Chance had stopped pulling his hair completely and now had a beautiful black coat. She thanked me profusely and told me I'd helped to provide a little miracle!

For Chance, the past year had been unusually difficult. No medication, no coaxing, no amount of love and attention had deterred this kitty from pulling out his hair. Fortunately for him, a 15-minute conversation and some mutual understanding was all he needed to help resolve his issues!

So imagine my surprise when I walked into the clinic once again three months later to find Tina carrying her cat, Chance, in one carrier while holding another carrier with her other hand.

She said, "Chance has been pulling on his hair again! But this time he seems really mad about something."

As soon as she made it into the office, I asked her to take Chance out of his carrier and found the right time to ask who was in the other carrier. "It's the new addition to our home," she said. "Froda is a girl kitty and she's three months old."

Chance was mad all right. Instead of his usual friendly self, he was hissing and growling. He wouldn't meet my finger extended to say "Hi," nor would he step away from his plastic carrier. He complained very forcefully about the new kitten who, he said, had a very bad smell.

Tina agreed with Chance and explained to me that the kitten suffered from diarrhea off and on since she brought her home. She kept the kitten confined to a bathroom with a litter box, except, of course, when the kitten was supposed to be out playing with her daughter. It was at those times that Froda would then sneak into the living room and have an "accident" on the carpet, behind the sofas or in the corner.

Chance was adamant that he didn't like the smell of diarrhea, nor the fact that the kitten was being untidy. She was supposed to have better manners, but that wasn't all. Chance went on to explain to me that the kitten was emitting a funny odor. When I asked him to be more specific, he sent me a smell like ammonia. He said it was coming out of her body and that something was definitely wrong with Froda. It had nothing to do with her stools, rather it was coming from her skin. What he was telling me made me think of people with diabetes whose bodies sometimes emit a particular scent.

I told Mom as diplomatically as possible that her kitten wasn't well and it would be wise to have her checked out right away. Because Tina works in the same building as Dr. Sig, one my favorite veterinarians, she did just that immediately following our talk. It turned out Froda was quite anemic and her liver was also not functioning properly.

Froda is now well, and Chance, the diagnostician, once again stopped pulling his hair! Apparently knowing what behavior will get his mom's attention, Chance uses hair-pulling to let her know when something is wrong. Good for you Chance . . . you're meow-velous!!!

You see, when we listen to our animals, they can sometimes be their own best doctors! And, on occasion, they can even provide us with "diagnoses" for other pets in the family.

CHAPTER 13

PETS AND HEALING
(EVEN FROM THE OTHER SIDE)

Most of this book is about healing our animals, but did you know that animals themselves are often great healers too? Some research even shows that the healing benefits of living with an animal companion were recognized as far back as the 9th century.

More recently, having a pet in the household has been documented to lower blood pressure and anxiety, and reduce the need for doctor visits and medicines. Pets tend to keep a person mobile and they often help their human companions socialize more frequently. Some people even say their pets have been a strong motivation to help them recover from an illness or injury.

Companion animals also have an uncanny ability to see through the many layers of protection we build around ourselves. If we listen to them, they can often provide us with insights into our true selves, helping us to heal emotionally and spiritually.

As our confidants and teachers, they provide us with unconditional love and a kind of friendship for which there is no equal. In fact, in one study of nursing home residents, more than 65 percent of both men and women said their pets had been their only friends when they were living at home.

Our pets also teach us to pay attention to the little things. Dogs often remind us "to slow down and smell the roses," and cats often tell us to "stretch out and relax in the warmth of the sun."

Animals began to take on a more formal role as healers as early as the 1790s, when mentally ill patients were given the responsibility of caring for them as part of their therapeutic treatment at the York Retreat in England. Then in 1919, St. Elizabeth Hospital in Washington, D.C., began using dogs in the treatment of their mental health patients.

The participation of animals in therapeutic settings has become so widespread that Aubrey H. Fine wrote an entire book on the subject called, *Handbook on Animal-Assisted Therapy: Theoretical Foundations and Guidelines for Practice*. Today, animal-assisted therapy is considered one of the 21st century holistic healing methods.

If we consider that animals often facilitate healing for humans with whom they do *not* have a special and loving relationship, imagine what they can do for the people in their lives with whom they do have a special bond.

Though most people experience healing while their animals are actually living with them, the first three stories in this chapter are quite unique because they're about pets who provided healing, even though they'd already passed on. They were *still* helping the people, whom they loved so deeply, find the comfort and peace of spiritual and emotional healing, even after they were on the other side.

CHRISSY

I went to Henderson, Nevada to present a class on "How to Communicate with Your Pets." Henderson is a small city about ten minutes south of Las Vegas and it couldn't have been more different from what I was used to. Its clean and ample streets gave me a feeling of tranquility which I no longer experience when driving the busy streets and freeways of Southern California.

My host, Darlene, opened her home for me as well as some of her friends, for consultations on a Friday. A workshop followed on Saturday.

On the consultation day, I was able to talk to 19 animals. One of them, in particular, had a very special story.

I was given a photograph of a little dog perched on the seat of a dining room chair. The photo was of very poor quality, fuzzy and a little worn, but it was the only one Judy had. She said, "This is Chrissy and she's now on the other side. Could you still talk with her?"

"Sure," I replied. "Her essence is still around. Let me see if she's available."

Before I continued, I asked Judy to confirm the breed of her dog, and she replied that she was a Toy Poodle. She had only one question for Chrissy, "Do you forgive me for having to finally put you down?" she asked.

The answer came through so immediately and forcefully that it startled me for an instant.

Chrissy said, "How can you possibly ask me that question? I wasn't even supposed to have made it past the first couple of days of my life when I was born! It was thanks to you, and everything you did at the time, that I was able to live a happy life for 15 years. Don't you EVER think like that again!"

I was startled because she was telling me she'd once been so close to death, and because such a strong, determined and direct message was coming from such a sweet, little dog. I asked Mom to validate the message.

Judy said that Chrissy was born in her home. At the moment of birth, the mother dog wouldn't open the sac. After Judy helped, the mother dog then refused to clean the puppy or even move her, probably because of inexperience, since this was her first litter. Chrissy was born not breathing. Mom frantically called the dog breeder for help while someone else called the veterinarian on the other line. Using mouth-to-nose breathing, Chrissy was revived. Fed only with an eyedropper during the first few days of her life, she was eventually able to join her siblings at meal times.

When the breeder came to visit, she had the "pick of the litter," but when she chose Chrissy, Judy's heart dropped. She knew she couldn't give Chrissy away now. "How could I part with her after saving her life,"

Judy recalled. "She'd become a part of me." In tears, Judy begged the breeder, "Please don't take her." Seeing Judy's desperation, the breeder decided to choose another puppy instead.

Chrissy then became inseparable from Judy, going everywhere with Mom, including grocery shopping tucked inside her purse. They behaved as one heart until the last second of her long and happy 15-year life.

Toward the end of her 15th year, Chrissy was very sick with a terminal illness for which nothing more could be done. Because Judy didn't want her precious pet to be in pain for such a long time, she made the decision to euthanize Chrissy after exhausting all possible medical options. She so deeply regretted having to make that decision that she'd carried the guilt of it in her heart for ten years until the moment Chrissy spoke to her in spirit. Then it became clear to Judy that she need no longer harbor any feelings of guilt. A great sense of peace came over her, and even though we were all bathed in tears, it was indeed a happy ending!

Even from the other side, Chrissy was able to heal her human mom with her love and understanding, albeit in a stern little voice.

MARY ANNE

When a pet dies, the grief that follows can be emotionally, mentally, and even physically disabling. Frequently, people who've lost their pets want to communicate with their spirits on the other side. They're looking for some closure and for a way to say, "I love you," one more time.

During this type of conversation, I never know what a pet will say, that may bring about healing for the person I'm working with, nor do I know which messages in particular will give the much needed validation that it is *their pet* who is actually providing the information. Whenever a pet gives a very specific message, it always helps to reassure their human companions, especially the skeptics, that I'm not just saying something in general that popped into my mind.

Take for instance, the following consultation.

Mary Anne, a tri-color Shih-Tzu dog, had passed two weeks prior to our scheduled appointment, and her "parents" were still in shock from the events leading to her death. She was only 9½ years old, and they weren't ready for her to go. She hadn't been sick and was under excellent veterinary care.

On the morning of our scheduled phone call, I did a deep meditation and contacted Mary Anne. During my meditation, I took notes about the pictures she was sending and what my senses were picking up. This way, when I spoke to the family later in the day, it would be easy to remember everything she'd said and what the conversation felt like.

Mary Anne had come in very clearly. She wanted to tell her "parents" about how she was still around them, moving specific things and appearing in their dreams. I thought the messages were pretty specific, but I didn't get much feedback from the family as I relayed the information. I could almost "hear" their skepticism. "Any dog could say that . . . I only vaguely remember my dreams . . . I didn't notice things moving," etc., etc.

I took a deep breath and continued to read to Mom and Dad from my notes. We covered several questions they'd asked, and with each answer it was more apparent that their little girl had a lot to say.

I finally came to something that had puzzled me when I received it. "Mary Anne is talking about her collar," I said. "She's showing me a hand holding her collar with the tags hanging out, but she's not wearing it. I feel this is important because she continues to show me that her collar is still serving a purpose."

Dad, who'd been very quiet during our phone conversation, immediately burst out saying, "Since she died, I've been carrying her collar in my hand every day. I feel she's closer to me that way."

Men are usually more skeptical about the work I do, so coming from Dad, this was a particularly nice validation, but nothing like what was to come next.

"Good," I said, "but there's more. Mary Anne also showed me a little plaque with her name inscribed on it. She said it was in a prominent place in your home. The plate with her name on it is new and she can see it. Do you know what she's talking about?" I asked.

This time, it was Mom who practically screamed into the receiver. Crying, and in total amazement, she told me they'd placed a clock on the mantelpiece with its hands permanently set at the very time Mary Anne's heart stopped beating. In front of it, they'd placed a picture frame containing their favorite photograph of her. Attached to the frame itself was a little golden plate with her name newly inscribed on it — just her name, "Mary Anne."

Thanks to these two messages from their beloved pet, Mom and Dad were finally able to begin healing from their loss. Healing validations like this are not uncommon. When I connect with pets who are no longer in the physical realm, they tell me they're often still around the people they loved. They hear us talking and know what we did with their bodies, their ashes or their belongings, and they're aware of the changes we make!

It's a part of the healing process to continue to honor their lives by thinking about them, and talking about them, as well as talking *to* them, even when you're no longer mourning their loss. Know in your heart that they're always a part of you. They're your furry little angels watching over you. They can see you and feel your thoughts, and they're still loving you.

When a pet's messages are so clear that they stir up very strong emotions and bring about such wonderful healings for the people who love them, as in Mary Anne's story, I know then that my Life Assignment has been validated once again, and that my work is fruitful, even when, at first, I encounter some skepticism.

SUNSHINE

I don't believe in coincidences. To me everything happens for a reason, at the right time and in the right place. When we need to be healed because we're in pain, it's not unusual for exactly the right person to come into our lives, as happened in this next case.

We were spending a leisurely Saturday afternoon at home when one of my son's friends came to spend some time with us. He was living in Minnesota studying to be a doctor, but wanting to get away from the cold weather, he'd made a trip to California to visit his family and friends. Jon and my son had been best friends since childhood, having attended grammar school, high school and college together. Jon is also like part of our own family and we teasingly call him our third son.

As he sat on the sofa with his new wife, he was recalling for us the events of the previous day. While visiting other friends, he witnessed their beloved cat's death. As a member of the medical profession, he was very concerned about how this type of trauma might affect his friend's wife who was pregnant. He knew the sadness caused by the sudden loss of such a beloved pet couldn't help but have an effect on her.

I asked him if he'd like to send a copy of my first book to his friends as my gift to help them cope with their loss. After I explained that a couple of chapters in the book dealt with the death of pets, and how to cope with such a loss, he agreed to do it.

I didn't expect to receive an answer so soon, but a week later I received this letter:

Dear Dr. Monica,

I'm a good friend of Jon and he recently spoke to you about our situation over losing our precious cat of 13 years. Jon gave me a copy of your book that you so generously gave him to pass on to us because of our loss. Jon and Jen actually saw our Sunshine lying on the ground when we walked out with them to say goodbye.

Your book was beautifully written and it surely was a tear jerker for me. I cried through half of it. I finished it within four hours and I felt so much better. It really touched me.

My husband and I would love to talk with you about why this happened to Sunshine. I've been somewhat hesitant to start the communication with you because I know it means opening myself up to this, but I've been hurting so much from it . . . I'm 6½ months pregnant and know that too much hurt can't be good for the baby. So I decided to contact you for help now.

Monique

We set up an appointment and she sent me the following information to use as a guide when I talked to Sunshine:

Sunshine was a white and grey female cat, approximately 14-16 years old. She'd been in our family since 1989 and was found as a stray. We had her for 13 years.

1) She was probably hit by a car because we found her close to our front door. There was a lot of blood coming out of her mouth. She was so, so street smart it's very hard for us to understand how she could have gotten hit by a car. She was just too aware of them.

2) Will we ever see her again in the same body when we pass on?

3) Will she come to live with us as another cat or animal in the near future?

4) Her death was very unexpected. She loved kids! We'd always planned for her to meet our child. I'm having a hard time understanding how this dream could be stopped only months before the baby is due.

5) There's a lot of guilt on our side. We were busy paying attention to our guests. Maybe if we hadn't, we would have been paying more attention to Sunshine. We always brought our cats inside before it got dark. The odd thing is that Sunshine was a people person so why she would choose to go outside when we were all inside is beyond me. That wasn't a normal thing for her to do.

We love and miss her more than words can possibly express. She was and always will be a very important part of our lives, so much so that our baby's middle name will be in honor of her.

Usually I talk with the animals in the morning when the house is quiet and the day is just beginning, because I find it's the best time for me. Although every communication is different, I always make some kind of connection. Sometimes it's more specific than others, but for me it's always a wonderful feeling.

After my conversation with Sunshine, I then reviewed my notes with Monique and her husband later in the day. They were so emotional during our phone consultation that they said very little at the time. Mostly, they just listened to my translation and cried. I then sent them my notes, and a couple of days later I received some very revealing answers.

Here are my consultation notes followed by Monique's responses:

Monica: When I talked with Sunshine, she was extremely personable, open and sweet. She was a lover. I saw a picture of her with her face right next to someone else's face, as if she was rubbing her cheek against it. Her expression was that of pure enjoyment and delight.

Monique: I would use all of those words to describe her as well. You were right on.

Monica: She loved to bathe in the sun and take naps. She told me she's doing just that on the other side.

Monique: This is exactly why we named her Sunshine … every time we'd see her she'd managed to find a speck of sun coming into the house, no matter how small it was. She just loved to lie in the sun.

Monica: When I asked her what happened on her last day, she showed me a picture I didn't like. I saw someone, a man, kicking her in the abdomen. The shoe or boot he wore seemed to have a steel toe in it, and this could account for the severity of the kick. I can't tell you if it was a mistake or if it was done on purpose. But I do know that Sunshine wasn't doing anything wrong. She said she was only visiting.

NOTE: At this point in our talk, Monique was overcome with grief knowing her cat, Sunshine, had been harmed in this way. Through a flood of tears and gentle conversation, we talked about who could have done this awful deed. Monique, understandably, wanted to know the identity of the person. I explained, as best I could, that I only saw him from Sunshine's limited perspective. I only saw the boot, and therefore couldn't identify the person. Because this took place in an apartment or condo complex, numerous people came and went, so there was no way to know, for sure, who had done this to Sunshine.

Once Monique was able to process these thoughts, I asked her to focus on Sunshine and her friendly personality rather than on her death. I recalled how Sunshine enjoyed her visits as she strolled through the neighborhood, and Monique commented on how she liked to greet everyone she met.

Monique: She'd always visit people she didn't know; she was so sweet this way.

Monica: In any event, the kick apparently ruptured her spleen, and possibly something else, because her whole tummy was full of blood. It also got into her lungs and she could hardly breathe. She tried to make it back into the house, but she just couldn't breathe any longer. It was only a matter of minutes and it was already dark outside. She went to sleep because she felt very weak and tired. This was the last thing she remembered. When she opened her eyes again, she was already in her new sunny place. Nothing was hurting and she could breathe again. It didn't take her too long to understand that she was on the other side. She said a lot of souls she knew from before came to say "Hi," including a man whom she'd known from home.

Monique: This man has to be our neighbor from about five years ago whom Sunshine was very close to. He was 65 years old when he died in his house from a stroke, and Sunshine was the only one who was with him when he passed away. He was retired and lived alone and he and Sunshine would love to hang out together in his apartment. They did this daily for almost four years, eating, watching TV, and napping while my husband and I were at work.

Monica: When I asked her if you'll ever see her again in the same body, she said, "Of course, how else would you recognize me when you get to this side! It's so easy here, all you have to do is think of me and I can be next to you in a split second. I know I sometimes took a long time to come when you called me before, but this is much, much faster."

Monique: We used to call Sunshine's name when we were looking for her outside, but she'd only respond several hours later. She loved being outside and wanted to come in on her own time. We chuckled when we heard this because it was always difficult bringing her in. We knew she was ignoring us.

Monica: I asked Sunshine if she'd come to live with you in the future, to which she replied, "I can't come back for a few years. I have a lot of work to do on this side. Since I've been here, they've told me how important I am. I'm supposed to teach others on this side before they get to go down. There's such a need for good ones like me. I had no idea how important we were. The new souls going in have many more problems to help people with than those of us who came before, but at the same time they're teaching people a lot of things even faster than before."

Monique: I'm not surprised. She was so special. I've had dozens of cats as a child, but she was truly unique — she acted more human than cat at times. She was very, very smart.

Sunshine: "My job was to teach both of you to be responsible for another being, to be patient and understanding, but at the same time, know how to set simple rules. You did magnificently, and now it's your turn to do the same for the little girl who's coming through."

Monique: We both decided to wait until the birth to find out the gender of the baby, but we've both been leaning toward a girl.

Sunshine: "You know, I'm supposed to meet her again soon. She's so excited to come through. She said you're her perfect match."

Monique: This is so exciting!

Monica: Sunshine told me, "I need to tell Mom something about the nursery," and then she showed me a picture of a small crib close to a window.

Monique: We told you on the phone that we didn't have a crib, but actually we do have a bassinette in that room. Jason and I both thought it was positioned alongside the wall away from the window. We went in there to check after our phone call and discovered we'd both forgotten we'd moved it *right by the window*. We were so surprised!

Monica: Sunshine also talked about the baby being allergic to cats! Therefore, she had a sense of urgency to leave home in time for the smells and dander to dissipate.

Monique: When my husband came home from work he told me that the baby being allergic to Sunshine was an interesting thought because he'd been very allergic to her himself. He had a reaction to her dander/hair and his eyes would swell up, get itchy and red every time she slept in the bed right next to him. She didn't have that effect on me. Maybe that's why she usually slept right next to me instead. We have two other cats and he's not allergic to them. He thought maybe his allergy to Sunshine could be passed on to the baby. This was very interesting to us. I'd forgotten about it because he'd just deal with it like any other allergy.

Sunshine: "I need to be Mom's guardian angel from this side. I'll continue to be with her in her dreams. Now I understand there's a time for everything. It was time for me to come back here. That day was better because you were distracted. It would have caused you a lot more pain if you'd seen me struggling to breathe during the last few moments of my life. You shouldn't feel guilty! It was supposed to happen this way.

"When I left my first family, I knew there had to be something better for me. They were never 'my people.' But when I met you, the strangest thing happened. I felt comfortable around you, and decided you'd do just fine as my new family. I grew up knowing that I was being loved, not just by one of you, but equally by both of you, and that made my heart soar. I learned to be more people oriented, and everyone proved to me that, in general, people are better than we (cats) give them credit for. I like to hear you say you love me and miss me. I'm often around our home and if you're paying attention you can even feel me.

"I love both of you and wish for you all the happiness that is soon to come."

After this healing experience which Sunshine had provided, Monique then wrote:

Dr. Monica,

I can't thank you enough . . . I feel so fortunate to have had this opportunity to be closer to Sunshine because of you. It's helping me feel better about her leaving us. Thank you for the work you do. What a gift!

Love,

Monique

The last story in this chapter is about a pet who was still living, but was sometimes quite sad because *his* human mom had passed on. Initially, I thought *he* was the only one who needed healing. However, because he was willing to share something very important with me during our conversation, his information then became the catalyst for bringing about some much needed closure and healing for the very special people in his life also.

WOLFIE

When I had a consultation with Dorothy and her dog, Wolfie, a Golden Retriever who was about 15 years old, she told me she'd inherited him two years ago when her daughter, Brandi, died. That's all the information she shared with me before I started talking with Wolfie.

He'd been very sad after his mom passed on, even though Grandma Dorothy was very loving and gave him such good care. He showed me their long walks, playing ball in the park, and playing with other dogs and children. It was very clear from the pictures he was sending how much he truly loved those times. He also showed me he loved to ride in the car. He and Grandma Dorothy were practically inseparable. Still there were so many nights when Wolfie was downcast and very sad.

I was explaining something to him about death, and communicating to him that his mom was on the other side when he sent me a picture showing me he'd seen his mom. She'd come to visit with him several times at night while he was resting in his favorite place on Grandma's bed.

When I mentioned this, Dorothy immediately wanted Wolfie to provide *any* information possible about Brandi. In the picture Wolfie sent me, Brandi was kneeling next to him. It was as if she looked at me and said, "Tell her I'm still wearing pants." I didn't really understand the reason why she'd say something like that, but I let it go as one of those unique pieces of information for which I don't need an immediate explanation. Dorothy asked me to repeat it again, and as I did, I remember shrugging my shoulders and, with a faint smile saying, "That's exactly what she said, and I have no other clue."

Dorothy then moved on to another question she wanted Wolfie to answer. "What about the animals?" she asked. I tried to get her to clarify that question, but she'd only say pragmatically, "He'd know."

When I asked Wolfie, he said he'd been living on a farm with lots of different animals and he missed them very much. He wished he could be there, but he understands now that he can't. It's funny, but when I translated that to Grandma Dorothy, and she confirmed that indeed he had lived on a farm, I immediately "assumed" *that* was the reason why Brandi said she was wearing pants, but Dorothy said nothing.

At the end of our conversation with Wolfie, Dorothy asked me if I could please talk directly to Brandi. I explained to her that it's *not* part of my Life Assignment to communicate with humans. My life is devoted to working only with animals and there are many other wonderful intuitives available who regularly communicate with humans. However, it seemed so important for her to find closure about something which had initially come up in my conversation with Wolfie that I reluctantly agreed to continue.

Brandi told me she'd wanted to die for a very long time before she finally passed. She didn't want to stay around, but she couldn't do anything about it except wait it out. And there was really nothing Dorothy could have done to help her during that time.

Then, out of the blue, Brandi said, "Please tell her that I want to apologize for the way I treated her. That was so bad of me. Tell her I'm sorry. I am so sorry. I no longer blame her for anything at all."

Dorothy smiled broadly for the first time. Then she told me that Brandi had been born a boy, but chose to have surgery to become a woman. Throughout her ordeal, she'd separated herself from family and friends and tried to start a new life. But during the operation, she'd been infected with Hepatitis C, which caused her a lot of pain during the last few months of her life.

Brandi had often blamed Dorothy for a lot of her emotional problems and for her life in general. When I translated to Dorothy that Brandi was sorry, the message relieved so much of Dorothy's sorrow. She knew now that all the things she'd endured from Brandi, and all the hurtful feelings between them, were finally resolved. She was now at peace.

Dorothy then commented on something I'd translated during my conversation with Wolfie. She said she felt the expression, "I'm still wearing pants," meant that Brandi had gone back to being a male entity, something he'd fought against so much during all of his life.

Dorothy reassured me that this consultation was the best experience she could possibly have had and she was now relieved of a lot of emotional baggage and pain. In the meantime, Wolfie had been able to accept Brandi's passing and say goodbye to the farm.

Shortly after our consultation, I received this letter from Dorothy:

My Dear Monica:

I'm ever so grateful that I was told about you. It was so wonderful that you picked up about Brandi. That was a very nice surprise. It was amazing how Wolfie ran from the car to your door as if he knew you. He was thrilled to be there. It was also amazing how he told you about all his wonderful experiences, many of which I'd forgotten.

The meeting with you was so wonderful. Beyond all expectations! I believe this meeting brought us closer together and helped free all of our spirits.

My very fondest regards. God Bless. Dorothy and Brandi, with Wolfie's love

As you can see, nothing is ever routine in my talks with animals. They teach me the importance of *always* listening with an open mind, and my experience with Wolfie also reaffirmed the importance of not making assumptions. But most of all, because of their willingness to share their thoughts and experiences, they're often the ones who bring about a much needed healing in the lives of those they love.

As the stories in this chapter have so beautifully illustrated, our pets have an uncommon ability to help us heal in mind and spirit when our hearts have been broken for whatever reason. But there are many other ways in which pets also practice the art of healing.

Often, just by his or her loving presence, a pet helps a person heal more quickly after an illness or operation. People get well faster because they want so much to be able to take care of, and play with, their beloved pets once again. Or, a pet may help to lower someone's blood pressure by distracting the person from the stresses of everyday life, especially when the pet lets his or her human companion provide tender loving caresses.

Companion animals provide us with healing opportunities to forget about ourselves and our cares for awhile when they need to have us feed them, walk them and pet them. And when we need a friend to talk to, they're superb listeners, our best confidants, and the keepers of our deepest secrets. Often they're the ones who give us a reason to go on living.

Sometimes an animal even chooses to take on the same illness their special person has. The pet either wants to take that illness away from the person altogether, or is trying to get the person's attention to teach them a healing lesson. This was particularly true in the chapter about "Spiritual Healing" when Casey was trying to take on his dad's medical condition to relieve him of some of his pain, Max took on Kevin's seizures, and Misty gained weight in an effort to show Cheryl that even though she, too, had a weight problem she could still give and receive love.

If there's a lesson to be learned about pets as healers, it's this: Never underestimate the power of sharing your life with a pet.

CHAPTER 14

PETS WHO REINCARNATE

There are so many researched and recorded cases of people who've spent more than one lifetime on earth, that the subject of reincarnation can't be brushed aside lightly.

While every religion discusses the phenomena of birth and death, only some address the topic of reincarnation, or rebirth. Fewer still, with the exception of some of the eastern religions, believe that animal souls come back to spend another lifetime. However, in my own experience of communicating with animals, I've discovered that many of our pets have spent more than one lifetime on this earth.

When I do a consultation, especially over the phone, I never know, nor do I ask, about the person's religious orientation, nor do I know whether or not they believe in reincarnation. However, if a pet tells me that he or she will be coming back in another lifetime, or has already spent more than one lifetime with their special person, then I share that information with the client. More often than not, it's the client who's requesting information about whether his or her pet will ever be coming back again.

In this chapter, I'll share some reincarnation stories with you and then provide more details about the concept of reincarnation itself. In the first case study, the first consultation is about two Dachshunds, one no longer living and one near death. The second consultation with the same two pets takes place after both are together again in Spirit.

Fritz and Puggy

Kathy belongs to the Cushings for Dogs group where several people had shared their experiences with her after having an animal communicator speak with their pets. She researched this topic for herself, bought and read my book, and then sent me an e-mail from Florida.

She wanted me to talk to her 16-year-old Dachshund name Fritz who'd been diagnosed with Cushing's Disease. She also wanted to hear from her female Dachshund, Puggy, who'd died of kidney failure at the age of 15, in September, 2001.

Kathy called me on May 24, 2002 at our appointment time so I could tell her about my morning conversations with Fritz and Puggy.

During my talk with Fritz, he said his whole body hurt and he complained of having horrible headaches. He told me it was very hard for him to concentrate on any task or to follow through on anything.

Because he was suffering from cognitive canine disorder, it was even harder for him to focus on some of the more detailed questions Mom had wanted me to ask him. I felt Fritz was letting me know that it was time for him to go.

While my conversation with Fritz was fairly short, when it was Puggy's turn, she was practically unstoppable.

"When I realized that you were calling me I was so happy," she said. "My energy is 100 percent now, and I'm a very happy girl. I enjoyed every minute of my life with Fritz and Mom and Dad, but here, I'm very busy because my job is to be a greeter. I greet others who are making their transitions, who don't yet have anyone they know on this side. I love to greet new arrivals." Then she sent me a picture of herself running around and enjoying all of her freedom.

Puggy gave me the following message for her mom: "When you're ready to have another animal again, I'd love to return to you. You'd recognize me because my eyes were so expressive before, and I'd like to keep that trait so you'd have no doubt it's me."

She also said, "Tell Mom she shouldn't worry about Fritz. I'll take good care of him, and he'll be standing up on his hind legs to show off again soon." She then ran off to do her job.

Later, Kathy told me that the very next evening, Fritz had a massive stroke/seizure and never recovered. She said they helped him to "go over the Rainbow Bridge" the next day, Sunday, May 26, 2002.

Kathy requested a second consultation about three months later, wanting to check in on her two Dachshunds, both now on the other side.

Since I communicate with hundreds of animals every month, I simply don't remember the details of earlier conversations, especially when some time has passed. And, because I need to be available to so many clients, I've found it unrealistic and impractical to spend my time doing research. For this reason, I approach each appointment as if it were the first one.

When Kathy called me in August, she reminded me that we'd worked together in May, but during the second consultation, I couldn't consciously remember any of the information from our first visit. I could only translate to Kathy what I was actually receiving this time, without relating it to the information from our earlier conversation. This is what I shared with her in August:

I'm pleased to tell you that Fritz is very happy on the other side. He was standing on his hind legs, with his front legs up in the air, and said to me, "Look! Tell Mom I can do this again!"

He told me that Puggy was waiting for him on the other side of the light. She was soooo happy to see him. I could see them wagging their tails. They looked like twins, very similar. Neither one of them had a single white hair on their noses. They both looked young and vibrant.

Puggy sent me a picture to show me she often puts her face on top of Fritz's back and just rests it there. It's her way of saying to him how much she loves him. They're enjoying their time together so much and they both feel very excited that we can still talk with them.

Fritz doesn't want to talk a lot about his last few months on earth because he says they were hard on him, and also very hard on you. He's sorry you had to go through so much anguish, but at the same time, he feels it helped you to have to stay more focused on him than on yourself.

He says you have so much to give to others, and you need to work on believing in yourself a little more. You have great compassion and it's a shame you don't love yourself as much as you should.

He thinks you'd do just great if you brought another pet into your heart. He wants to stay on the other side for a while, but he knows someone else special who's coming your way. This is someone he knows in spirit from before.

Fritz says his friend is almost ready to come back and it shouldn't be too long now. When the conditions are right, it'll become apparent to you that you're ready to go looking for him. It will be instant love and you'll have no doubt that this new puppy is meant to be your baby. Fritz says this is his present to you because you were so good to him throughout his life. Since he was so happy with you, he wants this new puppy to make you laugh and make you very happy, too.

Fritz then sent me several different pictures. In one, he was wearing a bow. In another, he was playing with a ball by rolling it with his nose. And in yet another, he showed me how much he enjoyed eating. He said the treats were the greatest, and he didn't mind doing tricks to get them.

In response to this consultation, I received the following thoughts in an e-mail from Kathy, accompanied by several pictures:

> August 6, 2002
>
> Dear Dr. Monica:
>
> I can't begin to thank you. I feel like a tremendous weight has been lifted from my heart. I'm sending some pictures to show Fritz "standing up" and Fritz and Puggy cuddling. That's how they usually

slept. They were almost always right next to each other. Many times their movements were actually synchronized! When they'd run, they'd run almost as one, but then Fritz was faster and would start to pull ahead, so Puggy would give him a "shove" with her butt as he passed.

I guess it's evident how very much I love those two, but again, they were my babies.

The picture of them on the bridge was taken several years ago. Fritz was afraid to go down on the bridge and Puggy seemed to be coaxing him down. He really didn't want to go — he remembered what had happened the last time he was on that bridge! The water in the pond was covered with duck weed and he was chasing a lizard. The lizard jumped off the bridge and scampered across the duck-weed covered pond. So, Fritz jumped right in after him, only to discover he'd jumped into the pond! I heard the splash and ran to rescue him! He was one very unhappy and scared little boy. He wouldn't go back down on that bridge.

Thanks again! I'll let you know when we get new babies!

Kathy Sheppard

I'd never seen any pictures of Fritz and Puggy until now, so during both the first and second consultations, I was simply translating exactly what I was seeing at the moment when Fritz stood on his hind legs, and Puggy rested her head on Fritz's back. When Kathy sent me the pictures, after the second consultation, it was a lovely moment for me because the pictures validated so perfectly exactly what I'd seen in my mind's eye. (See photos in the Photo Section, Fritz and Puggy, #1, #2 and #3.)

A year later in August, 2003, Kathy sent me an e-mail telling me they were almost ready to adopt new puppies. They were remodeling their home and getting it all ready for the pups, including the right kind of flooring and dog-proofing for the cabinet doors. Her husband wanted to wait until fall so the weather would be a little cooler and it would be easier to house-train them.

Kathy had been "seeing" Puggy out of the corner of her eye for several weeks before she contacted me. She knew this was her cue and the right time had come, but she had a lot of questions. Kathy wanted a reading with both Fritz and Puggy to enlist their help with the process of finding the right puppies.

Before we go on, I need to explain something very important. Although I do receive frequent requests to speak with animals who've already made their transitions, I rarely ever receive a request to ask them to directly help guide their person to a specific litter and specific puppies. I've always felt that this was a very personal thing and not up to someone else to point out. But Kathy was so determined not to miss the puppies who were meant for her that I decided to help her as best I could.

She had several specific questions for our third consultation:

1) Are they ready to come back?
2) We selected the names Daisy Mae and Norton Buster. Do they like them?
3) Where will I find them — with Patti, Jeanne or where?
4) How will I know them — will Puggy still have the kink in her tail and her big beautiful eyes? What about Fritz?

These are the notes from the consultation I did for Kathy on August 27 2003, in response to her questions:

Puggy is such a happy girl and has no problems communicating with me. She's still very outgoing and she's wagging her tail furiously as we start to exchange pictures. She's very happy that you're getting her message and she knows that now you're ready to start giving your love again. She's been eager to come back and was waiting for just the right time. She says that she's being born almost as we speak.

When I asked her how you'd be able to recognize her, she said this time she'll have some dark brown on her top coat. She'll be special and different from the others in her litter, and therefore you can't miss her.

She loves the name Daisy Mae because it has the sound of a proper lady. It also reminds her how much she loves the outdoors, which is one of the things she'll enjoy when she comes back. She sent me a picture of flowers and a beautiful garden to emphasize her feelings.

Puggy says she doesn't think you know the person who has her new mother and therefore she can't tell you her name. But she tells me that if you look for her (and I see you reading something like a newspaper) you'll be able to locate her. You shouldn't worry about *not* finding her. She'll make sure you're together again.

She also wants to tell you that Fritz decided not to come back with her. They're still good friends, but he decided he wanted to stay on the other side a while longer. He's sending someone else in his place.

All of a sudden Fritz started to talk without an introduction or even a warning. It almost felt as if he'd been listening all the time, and suddenly he got upset that Puggy was talking about him, so he decided to start talking for himself. He says that, personality wise, the new puppy is more adaptable and he'll make you laugh.

Fritz was laughing because he was trying to tell the new arrival he'd have to stand on his hind legs, but the new little boy was having a lot of trouble understanding how he'd *ever* be able to balance such a long body in that position for any length of time. (He apparently had never had any experience as a Dachshund before.) Fritz didn't know if he'd be successful at doing this trick unless Mom and Dad put a lot of effort into teaching him.

Again Fritz made the comment that the new puppy will make you laugh! He also says he won't leave you. He'll always be watching from the other side, and now more than ever, he wants to make sure the new kids will be OK.

Later, Kathy wrote to me:

> Dr. Monica
> I located a litter that had pups exactly like the description. They were so very precious. They ran to us and began covering us with

kisses. My husband and I felt that these were the ones for us.

When we arrived home, one of them did so many of the things that Puggy had done as a pup. I feel sure this one is Puggy reincarnated. These little guys are so mellow and loving! They've certainly made me happy! We just sit and laugh at their antics.

Kathy

It's important to note that this couple didn't rush the process even though they looked forward to enjoying the preciousness of their fur babies once again, albeit as different personalities. They first needed to be ready within themselves to give of their time and love to the new puppies. After the house had been put in order and the weather was milder, Kathy became aware of the clues she'd been experiencing and knew it was time to look for them. She listened to her intuition and followed her heart. Though it was about a year later, she was convinced this was meant to be, and she and her husband absolutely love these new babies. (See photo in Photo Section, Fritz and Puggy, #4)

Aicha

Diane had lost her special little girl early in the year. This was the best dog she'd ever had and she could hardly get over losing her. Though not easily, as time passed, she finally did accept the fact her precious pet was gone forever.

Then one day, out of the blue, she had a "knowing" — one of those moments when you just *know* something is true. Her inner voice was telling her it was time to get another dog. And not just any dog, but it would be Aicha coming back again as a different personality. Diane just knew this was a message sent from above because she had no hesitation and no doubt, so she set out to find this precious soul once again.

Before contacting me, she worked with another animal communicator who told her that her little girl was waiting for a Papillion body. But then Aicha decided that body was a very sick one and it would be better if she waited just a little bit longer for a litter of Cocker Spaniels, the very same breed Aicha had been before.

Diane did a lot of homework before calling me. She contacted all the breeders in her area and made a list of the upcoming births for all the different bitches who were pregnant. She compiled a list of the breeders' names and addresses, the bitches' names, the colors of both parents, the expected colors of the puppies, and how many litters the parents had already produced.

Armed with this information, she wanted to know how and where to find her Aicha. She didn't want to miss this opportunity and was now counting on me to help her out. I remember our first phone conversation. Diane wanted to make sure I'd done this before. She wanted to be certain I'd be able to find her little girl.

I told her I'd previously been able to obtain information about pets who were going to reincarnate, but I didn't know how much information Aicha would provide until I actually talked with her.

Diane decided to give me a try, and sent me a picture of Aicha and a list of her questions. We had our visit on *8/18,* and it became interesting how many times the number eight came up. *It seemed eight was quite a significant number in their lives.* This is how the consultation developed with Diane on the phone:

The picture Diane sent me was one of Aicha taken during her final days when her coat had been shaved. Aicha started right out by saying, "I wish Mom would have sent you a better picture of me. I used to be so beautiful. My ears grew long and silky, though Mom didn't like it when they'd rub on the floor and get dirty. I was such a good girl before, but I fear she may be disappointed in the new me.

"There's so much Mom needs to learn now that I've decided to come back and finish what I started. She learned how to love because of me the first time. Now she needs to learn how to be patient. That's a huge task for her. Mom's not very good at being patient.

"Please tell her I love her and not to worry so much. I'll make sure to find her. She'll know. Since she has a lot of questions, I'll try to answer them the best I can. I'm excited about this."

1) Is Aicha still coming back as a female?

Aicha: Of course, you don't like boys that much, remember?

Diane on the phone: She's absolutely right, I always had females!

2) Is she still coming back as a Cocker Spaniel?

Aicha: Is there any other breed that would be as good? You already know the answer to this question. I've been talking to you in your dreams for awhile now. You just saw me!

Diane: She's right. I've been praying so hard for her to be a Cocker Spaniel just like Aicha was before, because I just love the breed, and I've been feeling her around me as she used to be.

3) What color is Aicha going to be when she's born this time?

Monica: I think the best way to describe her color from the picture she's sending me is a combination of soft red and light buff. As she grows older, the color of red will be deeper at first and then will fade out. She'll be a beautiful strawberry blond, with long ears and long eyelashes.

4) What month is Aicha going to be born? And will it be the beginning, middle or end *of the month?*

Monica: She'll be born towards the end of this month. *I keep seeing the number eight. It could mean that she'll be one of eight puppies.*

5 and 6) Diane had two questions next for which I couldn't get answers because I rarely ever get names: Where is the breeder located? And what is the breeder's first name?

7) What month will I go to pick her out?

Monica: Aicha says she'd like to stay with her dog mother *until she's at least eight weeks old.* She wants to be very close to her birth mom. She says if you take her before that, she wouldn't have the opportunity to learn things she needs to know and she'll grow very needy of you. She wants to take her time to learn as much as she can. She said to tell you, remember patience! On the other hand, she's almost convinced you won't have the patience to wait that long and jokingly she says you *will* pay for it later.

8) How will I pick her out from a litter of puppies?

Aicha: Don't worry, this is the time, and we'll find each other. You can't go wrong.

9) Will Aicha remember me when I go to pick her out?

Aicha: I'll know you because our souls will recognize each other.

Then Aicha said to me, "Please tell Mom to realize that although I'm the same soul, I'm not going to be the same personality. This time I have more things to teach her and my agenda is full. Therefore I'll need to be a little more reckless and allow myself more freedom to express my feelings. We're already starting out on a good note. Tell her I'm so proud of her for taking the first step."

While Diane and I were on the phone reviewing my conversation with Aicha, Diane asked me what my feeling was regarding the breeder. Could I tell just by looking at the enclosed list of *eight breeders* which one would be the right one? I told her that although Aicha had not pinpointed anyone, I had a "feeling" that the mother would be Miss Jenny, who belonged to the second breeder and was one of her two dogs who were expecting.

Diane's voice jumped a few octaves as she almost screamed, "Me too, me too, I have the same feeling! Thanks! I needed to hear you say that! I hope she has her puppies on my husband's birthday, August 24, although her due date is August 26."

A week later I received a card from Diane:

Dear Dr. Monica:

Thank you so much for the reading with Aicha. The notes have especially helped as I like to read them over from time to time. Let me tell you the latest news — not all of it's good though. Miss Jenny gave birth to nine puppies — one has already died. *Four* of them are severely dehydrated *and* the other *four* are OK. I've said prayers everyday to let all the puppies survive. I sure hope Aicha is among the healthy ones. She's come to visit me a couple of times late in the night. I hope she didn't change her mind.

As a special thank you I've enclosed a St. Francis pet tag. Thanks for everything,

Love,

Diane

I called Diane ten weeks later. She'd chosen puppy number *eight*, the runt of the litter, and named her Arina. The puppies were born on *8/28*. When she was with all of the puppies, she looked into Arina's eyes and knew beyond the shadow of a doubt that this little girl was hers. Diane said that Arina has a lot of the same personality traits and does the same things as Aicha used to do, including watching TV at this young age, especially when there're whales or children on the screen. Arina is nine weeks old now but she was taken from her birth mom at five weeks of age because of health issues with her mother. Consequently, just as promised, Diane is having some issues with Arina!

The first thing Diane said to me when we talked is that she remembered how Aicha emphasized how important it was for Diane to be patient. "That is an understatement!" said Diane. But she loves her little girl just the same and wouldn't change what happened for anything.

Diane is convinced the reason they recognized each other right away is because they've already spent many lifetimes together.

REINCARNATION

The study of metaphysics has helped me clarify in my own mind how reincarnation works, and I'll try to explain it for you in easy, visual terms as it's been taught to me.

We all come from one single source. You may call it God, the Divine, All That Is, the Source of our Being, or whatever name you're comfortable with. But imagine if you will, just for this illustration, that the single source from which we *all* come is an Ocean where the waters are absolutely pure and perfect.

Then imagine that some of this very pure water from the ocean has been placed in a large receptacle, which we'll call a bucket.

Some of this water has then been taken out of the bucket and placed in a pitcher. The water in the pitcher is then transferred to a glass.

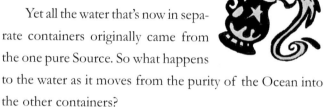

Yet all the water that's now in separate containers originally came from the one pure Source. So what happens to the water as it moves from the purity of the Ocean into the other containers?

In this example, the water inside the glass represents your soul, or your essence, while it's in human experience as an individual personality.

While you're here on earth, there are many varieties of glasses you might use to house your soul. The type you choose, in our example, reflects your personality and sense of values. For instance, yours may be a clear drinking glass (a no-nonsense type of individual who knows what he or she wants in life); a plastic cup with gaudy colors and decorations (someone who doesn't take life very seriously, who's all play and no work); a beautifully shaped glass with artistic designs on it (someone who's very creative and expressive); a champagne glass (someone who wants more than he or she can afford and is focused only on the material things in life); or a wine glass (a refined person who aspires to the higher things in life). But whatever type of glass represents your personality, it's only a temporary housing for your soul.

And what is a soul? It's the essence of who you are, not your personality with an ego, but the real you, who's growing and learning in each experience, in each lifetime.

As an individual soul, you're given the freedom to make your own choices. But when your soul temporarily becomes one with physical form, and acts as an individual personality during an earthly experience, you're free to make either soul choices or ego choices. If you make soul (good) choices, the water in your glass remains clear. If you make ego (bad) choices, the water becomes cloudy.

If the water in your glass has become cloudy, you then need to have other opportunities to make wise choices, ones which will bring you back into attunement with your Source, so that the water in your glass can become clear once again.

In order to reach this state of attunement, you're given all of the lifetimes necessary to learn to make wise choices, to learn many lessons, so that you finally *do* remember who you are in relation to your Source. But in order to remember this, you need to stop listening to the loud voice from the ego of your personality and start paying full attention to the gentle whispers from your Higher Self.

You may work on only one lesson during a lifetime, or you may be working on several at a time. If you don't learn the lesson, or lessons, during one experience, you'll be given as many other opportunities, or lifetimes, as you need, in which to learn them. And as you master each of these lessons, and begin to remember who you are in relation to the Source of Your Being, the cloudy water will become more and more clear. The learning process takes time because the soul is experiencing its lessons, *not with the complete freedom of spirit, but within the limitations of the consciousness of each human experience.*

When your glass (the body you used while you were here on earth) ceases to exist, your essence then goes back to the pitcher where the water represents your Higher Self whenever you're not in human experience.

When we talk about the Higher Self, we mean the part of you that was created perfectly. Your Higher Self makes choices that reflect your connection with the Source of your Being. It's the part of you which can comprehend what goodness is. Your Higher Self has the essence of the divine in it and is *always* connected to your Source. It's in your Higher Self, that all of your experiences from different lifetimes come together to help you remember this connection.

An example from the world of the ocean might help to illustrate this. Think of your Higher Self as the head of an octopus and think of each tentacle as a representation of a different lifetime you experience. The head of the octopus knows everything that's going on and directs each one of the tentacles. It knows where each tentacle is and what it's doing, which one is active and which one is at rest. The only tie each one of the tentacles has is to the head, or Higher Self. Each tentacle is independent of all of the others and it can learn different things based on the activities of its particular experiences. But it's the head, or the Higher Self, which puts everything together and combines all of the lessons learned by each of the tentacles, or, in other words, in each of the lifetimes.

When, in time, you've fulfilled all of the earthly reincarnations you need in order to learn all the necessary lessons, the water in your pitcher will be clear once again. You can then rejoin the next higher level and merge the water from your pitcher with the water in the large container.

The large container of water represents the Universal Soul. It's a communal place where all individual souls meet to work together toward the highest good of the world, maybe even of the Universe.

At the end of time, you'll eventually rejoin the pure and clear Ocean, or the "All that Is," our Maker, our God.

The main point to keep in mind is that the essence of each one of us is made of the same water, or essence, as the Ocean, or the Divine. The Bible says we all have a spark of the Divine and we're always connected to our Source.

While this is a very simplistic explanation of reincarnation, in general, it covers the essential points. But there's an important fact to keep in mind about reincarnation, especially as it applies to our pets.

When we, as people, come back to live another life, we're put in different positions each time by the circumstances of our new lives: family, money, social status or the new era in which we live. We have different experiences and we go through them as different personalities.

For our animals, it's the same. When we talk about an animal reincarnating, you need to fully understand that the soul of your pet is not going to be coming back exactly as the same personality of the pet you knew before.

Choosing to believe that a new pet is the exact replica of another beloved pet not only sets you up for disappointment, but it's also quite disrespectful and does a disservice to the new pet. Trying to repeat an experience, or have the same exact animal, is as impossible as cloning yourself and expecting you to make the same choices in your new life under an entirely different set of circumstances.

Because the new pet has a different personality, you might at first tend to miss the slight clues he or she gives to show you that the essence of your former pet, which you loved so much, is back. But your heart and intuitive knowing will recognize this precious soul in time, even if that recognition isn't immediate.

Each lifetime an animal shares with us is special because of what he or she is able to teach us. Though their lives are so much shorter than ours, and it hurts so much to see them go, it's still very important for us to learn to love again, so that our lives can be enriched by the lessons a new pet has to teach us, whether it's a new soul who'll be sharing our lives, or the soul of one of our former pets reincarnated.

CHAPTER 15

PETS AS SOUL MATES

A soul mate is someone with whom you have such a deep spiritual connection, that when you meet again, you both feel as if
you've known each other forever. The two of you are so
attuned to one another, you usually know each other's thoughts, even
when they're not spoken aloud. A soul mate is someone you can't imagine ever spending the rest of your life without. You seem to complete
one another. It's as if the love the two of you share is something beyond
the limits of space and time, beyond life and death.

For those lucky enough to have found their soul mates, they say it
feels like an eternal love which only has to be remembered to be renewed.
Upon meeting this other soul, a kind of genetic memory or instinctual
recall occurs, for which there seems to be no explanation. It's immediate
and both souls recognize each other from a time long past.

If we believe in reincarnation and how it works, then we can understand that eternal love has a way of finding us again and again, throughout our lives.

The idea of soul mates is as old as ancient history and mythology.
Plato, in his *Symposium (A Discourse on 'Love')* describes how Aristophanes
sees the Nature of Man. He says that, in ancient times, there were not just
two sexes, but that there was a third, a union of the two.

This individual was round, with a back and sides forming a circle. There were four hands and four feet, with one head and two faces, each looking the opposite way. This union of male and female made them extremely powerful, and they started to defy their deities.

Olympus wasn't a place where the gods were going to allow men to be rebels, so they decided to kill all humans. At the last minute, the god Zeus had a change of heart saying something like, "If we kill everyone, we won't have anybody left to adore us or to offer sacrifices to us." Zeus then offered a solution suggesting, "I'll cut each of these humans in two halves and allow them to live. Thus their strength will subside and we'll have no more disobedience."

The other gods applauded this decision and the divisions took place. Apollo turned the faces forward and rendered their scars invisible. The humans were divided into males and females and started to populate the earth.

Moreover, the legend continues, as much as the whole of Olympus tried to have humans forget about their beginnings, they couldn't prevent at least some memory of that original unity. This is the reason sometimes given why humans, to this day, continue to search for their other half, to once again become powerful and to feel complete. It's why we're always looking for the yin and the yang. The perfect balance, the perfect circle!

An important point I'd like to make is that soul mates have a spiritual connection regardless of what sex they are. You can have a soul mate in a friend of the same sex, just as well as you can have a soul mate in your marriage partner. It's something of the spirit, not of the body. A soul mate is a spiritual partner. The love of soul mates is an expression of Universal Love.

But what if I tell you that some people have found their soul mate in an animal friend? Is this such a far-fetched concept? What if a person has never been fulfilled spiritually or emotionally by another person, but they're able to find their solace in their beloved animal companion who loves them unconditionally? And what if the animal has such a strong bond with the person that only being with that particular person will do?

The next three cases are about people who found soul mates in their pets.

Boo

I went to a home to do a consultation for two friends and their dogs. One was a white Bichon Frise whose usually long curly hair was trimmed very short. He was a skinny thing, a little shy, and he hid behind Mom most of the time I was there. His mom, Sandy, had picked him out from the shelter and wasn't sure how old he was or what his past experiences had been.

Boo, although shy, was very eager to answer the questions Mom was asking of him.

He told her he was a very old soul who spoke to her through her heart. He always understood whatever she said to him in a special way.

Sandy wanted to know if he'd been abused before and he replied, "I know you think I was abused, but I wasn't in the way you think. The other people treated me just like an animal and never spoke to me. So I left them and was on a mission to find you. There were a lot of people interested in me at the adoption place, but I was waiting for you. I made sure you knew I was the one you should pick."

"Does he feel abandoned when I leave, does he think I'm not coming back?" Sandy asked. Boo replied, "Never do I feel abandoned . . . how could I? You only tell me a million times you're coming back!" Sandy broke into a very hearty laugh. "I do," she said. "I tell him things over and over again, because I want him to know."

Boo continued, "I feel what you feel. When you're sad, I become sad too. I do things purposely to make you laugh, to make you change how you feel. I understand everything you're saying — words, sentences, and pictures. We have a long history together. We've met many times before. I'm here to let you know I'm the one you seek. I'm your other half."

Sandy told me she had a special feeling for this little guy. It wasn't just love for an animal companion. She felt something deeper, as if their souls were one. She couldn't explain it, but Sandy knew Boo felt the same way she did. She often sensed this special connection when he'd shower her with kisses. He'd only kiss her on her lips, never on her hands or arms or face.

Sandy said, "I wouldn't tell this to any other person, but I know *you'll* understand me when I say I feel as if he's my soul mate, and he's come once again to look for me. That I found him at a particular moment in time when I was feeling so down on myself, is incredible. I wasn't looking for a dog. It just happened that I couldn't take my eyes off of him . . . or my heart. It was more than love at first sight. It was a knowing, a remembering. It was meant to be."

In the story above, it's easy to see how one soul completes the other. This "completion" is an important aspect of the relationship — whether it's between humans or between humans and animals. It's validated by one's inner thoughts, feelings, and emotions.

The story below is also a reflection of this "completeness." The next pet provided healing not only for his special person, but for many other people as well.

TRAGER

Denise came to see me with three of her furry friends and a picture of one who was in Spirit. His name was Trager. He was a German Shepherd who'd died at the age of six.

I was able to tell Denise what a special soul this animal was and that he'd come to her with a special agenda. He told me he'd been her soul mate and that it was thanks to him that today Denise had other animal friends. I just translated what I saw but didn't know the extent of the story until Denise wrote it down for me.

> Dear Dr. Monica,
>
> I met my canine soul mate on March 16, 1998. I was visiting a colleague friend of mine who's an intuitive counselor. She's also a foster parent for German Shepherd Rescue and Service Dogs for Victims of Assault. She had a lot of dogs with her, as usual. One very large, beautiful black and tan shepherd, with haunting yellow eyes kept circling the perimeter of the room — watchful, shy, suspicious — watching me all the time.

There was something about him which just kept drawing my attention so that I could barely keep my focus on my friend, even though she was trying to tell me about the course and direction of my future!

I remember her telling me she'd named him Trager, after a man who discovered how working with people's deep muscle tissue healed them on a very, very deep level.

She felt that Trager was here to be a deep healer also. He was so darned smart. In only a day at her office, he was already able to find where she hides the treats.

I can't explain what came over me as I watched him circle. I'd never had a pet as an adult because I had allergies to dogs and cats from the time I was three days old and had been conditioned to the idea that owning a pet wasn't a good idea for me. But there was just something about those eyes. . . .

Impulsively, I asked my friend if he was up for adoption, and what did she think of me adopting him. She decided to use a Tarot card deck that she kept close by and after shuffling, drew, no kidding, the Lover's card when it came to Trager and me. This is a woman who's not usually overly emotional and there she was with tears in her eyes saying. "It's a love match!" I was covered with goose bumps, even before hearing her words.

Off we went, Trager and me. He rode in the back of my Altima, seated, panting, looking at me in my rearview mirror — direct eye contact. If you know dogs, you know how unusual it is for them to make eye contact for any long period of time. I stared back at him as much as I could, given that I was driving. Several times I just shook my head and said to him, "Well, Trager boy, I sure don't know what we've gotten ourselves into!" He just continued to stare.

This was the beginning of my life with my canine soul mate. I took him through obedience training — he was a champ. Later I'd know beyond a shadow of a doubt, he was truly my champion.

As time went on, he never needed a leash as long as I was there. He heeled next to me without words spoken between us. He kept watch over me every night until I fell asleep. He was there, vigilant, every morning when I opened my eyes. He didn't crowd me; he was just always, always, the shepherd who watched over me.

I brought him to my psychotherapy office all the time and he both shielded me with his body from people whose thoughts were very negative, and provided deep comfort and healing for many, many of my clients. I keep a picture of him in my office and people who experienced him, and the two of us together, are still reverent when they see it.

I lost him after complications from surgery on October 23, 2002. A part of my heart died that night. To know this kind of love and devotion is to be blessed for a lifetime. When I thought back, I remembered that on the day of his surgery, I was sitting on some stairs across from him, praying that he'd do well during the operation. He walked back over to me from the door that led to the surgical room, and laid his head in my lap. Trager never, never laid his head on my lap because it was too unmanly for him. My heart filled with love for him and I told him everything would be OK. I was wrong. He seemed to know better.

Dr. Monica — I am so grateful for the reading you did on all my animals, as well as Trager. It brought me peace of mind and a greater understanding of our relationship.

With love and respect,

Denise and Trager

This next story is about a love that had to overcome many obstacles before these two soul mates could be together again.

SARAHORSIE

I wasn't Pamela's first choice when she selected an animal communicator to work with her horse this time. In fact, she didn't even know me, but the person she'd originally called had to cancel and had given Pamela my name as a substitute. I was happy to come to see them because I don't have the opportunity to "talk" with many horses.

Pamela had already consulted with another animal communicator many years before and she was now anxious to receive even more information from her 18-year-old female horse. This precious soul, whom she'd named Sarahorsie, was mahogany bay in color and 16 hands tall.

I arrived at her home and walked to the barn with Pamela's husband, Glenn, where Pamela and Sarahorsie were waiting for me. The first thing Pamela said to me was that Sarahorsie seemed to anticipate my arrival because, instead of walking around her huge corral, she'd remained calm and "waiting" on the cement patio under the awning. This was something unusual for her, I was told. I always send a message to the animal I'm going to see before my visit so that he or she will recognize me when I arrive. Apparently Sarahorsie had received and understood the message I sent her very well!

Glenn busied himself around the barn to give Pamela a little privacy. Pamela wanted to record our session and we started promptly. But it soon became apparent that both of them needed to hear what Sarahorsie was saying, so Glenn came a little closer to our group.

We had an active consultation with a lot of questions, and Sarahorsie explained the reasons for some of her behaviors. For instance, she explained she was refusing to walk pathways she'd walked in the past because she felt uneasy about the terrain. She was also reacting to Pamela's anxiety about lack of control, so I suggested Pamela act more assertively to reassure her horse that, in fact, *she's* the one who's in control. Sarahorsie then told us she was afraid of barking dogs coming toward her because she'd been attacked before by a mean barking dog. These were all behaviors Pamela hoped to improve, so it was nice to "hear" the reasons for them from her own horse.

We were approaching the end of Pamela's extensive list of questions, and she was already pleased with the outcome of our talk. Still, she had one last question she wanted me to ask her horse: "What does she want me to know about our relationship and life overall?" This of course, is not an unusual question, but the answer left all three of us stunned.

Immediately, Sarahorsie started to send information which I translated to Pamela: "We share a very special relationship because we've met before in another time and place where we don't have bodies but are only in Spirit. We were very close then and we'd pledged to find one another again. I want to thank you for being persistent in this life. You recognized my soul right away, as I recognized yours. We knew we couldn't live without one another, and you waited for me and fought for me so that we *could* be together again. I thank you for that because we're meant to be with each other. We're soul mates, we understand each other, we need each other, we love each other. I wouldn't be here today if it wasn't for your love and persistence. Thank you!"

Pamela's jaw dropped in awe, but not for very long. She immediately shared Sarahorsie's story with me:

Pamela had been suffering from depression and found the only thing that made her happy was to watch horses. Glenn would take her to the park where they'd sit and wait for the horses to walk by. One day Pamela saw Sarahorsie (then named Sara), and felt an immediate attraction which she couldn't understand. She felt compelled to get up and approach this horse so that she could touch her and talk with her. The bond was sealed and they became best friends. Pamela would go to Sara's stall to visit with her almost daily. When Sara was put up for sale, Pamela immediately wanted to buy her, but the owner refused, telling her that she didn't have enough know-how to deal with a horse of that caliber.

Sara was sold to another woman who, overnight, moved her across town. Pamela felt sick not knowing where Sara was, and Glenn was desperate to help. They both needed to find Sara again. After six weeks of searching, they came across yet another barn and went from stall to stall reading the names of the horses and the owners which were posted on signs outside each space. They stopped when they read "Licorice Twist Sara" and the name of the owner. They thought for sure this was "their" Sara. But it was dark and they couldn't see inside the stall because it had bars on the door. Pamela decided to call out Sara's name in a sing-song way, something she'd done during the years they'd already known each other. Suddenly, Sara nickered. Pamela had her answer. This *was* "her" horse!

Pamela knew the new owner didn't want her around so she'd go visit Sarahorsie at night just to be close to her. When eventually she was put up for sale again, Pamela and Glenn left a note on the door of her stall asking to buy her. But once again they were turned down because they didn't have sufficient knowledge about horses, and Sara was considered to be a "difficult" one.

As a last resort, Pamela and Glenn finally asked a friend to buy Sarahorsie from this woman, and the friend agreed. Thanks to this arrangement, Sarahorsie has been with Pamela and Glenn for the last 11 years. Persistence indeed paid off. These soul mates could not be denied their togetherness.

FINDING YOUR SOUL MATE

You don't find a soul mate just by wanting one. As with everything worthwhile in life, you have to work at it. You visualize, you pray, you write down your expectations, giving this relationship a reality in your mind that your essence, your Higher Self, will look for. Take a few moments each day to do this. Be regular. Do it every day at the same time and in the same place. Or do it several times a day. Use the same internal pictures or visualization technique, or use the same prayer. Keep it simple, yet organized in your mind, so you know what it is you're asking for.

Through meditation, communicate to your subconscious mind exactly what you want. Don't underestimate the power of your thoughts, or the love in your heart. If you're not finding someone as quickly as you'd like, maybe there's something else you still need to learn before the two of you are ready to be together again.

If you're looking for a person, be very specific about the traits and qualities you're looking for. Say when or where you'd like to find this person. Give a location, a country, a state, or a city. Define the qualities you're looking for in this person.

If you're looking for a pet soul mate, name any specific species, breed, sex, color, or markings. Note the qualities you'd like your pet soul mate to have. Make a list and keep it handy. Start believing that everything you ask for will materialize. Know that your Higher Self is always working to manifest what you need or want, if it's for your highest good.

A FINAL THOUGHT

Most of the time, finding a pet as a soul mate comes as a complete surprise for my clients. They weren't prepared ahead of time for such a soul-stirring encounter, although inevitably, they all "knew" that something special was going on the minute they met. They just never thought a pet could bring so much love and happiness into their lives, and affect them so strongly at such a deep level.

Sometimes when I talk to my clients about an animal who's passed on, they don't want to tell me how significant their love for their animal was until after I've been able to make a connection with the spirit of the animal and verify that they have, in fact, had other lifetimes together. I think most people are afraid to express that kind of love aloud for fear that someone will think less of them, or even think they're crazy. Please don't! If you've had a very special relationship with your animal, one that goes beyond the regular human/animal bond, you're indeed counted among those few who are extremely blessed.

Finding a soul mate is rare. Most people search a lifetime and never do. If your heart and soul are telling you that this relationship you have now, or had before, with a special animal is more than just an ordinary person/pet bond, give yourself the gift of acknowledging it. Yes, you are special; you are loved beyond the physical. Yes, you will continue to be loved eternally. Yes, the promise you've made to each other of finding the other again has or will come true. Yes, even if it was only for a short time (by our standards), you were COMPLETE.

CHAPTER 16

PETS AND ENERGY IMPRINTING
UNDERSTANDING LIFE, ENERGY, PHYSICAL EXPERIENCE AND AURAS

I'm frequently asked by my students and clients why their new pets seem to take on some of the exact behaviors of their deceased pets, even though it doesn't look as if it's a case of reincarnation.

They may ask: "How come my new dog is doing unusual things that my previous one used to do? He's displaying *exactly* the same behavior as the dog I had before him, with no encouragement from me. But I got him one month *after* my first dog died, and he was *already* six months old at the time!" How could that be reincarnation?

Or, "I got an *older* cat after my first one died because I didn't like being alone, but this one is picking up all the same characteristics, behavioral patterns and mannerisms as my past friend. If this isn't reincarnation, then what's happening?"

They're not talking about common things most animals do, like circling several times before lying down, routinely begging for food, or jumping on the sofa. Instead, they're talking about unique behaviors.

When I was teaching a class on "How to Communicate With Your Pets," one of my students told me she'd gone to one of the biggest bookstores in California searching for information about animals coming into a new home who seem to "pick up" traits of a recently deceased pet. She was told there were no books on the subject.

During class, she asked me about this unusual pet behavior. As I was relating the details of my beliefs on the subject, she wanted to know what this process was called. "I don't know," I said. "I can't really recall if I've ever seen it identified." So I decided to give this unique process a name. I called it *Energy Imprinting.*

Understanding Energy Imprinting may help answer some questions about the unusual behaviors of new pets which aren't explained by reincarnation. I'll explain more about Energy Imprinting in a moment, but first let me share with you what Tammy, one of my students, experienced with two older cats who came to live with her.

Chat and Thimble

A little more than a year after both of her own cats died, Tammy inherited her sister's two cats, Chat and Thimble, one boy and one girl, siblings, 12 years old. They'd never been in Tammy's home or spent any time with Tammy's former cats. She soon realized, though, that both Chat and Thimble had adopted the same behavior patterns as her two deceased cats.

For instance Chat, the boy, who'd never begged for food before, would now stand meowing in front of the refrigerator and would only become quiet the minute Tammy opened the refrigerator door and pulled out a *can of whipping cream.* As unusual as this may sound, it was the exact behavior of her previous female cat.

In addition, there were other unique behaviors, like choosing the exact same spot to sleep (the top northwest corner of the headboard) rather than anywhere else in the house, pushing open the door of the shower and drinking from the dripping water faucet, meowing to be let *inside* the closet, sleeping under the covers, and stretching out on the hall carpet using his front paws to dig down while at the same time letting his hind legs extend straight out behind him and stretching his body full-length. All these traits were exactly like her first female cat, and they were ones Chat had never before exhibited when he was living with Tammy's sister.

Thimble was also changing. She was now sleeping across Tammy's right arm next to her head (like the male before her). She'd also come when she wanted love and attention, and then lead Tammy to the kitchen wanting to be fed. Thimble had never shown any of these behaviors before she came to live with Tammy.

Tammy had known these two cats for 12 years and knew with certainty that it wasn't until they moved into her home that these new behaviors appeared.

Her story is a good illustration of what I hear time and time again from my students and clients. How could it be possible that after one of our animal friends dies, another will exhibit the very same unique characteristics, manners, and habits — behaviors that are not common to all animals?

They may sleep in the same unusual spot, beg for a treat by performing the same trick without being prompted, pace alongside the refrigerator when they want something unusual that's inside, carry their leash without being taught, drink from the same faucet, bark in the same manner to get your attention for something you're doing or not doing, or lie on top of you in the very same way your beloved pet did before.

It seems that the reason for these unique behaviors must be something different from reincarnation because often the "new" animal is already older, and may even have been alive at the same time as the original pet, albeit living in a different home or environment.

As in the story above, the 12-year-old cats were alive at the same time as Tammy's first two cats, but they belonged to Tammy's sister and they lived only with her. Since all four animals were in physical experience at the same time, our linear thinking tells us this would not be considered a case of reincarnation.

But how is it that Energy Imprinting takes place? To answer that question, I first need to explain several very important concepts — Life, energy, physical experience, and auras.

First, we must clearly understand something very profound, yet ever so simple — we must understand the difference between *Life* and *physical experience*.

Life is the real and eternal part of each living being. *Life is eternal energy*. It's the *essence* of every living being, and it goes on forever. *Life leaves physical experience (or physical form), but it never ever dies*. Some people might refer to this as the Eternal Soul. I often say it's the Divine Spark from which all beings and things emanate.

On the other hand, if we can touch or see something, or experience it in any way with our five senses, what we're seeing, touching or experiencing *physically*, is only the *temporary* part of our human or animal experience on this earth.

What we see, touch, or experience, which is in physical form, *will* go away (or you might say "die"). This happens when the Life Force, the essence, or the energy of a living being makes its transition out of physical experience and form, back to Spirit.

While we're in physical experience, we interact with each other by mingling our auras. And what is an aura? Our physical bodies (the temporary part of us) are surrounded by an energy field (the eternal part of us). This field is like a large sphere of light. It has colors which are the reflection of our Soul. This light, or aura, that surrounds us is Universal Light or Energy, and it's eternal.

When we have a deep love for another human or animal, our auras or energies are constantly touching and blending with each other. The stronger our love, the more attached we become. In fact, we often feel much better when we're physically close to someone we love. Our pets reflect this when they follow us around the house and settle down wherever we may be. It just *feels* better to them when they're close to us.

When the eternal part of a person or animal is ready to leave earthly experience, the aura around the body begins to fade because the essence or energy is moving *away* from physical form and closer and closer to Spirit. At the end of our stay here on earth, the body goes back to Mother Earth while the soul moves up to a higher energy vibration or dimension.

After the Life Force, or energy, of a person or an animal leaves this temporary physical experience, a human or pet making the transition into Spirit then has to adjust to a spiritual level of living.

When a person or animal dies, because their aura was so lovingly intermingled with ours, the sudden separation of the auras results in a deep sense of loss for those of us who remain in physical form. The entire nervous system and vibrational frequency of our physical, mental, and spiritual bodies are affected.

It means we must then take time to readjust and realign so that once again we become centered within our own individual auras. This transformation is not only mental (adjusting to being without the one we loved so much) but it's also physical because our bodies need to adjust as well.

The longer and more intimate the time spent together, the greater the energy exchange has been. The closer and more intimate the relationship, the longer the separation of auras may take. There's usually a vague sense of emptiness as the energy of the deceased person or pet disengages itself and withdraws from those who are still in the physical world.

But whether it's a person or a pet who dies, even after their transition out of earthly experience, they leave part of themselves with us. Part of the *energy* that existed while they were in physical form remains connected to, and is a part of, the people and animals they left behind because of the bond of Love.

Even when we *know* the physical body no longer exists, we may still have those moments when we *feel* the presence of the person or pet who's gone, as if he or she is actually physically close to us. In those moments, what we're feeling is his or her energy body (more specifically, the etheric body) which usually remains behind for a time, until we've become better adjusted to our loss. Once an animal has left physical experience, you may even get a glimpse of, or "*see*," his or her essence, or physical double, out of the corner of your eye.

When we feel a connection to a person or a pet deep within the most sensitive part of our "selves," whether or not another person or animal is physically present with us, then what we're feeling is their *essence, their energy, the real part* of them, which is eternal.

This same essence is what people experience when they *feel* the presence of their beloved pets, even when they're no longer here. For example, you may feel the bed move and you sense that the animal is there by your side, or you think your cat is rubbing against your leg, but when you look, he's not visibly there.

Some dogs, and especially cats, can see this essence. You may notice them staring attentively at the ceiling, or meowing at a specific area of the house even though *you* can't see anything unusual going on.

It's also this same essence which a new animal senses when he or she first moves into your home. Without any regard to gender, the essence of one or more of your beloved animal friends who've made their transition is passed on to the "new" animal. The new animal absorbs this essence and makes it part of his or her own self. This is the process I call Energy Imprinting.

It's because of this Energy Imprint that your new animal friend begins to display the same distinctive characteristics, personality traits, behaviors, habits, or quirks as your previous pet did. The new pet exhibits these familiar characteristics in order to be accepted, to please, to comfort his new family and to feel more at home. This Energy Imprint now becomes part of his identity and it paves the way for a smooth transition into his new family.

Why? Because the new soul is there to remind you of the eternal bond of love you created with your previous animal friend. The love you had for your previous pet is eternal, and the best way your new animal friend can remind you of that, is by reflecting that love back to you through familiar behaviors.

You may also ask, "Is it possible to un-do the Energy Imprint?" The answer is not a clear yes or no, but what's more important, I've not yet dealt with anyone interested in trying. My clients and students have expressed that the Energy Imprint process made them feel as if their beloved animal friend was watching over them, was still with them, and was very much present in their lives. Some even feel as if their beloved pet never departed. It's a very comforting feeling for those families whose animal friends have made their transition.

For clarity's sake, I'm providing a list of differences between Reincarnation and Energy Imprinting for you to use as a guideline:

REINCARNATION:

1) You feel you already *know* the pet and immediately have deep feelings for him or her.
2) The pet knows you immediately after seeing you and clearly wants to go home with you.
3) He or she can pick you out of a crowd and vice versa.
4) If you're looking at a new litter, one pet will come to you wagging its tail or mewling softly as if he or she knows who you are.
5) The pet displays atypical behavior towards you (e.g., a shy cat who won't go to anyone else comes running to you and cuddles in your arms).

6) You have an intuitive or gut feeling, something pulling your heart strings, or maybe a feeling of *déjà vu.*

7) The reincarnation cycle in animals is believed to be five to seven years, unless death was an accident and/or its original Life Assignment was not completed.

ENERGY IMPRINTING

1) The animal is new to the family but is not usually a very young puppy or kitten. The animal could be an adult and has had completely different experiences with his or her first family.

2) The new pet takes on characteristics, personality traits, and habits almost immediately upon arriving in your home.

3) The new pet develops the same tastes in uncommon foods. (The new dog loves carrots, bananas, green olives. The new cat likes lettuce, toast, whipped cream, etc.)

4) The new pet does the same tricks without being prompted.

5) The new pet acts exactly like the other pet when introduced to a similar situation.

6) Energy Imprinting happens soon after another animal's death.

7) Energy Imprinting is usually seen in the same species — dog with a new dog, cat with a new cat — but the gender of the pet doesn't matter.

These are just some guidelines to help you understand the differences between Reincarnation and Energy Imprinting. Hopefully, you'll find them useful and a springboard for thought.

The Energy Imprint process almost becomes a healing process in that it makes you feel like your beloved animal friend never left your side. This process has helped many families realize that they'll always be connected with their loved ones, person or pet, because their essence and their spirit will always be with them.

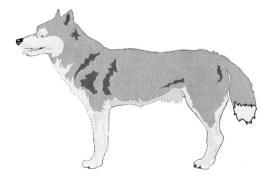

CHAPTER 17

RELEASING OUR PETS WHEN IT'S TIME
AND COPING WITH OUR OWN FEELINGS

Every pet comes into our lives at exactly the right time, and leaves at exactly the right time, whether or not it *seems* so to us at the moment.

Sometimes it even becomes our responsibility to help them make their transition so they won't have to suffer unnecessarily.

What do we need to know to help us make wise decisions for our pets when their lives are nearing the end? And how do we cope with our own feelings? Often, knowing we're doing what our pet needs and wants, helps to alleviate some of our own pain.

Part of my Life Assignment is to help my clients understand their pets' needs and feelings at this point in their lives. How does the pet feel about staying or leaving? What would make things easier for them? What do they need from us most of all?

The stories in this chapter may help answer some of those questions. Then we'll also talk about coping with the loss of a pet and learning to love again.

SYLER

Cindy called me to find out *exactly* what it is that I do. She told me she didn't want to talk to someone who wouldn't be "for real," or who'd simply tell her anything she wanted to hear. She purposely didn't say anything specific about her situation, but instead, asked me what kind of information I could get from her older pet.

I explained that animals have feelings and sometimes they're able to tell me where and how it hurts, what they want and need from their humans, and ultimately, when or if they're ready to make their transition. She seemed satisfied with my answers and made an appointment for me to come to her home to see her 13-year-old female German Shepherd mix.

As soon as I arrived, Cindy took me in to see Syler who was lying down on the bedroom floor. She introduced me to her husband, and without saying a word, she sat down on the bed and waited to see what I'd do. Sensing how eager they were to hear something from their pet, I immediately seated myself on the floor, closed my eyes and went to work.

After introducing myself to Syler and telling her that I'd come to talk with her, and with her mom and dad, she immediately sent me a picture. In it, she told me she'd been with her daddy all of her life but that Mom came into their lives later. She made me feel she was Daddy's girl first, and that Mom didn't know her quite as well as Dad did. It didn't make her love Mom any less. It was just a fact.

When I told them this was Syler's way to validate her identity, they were amazed at the accuracy. Mom had been with Syler for a little less than two years and Syler was, in fact, Daddy's little girl!

This is a good example of one kind of message pets may use to let their humans know they're the ones who're actually doing the talking, and that I'm not just making up the information as I go. I didn't know this fact about their family in advance, and it delighted me to learn it from Syler herself first.

The consultation went on and Syler was able to relate to her parents how badly she was feeling and how and where it was hurting. She requested they try to find another way to lift her up when they needed to move her outside to relieve herself two or three times a day.

Even more important, she told them how difficult it was for her to go on living and she didn't want to stay around much longer. She wanted to ask her daddy to "let her go," though she realized this was something he simply wasn't yet ready to do. She tried to make it as clear as possible that she didn't have too much time to live and wanted me to let them know she was ready to die. Syler took the opportunity to tell her daddy how very much she loved him and that she'd lived a happy and fulfilled life. But she insisted her life was coming to an end and she couldn't feel joyful about staying much longer.

Tears were rolling down both their faces when I finally turned around to look at them. Dad was impressed and shook my hand to thank me. Mom walked me out to my car, and she was relieved and somewhat happy to know the truth. "Dr. Monica, thank you," she said. "That is some of the best money I've ever spent."

RAMBO

Paula came in on a Saturday morning to see me with Rambo, a male Maltese, who was 12 years old. He'd been diagnosed with skin cancer and I was surprised to see him in such a bad state. He had scabs all over his body and the skin was so red it looked burned.

Even in this condition, his demeanor was calm and his eyes were focused on me.

Because of his situation, Mom took him with her everywhere she went and she'd always wrap him gently in a blanket because she felt it was the best way to transport him. Rambo was now lying on the floor on that blanket, waiting to talk with me. Little did either of us know what he would soon have to say about his ever-present blanket.

Mom couldn't bring herself to ask him any specific questions. "I just want to know how he feels," she said.

Rambo, on the other hand, was very specific and wasted no time telling me all about his feelings. "Tell her I've had enough," he said. "This is no way to live. I can't stand up because it hurts when my skin stretches. I can't lie down comfortably because I can't stand the feel of the blanket. I'm so tired I fall asleep on my feet, and when I do, I sway and fall down. I know she loves me, but this is not what I want."

He continued, "Even when she touches me, it bothers me. Lately I've been so upset that I've started to growl at everyone who even comes close to me. It's my warning. I DO NOT WANT TO BE TOUCHED! What else can I do? Is she listening to me?"

As tactfully as I could, I explained to Paula everything that Rambo was communicating to me. He wanted to leave now, but he couldn't do it on his own. She was his only hope.

Most people don't feel ready to listen to what their animals are telling them when the animals want to leave. However, somewhere deep inside, they usually know. My role is to translate the information for them, and often it simply confirms what they already know or feel intuitively. Once they hear it said out loud, and they know what their pet really wants from them, they're usually better able to cope with what they need to do to relieve their pet's suffering.

Though she was drowning in tears, Paula thanked me for letting her know exactly what Rambo's wishes were.

The following week, in between consultations, I spoke with Paula briefly over the phone.

"I wanted to thank you so much for what you did for us!" she said. "Rambo was put to sleep on Sunday morning after our Saturday talk. In the morning after a good breakfast, we went out to his favorite spots for a nice long walk. I talked with him and told him we were going to visit Dr. Harding, something he dreaded doing during his treatment. But as I continued to explain what was going to happen, he seemed to understand everything. For the first time in months, he jumped into the car without wearing his leash and being prompted, or almost dragged by me. He was ready. I had no doubt in my heart. I want to thank you because you gave me so much comfort and the strength to do what I knew was necessary."

———

Sometimes when our pets are approaching death, we want them to wait at least a little longer for our benefit. We love them too much to let them go just yet. And when two people must agree on the final decision, it can make matters even more difficult. This was the case with Greg and George, who couldn't agree, at first, on what should be done for their cat, Buster, who was dying.

BUSTER

This consultation was done on the phone while both "parents" were on the line.

I said to them, "Buster's very slow in answering my request for his comments. He's upset. I'll even venture to say he's angry." He's telling me, "My time is up and everyone knows it but Greg. My insides are shutting down little by little and I'm no longer able to enjoy the things I always did.

"Getting up from one place to walk to another is a major endeavor. My throat has become swollen and it's hard to swallow anything, including water. I absolutely hate it when you force feed me because it makes me gag, no matter how gentle you are."

"This is hard," I told them, "but he's siding with George."

"George knows better because he can feel it not only with his heart, but also in his gut," Buster continued. "I've had a wonderful life. I've been the center of attention and love, and I've enjoyed your company and loved both of you, even when you've been stressed out.

"I've tried to fight for a while but my body's not helping. I despise the needles in my back, and there's no way I can continue to swallow pills when I can hardly lick water."

I let Greg and George know that Buster mentioned he'd wanted to release himself from his body when they were away for a few days of vacation and Buster was boarded at a veterinary clinic, but it didn't happen. He also said, "I don't like being outside my home and far from my friends. I'm very serious when I ask you not to send me back to stay at the hospital. I'm tired of hurting and tired of fighting. I need you to be brave for me and help me to release. I don't have very much time anyway, but I'd really appreciate your help."

I told both Greg and George that Buster didn't want them to grieve for him. His life was full. He received a lot of love and he always felt he was very special to them.

"Is there any way," Buster asked, "that you can have someone come to the house? That would be ideal."

I added, "He says he keeps telling Ally (their female cat) that he can't cope anymore. She's been very gracious toward him. He also asked her to be more loving toward the two of you when he's gone, and she seems to be up for the challenge."

It was very difficult for both of them to hear how much their beloved cat wanted to be released from his suffering, but they understood his feelings. I didn't know what happened until much later when I received a card from them saying:

Dear Dr. Monica:

It's been several months since your reading with our cat, Buster. Your communication helped us accept that Buster was, indeed, very close to the end, and that he just wanted to be released from all his suffering. As much as I'd resisted, I finally let go of my own needs, and the next day we asked our vet and neighbor to help us out. He came to our house where we'd put Buster on a comfortable hassock, surrounded by the roses he loved (to eat!) so much. We were with him at the end, stroking and nuzzling him. He was such a loving cat. It was difficult, but loving and peaceful.

Unfortunately, our other cat, Ally, who was much older, lasted only a few more months herself — after enjoying being the only cat in the house! It was easier to let her go after Buster, and we took care of her beautifully.

Thanks again for helping us to hear our animals — and to listen.

Greg and George

COPING WITH OUR FEELINGS OF LOSS

While we often have to make the decision about the right time to release our terminally ill pets, once we've done so, we then need to cope with the many feelings that follow, especially our sense of loss.

Human death is buffered by everything from time off work, the support of family and friends, and funeral services or memorials. It's not the same when our pets pass on. Dealing with a pet's death can be a far more traumatic event. Society doesn't know how to handle this kind of sorrow. Many times, even friends or family don't understand the close bond you had with a pet and they come up with the only line they know, "It's only a dog," or, "It's only a cat! You can get another one."

But anyone who's ever loved an animal will tell you that there's something very, very special about each one. No two dogs or cats are ever the same. A pet who's been with you through thick and thin is part of your family. They understand you even better than your best friend. In fact, they may be your best friend.

No matter what your beliefs, your creed, your religion, your height, your weight, the color of your skin, or how intelligent you may be, your pet always accepts you and never judges.

An obediently trained pet may make you feel successful as an individual. Their respect may give you a sense of self-esteem which you rarely experience otherwise in life. There's no need to lie to them about anything. You can be yourself at all times.

So close are we to our animals that many of my clients refer to their pets as their "furry children," and — as we've read throughout the book — to themselves as "Mom" or "Dad."

After a pet leaves us, it's a time when rituals are a blessing and an essential part of the healing process. Having a memorial service can be a beautiful experience of healing, and a celebration of the wonderful life your pet lived. You may also feel the joy of releasing into the peace of Spirit someone who was suffering and in pain. For our pets, as we do for people, keeping their ashes in a beautiful container or giving them a gravesite, are wonderful expressions of love. Setting up a space of remembrance where you can have their picture, and a candle or flowers, and possibly an urn with their ashes in it, is a beautiful visual way of also bringing healing to your heart.

As time passes, you'll actively be able to turn your grief into joyful remembrance of your precious pet if you'll just *train* yourself to focus on their *life* instead of on their death. Instead of thinking about the difficult time toward the end, remember the wonderful years of joy they gave you. Even if your pets lived only a short time, focus on the good times. Remember the cute things they did, the way they played, the love they gave, and the joy that filled your heart. When you can do this, you're honoring the unconditional love they always gave you.

Working Through Difficult Feelings

Before you reach a point of loving acceptance, you may find yourself experiencing a multitude of other feelings including anger, guilt, depression, and a sense of failure. Not knowing for certain what caused the pet's death, or wondering if there is life after death, can cause feelings of anxiety and sorrow. Hopefully this book has reassured you, there *is* life after death. Yet, you may still experience any or all of these strong feelings. It's important for you to know, they're normal human reactions to the loss of each person or pet.

But what are we supposed to *do* with all those awful feelings? First and foremost, don't deny them, and don't try to harshly shut them off. Grieving is a process we must move through *gently*. Acknowledge each feeling as it arises, thank it for the lessons it's teaching you, and then tell it you freely release it so that it can be changed into the energy of love. As you gently release each feeling of anxiety, sorrow, anger, guilt, depression or failure, you open up another place in your heart through which love can flow.

So often, we feel that we should've done something more or something different. We go through the "if only" and "why" stages — "If only I'd known, if only I'd tried this, if only I hadn't done that, why couldn't he have lived longer, why did she have to leave so soon, why wasn't I paying better attention to him, why did she have to get sick when we took such good care of her?" — and these questions make us feel a sense of failure or a sense of guilt. You'll probably go through at least some of these feelings, but the key is not to get stuck in them.

Realize that you probably *were* doing all of the things you were *supposed* to be doing for this particular pet, according to what you knew at the time. After your pet has passed on, if you discover things you might have done differently, thank your pet for helping you learn this new lesson, and embrace the new information as something you can use to take care of the next pet you have, or share that information in a positive way with someone else who needs to know.

Many people find it very comforting to reflect deeply on the thought at the beginning of this chapter: Everyone comes in at exactly the right time and everyone leaves at exactly the right time. It may not *feel* like the right time to you, but you need to *know* at the center of your being, that no matter what the circumstances appeared to be, your pet left at the right time for him or her, and for you.

Maybe your pet's Life Assignment had been completed — yes, pets have them too. Or maybe you had to experience the death of a pet in order to learn how to move through grief into the joy of celebrating your pet's life. Or you needed to learn to let go, and then give love again to a new pet. Or your lesson with this beloved pet might have been to simply let yourself know pure and unconditional love in a way you'd never experienced it before.

Know that Life is meant for *living*, not for grieving or for blaming yourself endlessly. And know that you honor your pet's life in a special way as you move gently out of grief into the fullness of joy and living once again. One who knows how to grieve over a loss, and then *release* that sorrow, truly knows how to live and love.

LEARNING TO LOVE AGAIN

For most people, the question then arises about whether or not to welcome another pet into your home and heart.

When a beloved pet passes on, we experience first-hand how short their lives are in comparison to our own. Intellectually, we've always known their life cycle is so much shorter than ours, but emotionally, we're rarely ever ready to let go when the time comes. We sometimes feel as if we never want to love another pet that deeply again, because when the time comes to have to let them go, we already know how much it's going to hurt. We may even wonder if we'll *ever* be able to love that much again.

This thought causes many people to spend their lives trying to avoid pain by denying themselves the joy of loving someone else. They won't allow themselves to get too close to other people, or to another pet, because they fear having to endure the pain of loss again.

Love and pain are like two sides of a coin. When our emotions are awake and vibrant, they're sensitive to *all* feelings, including *both* love and pain. When you love and are loved, you're vulnerable to being hurt as well. When you detach yourself, you may not get hurt, but neither will you be giving or receiving love.

Because the ability to love comes from the very Source of our Being, we're endowed with an endless capacity for love. Everyone has a basic desire to give love and nurturing to another, whether it be to our children, family members, friends, our pets, or even to the world around us.

We see this innate need expressing itself very early in life when children provide nurturing care to their favorite dolls, younger brothers or sisters, or young friends. Later, we see it when they become young adults and provide love and care for their own children. And when children are gone from a household, it's not unusual for their parents to bring in a pet to fill that void. We *need* to be able to give love to another being. Equally and enormously rewarding is the feeling of having our love reciprocated with a pet's unconditional love.

So when *is* the best time to bring a new pet into your home? Definitely *after* you've taken sufficient time to work through your feelings about the pet who's just left. If you bring a new pet home too soon, you may not be ready to give that pet all the love he or she deserves because you'll still be experiencing such deep feelings about the first pet for some time to come. And you may always be making comparisons between the two of them, instead of learning to love the new pet for who he or she is.

Is it ever OK to bring home a new pet very soon after the first pet passes on? If you have another pet in the family who seems inconsolable without a companion, it may then be one of those rare occasions when it becomes necessary to find a new pet fairly soon to help the grieving pet recover. But, in general, it's best to wait for a while until everyone in the family is ready to welcome someone new. Then you can open your hearts to loving once again — even loving someone who'll only live a short life span.

Love, after all, is one of our great Absolutes. It's an energy that exists throughout the entire Universe. It's love that draws people and animals together into enduring relationships. Love is the greatest healer of all.

May our love for our pets be as eternal as their love for us is unconditional!

CHAPTER 18

LESSONS LEARNED

For some of us who've already completed a learning curve through the death of a beloved pet, there's the wisdom of hindsight. At first you review everything you did, both right and wrong. You mull over all the "whys" and "what ifs" and wish you had had just a little more time to do at least some things differently. But after figuratively beating yourself up for what you think you did wrong, or for what you didn't do that you wish you'd done, the light finally dawns. You begin to realize that, while you can't go back in time to change anything, you have in fact, learned some very valuable lessons along the way.

Some lessons are more difficult to learn, especially when they involve the serious illness and death of a precious pet, or a long relationship with a less than perfect pet. But you'll have mastered those lessons when you understand that this process we call Life is about living, loving and learning, embracing the synchronicity in all things that surround us, and being open to your intuitive feelings.

It's particularly rewarding for me when clients write about how their experiences with their terminally ill pets have helped them learn and grow and make important changes in the way they look at life. Their stories contain lessons for me to learn as well, and lessons that may also touch your heart and give you new insights into living life more fully and releasing your pets more peacefully. With their permission, I've included letters from two of my clients. These are their "Lessons Learned."

COLLEEN FOX

A resident of south Orange County, California for many years, Colleen has enjoyed successful careers in education, health care administrative management, and corporate telecommunications. She's now reveling in her fourth career of "life after work" which provides a peaceful environment for reading, writing and spiritual study, as well as the luxury of time to share her helping and care giving skills with family and friends. She also continues to teach a specialized program of phonics and spelling to individual students who benefit most from one-on-one lessons.

Colleen has always had a special affection for terriers, so several months after Benji, the family's 14 ½-year-old terrier poodle mix, passed on, she fell in love with an eight-week-old West Highland White Terrier whom she named Casey. Always a joy, Casey was a very wise, very self-assured and very much in-charge Westie.

When Casey was four years old, he and Colleen welcomed Peaches into the family. She was another very independent, very energetic and very loveable Westie who was already three years old. They enjoyed six wonderful years together until Casey passed on at the tender age of ten. This is their story as Colleen shared it with me in her letter.

CASEY

Dear Dr. Monica,

Casey, Peaches and I are very grateful to you for your loving support during his illness and transition. You've been a very special part of our lives, so I'd like to share with you some of the unique lessons which this experience with Casey helped me learn.

But even before the lessons began, there were two significant signs which were very important. Although I didn't understand their meaning at the time, I would later come to realize what they'd been trying to tell me.

About a year before Casey was diagnosed, I began having the same dream over and over again. In the dream, both our front door and the security screen door were wide open, and Casey was gone. Not both Peaches and Casey, just Casey.

The dream was so vivid that several times, in real life, I flew out of bed, wide awake with my heart pounding. On these occasions, when I checked our front entrance, both doors were always securely closed, and Casey and Peaches were always safely sleeping in their favorite places in the bedroom.

Every time the dream happened, it was like a snapshot of a single moment in time, and each time, in the dream, even though he was gone, I felt certain that wherever he was, he was somehow OK, and his life was still safe. Yet, in the dream, I always had a sense that he wasn't coming back, that I'd never see him again.

Each time I awakened, I'd always have a very unsettled feeling which would leave after awhile, but would always return the next time the dream occurred. I thought the dream was telling me I should use extra care whenever doors to the outside were open, but it would prove to be much more symbolic than that.

Something else happened during this same period of time which I didn't associate with the dream until much later. Occasionally at night when Casey walked into his carrier, settled down, and looked back up at me, he did it in such an unusual way that it made me stop short and ask him, "Are you OK?"

Though intuitively I felt something was not quite right, there was never anything I, nor our veterinarian, nor laboratory testing, could pinpoint to confirm that anything was wrong.

However, one evening in late July, I discovered that his abdomen was very firm and distended and he'd gained almost two pounds of weight, literally overnight. After several days of lab work, ultrasound testing, and consultations, we had a definitive diagnosis: end-stage liver disease.

After the diagnosis, I never had the dream again, and the reason my intuition had been so heightened was clear to me now. I understood that both the dream and the intuition had been trying to tell me that Casey would, in fact, be leaving, but his life would still be safe. The third lesson, which was still to come, would help me understand much more deeply why this was so.

Through an unusual set of circumstances, we saw a different veterinarian each day while he was being tested, or when we were reviewing test results. Though none of the veterinarians who saw him would be specific, I had a strong sense that each doctor felt Casey might not see his tenth birthday which was only about six weeks away.

As you know, Westies usually live to be at least 14, so the fact that he might leave before he was even ten seemed way too soon. Yet, even as I was listening to the prognosis, there was a place in my heart where I knew we still had more than just a few weeks left together.

But should I commit wholeheartedly to an expectation that we might see significant improvement if we used certain treatments? Or should I just accept that the rest of his time was very short, and not use any alternative means to try to improve his condition? Did I simply need to start preparing for our eventual separation by making the time we had left as special as possible? The answer was to do each of these things at the appropriate times.

And so began a six-month learning curve, full of lessons and insights, which helped to bring moments of peace and calm where, otherwise, there would have been only a sense of impending loss and grief.

And of course, it was Casey who was my best teacher during this time, as he'd always been throughout his entire life. From a very young age, as most of our pets do, he had me well-trained to his comfort and convenience. But since I'd long ago mastered the basics, he was now going to guide me through a very advanced course of spiritual study and growth, as he patiently endured his final illness and prepared to make his transition.

The First Lesson

The first major lesson involved making a *conscious* choice to learn to live in the present moment. Was I was going to let myself feel sad every time I looked at him, thinking only about how much time we might *not* have left? Or would I freely and happily let myself experience and treasure the enjoyment of each and every precious moment of the rest of our time together?

You and I both know that any feelings we experience come directly from the thoughts we're holding onto. We also know that we have this wonderful ability to *choose* those thoughts, and therefore to *choose* our feelings. So I made a conscious decision to acknowledge the sad thoughts only very briefly. I'd replace those sad thoughts as quickly as possible by thinking about all the good things in our lives that Casey and I were still able to enjoy right now. He was still here, and I could hold him and hug him and love him every day. I soon found myself experiencing feelings of comfort and peace, and smiling with joy every time I looked at him, instead of always welling up with tears.

I discovered that by *consciously* choosing to be aware of all the good things that were still happening, I was free to notice and enjoy all of the cute, funny, and happy experiences of our life together, and to tenderly preserve each one of those precious moments in a special place in my heart. By doing it this way, I didn't miss out on any of the abundant good times which were still ours to enjoy.

Replacing sad thoughts with happy thoughts was a very difficult thing to do at first, but I *worked* at doing this, *because I wasn't willing to let the sad thoughts steal all the joy I could still have.* I was finally learning to live in the present moment, and to make the most of each and every precious one.

Consciously choosing the happy thoughts, however, didn't mean that all of the sad feelings eventually disappeared. On the contrary, sad thoughts would pop into my consciousness, sometimes with an intensity I couldn't ignore. When those feelings did come up, often accompanied by a flood of tears, I let myself embrace them because they were an important part of my human experience which I needed to honor at that moment.

But after a few moments of cleansing tears, I'd ask myself: do I need to stay in this sadness, where the focus is on me and what I'm feeling? Or do I want to move into feelings of love and peace because Casey is still here for me to enjoy right now? *More importantly, what do I want* his *experience of* me *to be during* his *last months — one of love and happiness, or one of continual sadness and tears?*

This meant that if there appeared to be a crisis, I had to look at his condition objectively each time, instead of collapsing into a sense of fear, and dwelling on the thought that this might be the end. I discovered that becoming objective, instead of frantic and fearful, allowed me to express more love and tender care for Casey at those times, and this helped him to be more relaxed and to go through any temporary discomfort in a calm, peaceful environment.

Sometimes during a minor crisis, I had to content myself with simply recognizing that he was still breathing, his heart was still beating, he wasn't in severe distress, and he was still here for me to love. Instead of letting myself think about the worst case scenario each time this happened, I needed to stay focused on patiently and expectantly waiting for things to improve. And in each of the minor crisis events, things *did* improve, which confirmed for me that my energy was much better spent on loving and caring thoughts, than being spent on fearful or grieving thoughts.

During those moments, I would gently pet Casey and tell him how much I loved him and how proud I was of him for the strength and courage he was showing. I'd also tell him we wanted him to stay as long as he possibly could, but he was free to leave whenever he needed to go, and I would help him make his transition if he wanted me to do so.

Most of the time, though, I could rejoice in his overall quality of life which he best showed by his continued spirit of independence and his zest for certain activities of his daily life.

The Second Lesson

The second major lesson required letting go of my desire to do everything I possibly could which might continue to improve Casey's condition. The time would come when I needed to honor his wishes as respectfully as he'd been honoring mine.

When he was first diagnosed, I felt it would be beneficial to give his liver some intensive nutritional support. With the help of two holistic veterinarians, we developed a plan using special dietary supplements with his meals, and *therapeutic grade* essential oils which were applied to his tummy. In less than two weeks, one of our veterinarians saw an incredible 85 percent improvement in Casey's condition.

We continued using nutritional supplements, therapeutic grade essential oils, and a couple of medications for four months with apparent good results and, more importantly, with Casey's cooperation. But after four months, there was about to be a major change, and Casey would definitely make his wishes known.

When we came to visit you in early December, I didn't want to share too much information with you before you talked to him, so initially, I only told you he had liver disease, severe bloating, and a poor appetite, and I wanted to know whatever he wanted to tell me, now that we were four months into his illness.

I was stunned in one way, though not surprised in another, by how specific he was in his second message. After first telling you he wasn't ready to leave yet, the next thing Casey conveyed to you was something you couldn't possibly have known in advance. He said, "I'm soooooooo tired of taking all . . . those . . . capsules . . . I don't want to be fed by hand . . . I just want to eat by myself."

I then explained to you that when we first began treatment, I used to mix his nutritional supplements and medications into a gravy as part of his dinner, and he'd gobble them down.

Later, he began to refuse regular meals, or even the gravy by itself, so to get at least *some* nutrition into him, I tried putting the supplements and medications into empty gelatin capsules and wrapping them with a little moist food like a treat.

I'd then feed the capsules to him by hand to be certain he took all of them, and didn't just lick off the moist food without swallowing the important stuff. It took about 14 capsules each day, given at different times, but this way he was getting at least *some* nutrition and his medications. He always accepted these treats with a reasonable degree of willingness . . . until now.

He'd already stopped eating a balanced diet, and if he wasn't willing to take the supplements and medications in any form, it meant he'd no longer be getting the nutrients necessary to support his liver.

For me, it was the beginning of the second major lesson — lovingly learning to accept, and do, whatever he now wanted and needed to have me do, even if it wasn't my first choice. The time had come for me to let go of my wishes in favor of doing whatever would make Casey happiest.

This meant giving up the possibility he might improve further, accepting the fact he'd now be happier and more comfortable letting nature take its course, and making peace with the fact that the end of that course would probably come sooner rather than later.

When Casey was first diagnosed, I knew without question, as every good doggy mom does, that I'd do everything in my power to make the remainder of his days as comfortable as possible, but I wouldn't try to prolong his life in any way that didn't bring him comfort and happiness.

So together, we moved into the next stage of his care which meant letting him direct all of the choices from now on. I had the peace of knowing I'd done everything which could reasonably be done from a health care perspective, but I also knew in my heart that it was OK to stop doing those things now because that was *his* wish.

Essentially, we were transitioning from intensive care to hospice care and it was acceptable and peaceful for both of us. By this time, we'd already enjoyed four wonderful months together which we might not otherwise have had, and even though we didn't know it, we still had two more precious months left to share the joy of each other's company.

Throughout the remaining months, Casey continued to maintain his basic independence and enjoy at least a reasonable quality of life. His appetite for moist food even improved for a time, though he still wouldn't take any medications or nutritional supplements.

One of my most treasured memories from our last two months together will always be the deep down joy I felt each day as I observed the exquisitely profound pleasure he experienced from one of our special daily activities.

Since he no longer had the energy to walk for any distance outdoors, the highlight of his day now became cruising through his neighborhood every afternoon in the flat bed of a baby stroller.

He could have stretched out and relaxed, or been sitting down, but instead, he'd usually stand steadily for the entire ride, even when we went up and down steps and curbs, or rolled over some bumpy cobblestones. And whenever we'd meet his tall doggy friends, he seemed delighted to have the advantage of now being eye-to-eye with them!

One of our neighbors used to describe him, in his walking-on-all-four-paws days, as always being such a "presence" in the neighborhood. And using this new form of transportation, he was *still* King of the Road!

The Third Lesson

It was always natural for me to use prayer and love in my treatment of Casey from the very beginning. And once he began refusing any medical or alternative means of support, prayer and love were all I *could* use.

I mentioned earlier, that in my recurring dream, I always knew Casey's life was still safe, even though, in the dream, I knew he was never coming back.

What I was about to learn next would help me experience this "knowing" that his life was still safe at a much deeper level of understanding than I'd ever experienced it before. And I realized the dream had, in fact, been preparing me for this third lesson about the *continuity* of Life.

In the quietness of meditation and study, I'd lovingly observe Casey as I prepared myself for his leaving. He was still so full of love and very much alive during this time that I found myself asking the question, *What is this thing called "life" which animates him so wonderfully now, but won't be visible to me after he makes his transition?*

While pondering the answer to that question, I realized that whenever we talk about *life*, we *usually* mean *only* that span of time which begins when we're born and ends when we die. But, we also talk about having eternal life.

So does this mean we have two *different* kinds of *life*, one that ends (human life) and one that doesn't end (eternal life)?

Or . . . do we have *one life* which is eternal? And within that *life*, do we have something which we should more appropriately call a human *experience*, because a human experience is something that *does* begin and end?

I've often read, or been told, that we're spiritual beings *having* a human experience and that idea always resonated with me every time I saw or heard it. But now it began to take on a more profound meaning for me.

This insight about *life* and *experience* was followed by yet another important perception. While I've always believed in the *concept* of eternal life, I was beginning to realize that, all these years, I only had an intellectual grasp of what "eternal" meant. I understood that God was eternal, with no beginning and no end, but somehow I'd grown up thinking about eternal life as something outside of me which I should aspire to, but it was something that would only "start" when I "died."

Now the reality was *finally* dawning on me, that if something's eternal, it's *always* "on." It can't have a beginning or an end. So if our *life* is eternal, we have it *before* we come into human experience, we have it *while* we're in human experience, and we continue that same life *when we leave* human experience.

For the first time, I was comprehending the real meaning of the word "eternal," and joyfully experiencing moments of deeply understanding the beauty of the continuity of life.

And now I also realized why, in the dream, I always had the feeling that Casey's *life* was still safe, even though he was no longer physically present and I wouldn't see him again.

In "A Parable of Immortality," Henry Van Dyke expresses this idea in a very comforting way. He writes:

I am standing upon the seashore. A ship at my side spreads her white sails to the morning breeze and starts for the blue ocean. She is an object of beauty and strength, and I stand and watch until at last she hangs like a speck of white cloud just where the sea and sky come down to mingle with each other. Then someone at my side says, "There! She's gone!"

Gone where? Gone from my sight . . . that is all. She is just as large in mast and hull and spar as she was when she left my side and just as able to bear her load of living freight to the place of destination. Her diminished size is in me, not in her. And just at the moment when someone at my side says, "There she goes!" there are other eyes watching her coming and other voices ready to take up the glad shout, "Here she comes!"

I feel that's such a wonderful way to describe the continuity of life!

All these thoughts helped me experience a profound knowing that we and our pets don't "die" in the traditional sense of the word. I didn't just know it intellectually now. I could feel, with a new clarity, that what we call "death" is only the end of an experience, not the end of Life.

I could *feel* that it's simply that moment in time, when the *eternal essence* of a person or pet, discards his or her tangible form, and leaves this human or doggy experience behind. Our beautiful eternal essence, that which animates us and makes us *soooo* special, simply makes a transition from earthly experience to spiritual experience, and continues living safely on in God's loving care.

These new insights made it possible for me to release Casey with a much greater sense of peace and comfort when the time came for his passing.

Meanwhile, he and I were blessed with six precious months altogether to prepare for the special moment of his transition from earthly experience. Many times, I lovingly recounted to him the truths:

~ That our illnesses, our experiences, and our tangible physical form are *not* the essence of us, they are *not* who we really are; and

~ That human and doggy *experience* have a beginning and an end, but our *Life*, our *essence*, is eternal and always safe with God, *whether we're in or out of tangible physical form.*

Some might ask: Couldn't Casey have been healed with prayer? I recently found an excellent answer to that question in the form of two letters which I came across in a magazine.

The first was written by a loving owner whose much older dog was diagnosed with medically untreatable cancer which had spread throughout his entire body. Prayer was the only treatment she could use and, in spite of a number of quite difficult times, in less than a year the dog had recovered completely.

The second letter, from the veterinarian who'd attended the dog since it was a puppy, verified the owner's account of the dog's healing. But he included a very important insight in his letter. He said in some cases healing depends on whether or not the patient has the will to live, or whether the patient feels his purpose in life is, or is not, finished.

If Casey's purpose was to bring me joy and delight and to be a special teacher in my life, then his purpose had already been magnificently fulfilled. But did he still have the will to live?

Seizures are often one of the consequences which are a part of severe liver disease. Casey had been experiencing only fairly minor ones for about three months, but one night in early February, he had a full blown episode. When you talked to him the following day, he told you he'd really tried to come back after the first major seizure the night before, but after each of the next episodes over several hours, he said it was just too difficult, and he no longer had the will to try.

And that was exactly what had happened. When we came home from the emergency hospital after the first seizure, he did seem to "come back again" and we enjoyed almost six hours of "normal" time together. But after the second and subsequent episodes in the early morning hours, he'd simply lie in my arms oblivious to the world around him. He seemed to just give in and not even try to come back.

This was a sign for me that the time had come for him to make his transition. Through your precious gift of being able to communicate with him, Casey then gave me confirmation that he *was* now ready to leave and he trusted me to help him. This was in direct contrast to what he'd clearly said to you in early December when he told you he wasn't ready to leave yet.

During my final visit with him at the hospital that evening, I recounted for him in a soft voice, and through gentle tears, each of the things I so dearly loved about him, and each of the lessons he'd helped me learn.

I told him that because his tangible body was no longer functioning properly and was now causing him serious discomfort, it was time for him to leave it behind, and joyfully go find everyone who would lovingly be waiting for him on the other side.

I let him know that he had Peaches' and my permission to leave this earthly experience and continue his life the way life is really meant to be lived — joyfully, fully, freely, eternally. His passing, with the gentle help of our veterinarian, was very peaceful and surrounded with so much love and kindness from everyone who was taking care of us.

The Final Lesson

After Casey left, as I'd also had to do after Benji made his transition 11 years earlier, there was one more choice I needed to make, another lesson I needed to learn, or re-learn, about how to live fully in this human experience.

Which option would I choose to hold onto now — a great sense of emptiness because Casey and Benji were no longer present, or a great sense of fullness and joy because of the tremendous love we'd shared?

In their own unique ways, each of my pets spent their entire lives letting me experience the beautiful qualities of vitality, energy, joy, freedom, goodness, understanding, intelligence, and unconditional love. These qualities were visible to me, through them, in a special way while they were here on earth, but I didn't have to give them up just because I couldn't see those two precious pets any longer.

Because those universal qualities are part of the Source of Our Being, they can be found in *everyone*. I could still enjoy those qualities as a special part of my life, every day, just by looking for them in Peaches, and in other pets, and in the people around me. Now whenever I do this, it's my way of saying to each of my pets, "You've taught me so much about love and life. Because of you, I always want to make these unique qualities be a special part of my experience."

And so, with loving gratitude to both Casey and Benji, to Cato and Bear who each temporarily shared their lives with me, to Gaysie, my very first dog from childhood, and to Peaches who still delights me every day, I choose the option to live with great fullness and joy as a tribute to each of them!

Casey's Legacy

Casey's zest for life, and his patient endurance of the challenging times, also touched the lives of so many others who knew him. This was made so beautifully clear to me by the outpouring of love and support which both he and I received at home, throughout our neighborhood, and at each of our two veterinary hospitals.

Spoken expressions of sympathy are usual when someone loses a pet, but after Casey made his transition, I received more than a dozen sympathy cards. And not just pre-printed cards with a signature. Each and every one, including those from each of our veterinarians, came with a personally handwritten and very thoughtful note in tribute to Casey. I also received several flowering plants, many phone calls, invitations to dinner, and many kind words and hugs as Peaches and I met friends on our walks.

One of the most touching gifts of all was the contribution made by one of our veterinarians to the Companion Animal Memorial Fund in Casey's memory. This fund at the UC Davis School of Veterinary Medicine supports finding ways to relieve pain and suffering among our companion animals. This wonderfully thoughtful gift brought me very special joy and still warms my heart every time I think about it.

As you can see, Dr. Monica, even though the last six months of Casey's life were not the easiest, they were still filled with a special peace and joy for both of us. Thank you so much for taking time to let me share with you some of the unique experiences I had, and the wonderful lessons I learned, while sharing my life with a very loveable Westie who was also my very special teacher.

Peaches and I both send you our gratitude for helping us with Casey, and also for helping to prepare Peaches for what was going to happen. Based on recommendations from both you and the doctors, shortly after Casey made his transition, our veterinarian gently placed his body on the floor on top of the soft cuddly comforter the hospital had provided for him.

Peaches was then brought into the room so she could say her goodbyes. She appeared to be very much at ease and seemed to understand that Casey was gone. When we returned home, she never even searched the house for him.

Although she now thoroughly enjoys having all of the attention for herself, I know the experience of Casey's passing was made much easier for her because you prepared her ahead of time to understand what would be happening.

Thank you again for being there for all us when we needed you and for being a special part of our lives in a very loving and caring way!

With love and gratitude,

Colleen

PURUSHA SHAKTI

Purusha Shakti* is a spiritual teacher, an energy healer, a performance artist, an author, and a painter. Purusha teaches various techniques in yoga, meditation, chanting, and hand drumming, to name just a few.

A former national and world champion skydiver with a career spanning 30 years and over 4,000 jumps to her credit, she says that her first jump was such a "high spiritual experience" that it convinced her that the only true purpose in life is to live a life of service to God.

Although she's now retired from the sport, Purusha is hard at work on her autobiography, *Flying Without Wings, An Autobiography of a Pioneer and World Champion Skydiver*, and at age 63, she still finds time to "fly" in the indoor wind tunnel at Perris, California. Here is her story, in her own words, about the lessons she learned from her cat, Flower.

* To learn more about Purusha Shakti, you can view her website at: www.purushashakti.com.

FLOWER

I adopted Flower and her brother, Butterfly, from the Lake Elsinore Animal Friends Shelter, in Lake Elsinore, California, on October 17, 1991. They were about eight weeks old the day I visited the shelter, and although there were some pedigree Siamese cats that had been advertised which I'd come to see, I kept coming back to look at Butterfly.

He sat separate from the rest of the litter of six tabby cats, and he was the tallest, most stately kitten I've ever seen. While the others played and romped together, Butterfly sat aloof, unaffected by the others. Having had many cats before, I prefer to get my animals in pairs because they seem to enjoy the company, so I finally decided to get Butterfly and one of his playful littermates, his sister Flower.

Ten years later, I would realize that I'd made a mistake. I should have taken Butterfly alone, or I should have taken Flower and one of the kittens she was playing with, because even though Butterfly and Flower were brother and sister, they never really got along very well.

The word "pet" as defined in the dictionary is, among other things: 1) any domesticated animal kept as a companion, 2) a person especially cherished or indulged, 3) a thing particularly cherished, 4) kept or treated as a pet, 5) cherished or indulged, as a child 6) favorite; preferred, 7) showing fondness or affection: pet names, 8) to treat as a pet; indulge, or 9) to fondle or caress amorously. I take this definition literally.

Butterfly was the perfect pet, and he got his name because of his markings, which brought to mind the beautiful patterns on a butterfly's wings. Butterfly never gave me a moment's trouble. He always ate whatever I put down for him, he was easy going and agreeable, he was affectionate, yet independent, he was quiet and docile yet he had a playful mischievous nature, and 5½ years later when I would adopt my first dog, Little Dove, to be followed 1½ years after that by Moon Feather, Butterfly got along just fine with the dogs. Flower on the other hand was just the opposite.

Flower was a fussy eater which had me constantly trying to find the perfect meal. She "talked" with a piercing voice non-stop which drove me up the wall most of the time and which tried my patience to the max. She was anti-social, spent the entire day hiding in the closet and would come out only to eat or cruise the backyard at night which made me wonder why she was called a "pet." She hated being petted and would always shake my hand away, which often had me questioning why I kept her, and she was always hissing or growling at something or someone, usually her sweet brother, which at times made me want to slap her. In short, Flower pushed all my negative buttons and I spent most of my time trying to control my disappointment, my anger, or often, my rage. We had the perfect love/hate relationship.

There were often times when I expressed my dislike or disapproval of her with my words, or my actions, sometimes throwing my own tantrums, and sometimes a water bowl or anything that might be handy that was not breakable (and not directly aimed at her, of course), and after such times, remorse would set in and my guilt, or my disappointment at having lost my temper would really get me down and make me realize how much further I had to go before I could call myself a really loving human being.

Butterfly contracted a rare form of lymphatic cancer which was diagnosed in March of 1999. We think he had it for quite some time because he started losing weight the year before, and although he had no other outward displays of the disease, he just started to look different to me. We managed to keep him comfortable with steroid drugs until December when he developed a tumor in his leg and it was then apparent that he'd started to go downhill.

Being a loving mother, I couldn't allow my baby to suffer, and I did what should be done and held and petted him while the sedative and then the lethal injection were administered. Butterfly passed with me chanting and praying and wishing him well in his next life. This was not done without the incredible pain of having to say goodbye to a loved one, and of course I suffered great sadness. I wondered where my strength came from to be able to endure such a thing, but of course I knew that the truth came from deep within me: There is no death.

After Butterfly's departure, Flower's behavior got even worse. She started howling in the middle of the night, every night, and from that time on, I'd never get a peaceful night's sleep. She continued to reject my attempts at petting her, spent her days in the closet, and in general made no positive contribution to our happy household. I was so mad at her for waking me up all the time, and for producing that anger in me, that I actually went to a "pet psychologist" to try to find some answers.

Dr. Monica said that Flower was very difficult to "read," but that she deduced that I had taken Flower away from her favorite sibling, a sister that she loved, when I'd adopted her from the shelter, and that was possibly why she has never been a happy cat. Dr. Monica didn't know the circumstances of Flower's adoption, so this was either a very lucky guess or she really did have some intuitive abilities.

At any rate, it certainly made sense to me and provided me with some explanation as to why I'd been blessed with such a neurotic cat. She suggested that I might try getting another kitten but could not guarantee that this would remedy the situation. She advised me to ask Flower in advance about this possible solution to my problem, by picturing in my mind a new kitten that was meant *especially for Flower to love and take care of.*

She explained that cats "see" things with pictures, rather than with words. Well, I spent months thinking about this, and sent these talking pictures to Flower, until one day in October 2002, a beautiful white kitten showed up at my door at work. It seemed as though the Universe had sent "Sparkle" as an affirmation. Perhaps this would finally bring peace and happiness to our household. I knew better than to bring her home at once, so instead I took Sparkle to the vet for a check up and an overnight stay so that I could prepare Flower, the dogs, and the house for a new baby.

Sparkle was another perfect cat. The vet said she was three months old and her solid white coat matched the Bichon Frise dogs exactly. She was sweet, friendly, playful, and she immediately bonded with the dogs and with Little Dove in particular. I've never seen the likes of this before and would never have thought it possible that a dog and a cat could have so much fun together.

Sparkle spent most of the day playing with the dogs, or climbing the tree in the backyard and jumping to the roof, (where she had to be rescued several times until I realized that she was going to have to figure out how to get down herself when I was at work, and of course she did), but she would always wind up curling up with the dogs for naps. During the first month that Sparkle came to live with us, I paid little attention to her, and gave all of my attention to Flower, so that she wouldn't feel envious, all the while sending those talking pictures to her about how Sparkle was her own personal kitten to love.

Flower would have nothing to do with Sparkle. As the days went on, Flower's dislike of the kitten became more and more apparent, and it was lucky that the kitten was a tree climber and Flower, in her senior years, was not. When I saw Flower sneak up and attack the kitten a few times when the kitten was sleeping, I knew I had to keep them separated.

At the same time that this was happening, Flower started having diarrhea, and my solution to both problems at that time was to keep Flower in the spare bedroom, where her favorite closet was, by using a child's gate across the doorway. In this way, Flower would still be a part of the rest of the household. I could monitor her bowels by keeping a litter box in that room, and Sparkle would be safe. I could then keep trying to convince Flower to become a mother to the kitten, since everyone I talked to about this was saying that in time Flower would come around and finally accept the kitten.

For a few weeks it seemed as though things were improving because Flower stopped hissing and she and the kitten would sniff each other through the openings in the child's gate. However, Flower's diarrhea wouldn't go away.

Flower spent an entire week in the hospital over Christmas. She was diagnosed with pancreatis, (I believe that she was so upset about the kitten that she made herself sick over it), but even more serious, we found that she had degenerative arthritis in her lower spine and hips. I realized, in retrospect, that this condition was probably congenital, and all the years that she didn't like being petted was because it hurt her! You can imagine how guilty I felt when I learned this news.

Upon Flower's return home from the hospital I put her in the spare room again so that she could enjoy the comfort of her closet, and in the meantime I knew that I would have to make a decision.

Although my logic told me that Sparkle and the rest of the family got on splendidly, and with Flower gone we would finally have peace in the house, not to mention nights of uninterrupted sleep for me, my heart and soul could not give up on Flower.

I might never be able to get through to this cat, and I might never have a moment's peace as long as she lived, but there was no way that I could abandon my little girl. Do you throw away a child because they don't live up to your expectations? Does a person's value depend upon their ability to please you? Do you reject a young soul because they don't see the world in the same way that you do? Do you cast away an elderly person because they can no longer fend for themselves? Do you love someone less when they get ill?

My girlfriend Linda agreed to adopt Sparkle. It was a sad parting the day I delivered Sparkle and all of her toys and dishes and other paraphernalia to her new mom, because my dream of creating the perfect solution to my problem with Flower went with her. I cried as I said goodbye, and I thought of how much Little Dove would miss playing with her, and how much joy she'd brought into our lives in just a couple of months.

When I returned home, I took the gate down and invited Flower into the kitchen to enjoy some supper. *From that moment on, our relationship shifted.* Flower continued to wake me up every night, but my reaction was totally different. Instead of being angry, I invited her to sleep in my arms, being ever so patient as she slowly and gently tried to lower herself to the mattress. I learned how to pet her where it didn't hurt (her chin, her cheeks, and her ears), and each night I would happily go back to sleep to the sound of her purring.

Flower's diarrhea went away, and to help with her arthritis I gave her medication every day, plus I made steps for her all over the house so that it would be less painful to climb up on the bed, or the couch, or her dinner table. I learned that she preferred two flavors of canned food, and fed her only those two from then on. She still spent most of her time in the closet, but that was OK with me. *She was OK with me.*

Two weeks ago, Flower started crying in pain whenever she had to get up from a lying position, and then she started crying when she had to climb her little steps to her table, or my bed, or the couch.

Yesterday, I told her that tomorrow would be a wonderful day. I told her that she'd go to sleep, and when she woke up she would be pain free.

At 7:45 am this morning I gave Flower 50 milligrams of Benedryl, as a mild sedative, as I'd been instructed by my veterinarian. I then sat beside Flower as she lay in her bed in the closet, and spent 40 minutes stroking her about her head and ears while she purred. When she was totally relaxed, I put her in the pet carrier and we drove to the vet.

They had a private room waiting for us, and with me petting her, the vet injected the first shot, which was a heavy sedative. With me continuing to stroke her, and telling her how much I loved her, Flower relaxed and serenaded me with her purr song one last time. At the appropriate moment, the vet administered the final injection. Flower never knew, and she never suffered, and as I'd promised, she went to sleep, I'm sure, to wake up in another place that was pain free.

After the vet checked to make sure that there was no longer a heartbeat, she invited me to stay with Flower as long as I wanted to, and I was left alone with my Flower. As is the case when the soul leaves the body, some bodily functions occur and fluids escape. I did my final motherly act and bathed my dear little girl, so that she was once again her sweet smelling self, and then I left.

As I said goodbye for the last time, I had the most wonderful revelation, and I sent Flower on her way with the highest of tributes. Because I realized that she was so much more than my pussycat; she was one of my greatest teachers in this life. She taught me the true meaning of unconditional love, sacrifice for the sake of love, and patience for love. It will be a lesson well learned, and one I shall never forget. In my unconditional love for her, and in my sacrifice and patience, I'd come to know the ultimate joy: love. Love is all there is. Love is the only reason why. Love is the highest high.

They'll prepare Flower for cremation. I'll keep her remains in the special little cedar box that they provide, the same as I did with Butterfly. In my Living Will there are instructions to have my skydiving friends release all of our ashes together, in free fall, when the time comes.

I'll be sad for a little while, but I'll never be without the lessons Flower taught me. She is certainly one of the most important loves of my life, one of my greatest teachers, and one of my dearest friends. I'm eternally grateful to God for my Flower.

God bless you Flower, wherever you are.

Mother Purusha Shakti

June 4, 2003

These two women have several things in common — the ability to adapt their outlook in response to new understandings, the commitment to persevere through difficult circumstances, the strength and determination to fulfill a promise made long ago, and of course, a spiritual understanding that keeps them in touch with the Source of their Being, and what they're here to do. This understanding, like Purusha said, is LOVE, and with love we can accomplish anything.

Our animals are often our best teachers and through them we can learn unconditional LOVE. May this LOVE be with us always.

Epilogue

Talking to animals, listening to them with empathy, understanding their feelings and wishes, and making some changes in your daily life to meet your pet's needs are all ways you can DO SOMETHING. They're opportunities for you to provide a more comfortable and satisfying experience for your pets at every stage of their lives.

People who've read my first book, *What Your Animals Tell Me*, say they now look at animals in a different light. They offer a friendly "Hi!" out loud when they meet them, something they'd never thought of doing before. And they're curious about how animals "feel" when they see them in different situations. Some say they can now "tell" how much a certain animal loves his or her human companion, or another animal companion. This is true for people who have pets, as well as for those who've never had an animal of their own before. Hopefully, this second book will encourage even more people to interact with animals at this deeper level of communication and understanding.

Those who already live with animals often yearn to find out if their pet is sad, upset, worried, lonely, bored, or in pain — all things, that until recently, few people knew animals could feel. Many have successfully begun to communicate with their own pets on a regular basis, or they've requested help from an experienced animal communicator. A few have even discovered their own Life Assignments and have become animal communicators themselves.

I said in my first book, that I can imagine a world where inter-species communication is the norm. Several years later, I still believe we can achieve this. Communicating with animals so that we can understand their needs is essential to *fully* integrating them into our society. Animal communicators, medical empaths, and healers will bridge the gap between animals and new medical technology. And pets, whose human companions learn to communicate with them, will no doubt lead longer, fuller, happier lives.

After completing my first book, I didn't think I had anything more to write about. I was wrong! The animals have continued to teach me, enlighten me, and amaze me with their courage and their stories which have filled this book. I hope you've had similar experiences of learning, enlightenment, and amazement while reading what they had to say.

As I worked on this book, I discovered that there was even more helpful information I wanted to share. While there are some tools within these chapters to help you get started, if you really want to DO SOME-THING, then you'll want to watch for my third book, to be published later in 2006 entitled, *For Pet's Sake, DO SOMETHING! Tools for Healing your Pets.*

In that book I'll provide detailed how-to information showing you specific techniques for communicating with your pets when it comes to both everyday things and their health challenges. I'll explain animal auras and chakras and spiritual healing techniques you can use, including Reiki, Cosmic Healing, and Absent or Remote Healing.

On a practical note, we'll talk about guidelines for good, better and best nutrition, as well as using vitamins, minerals, and other nutritional supplements.

For those who are interested in natural healing choices, you'll find information about using herbs, homeopathy, therapeutic grade essential oils, and flower essences for your pets. We'll also explore healing with crystals, color and sound, and we'll visit the topics of massage, acupressure, acupuncture, and chiropractic.

When you're ready, you can immerse yourself in these different techniques so that you can DO SOMETHING more for your pet's sake!

I look forward to meeting with you again with my next book!

ABOUT THE AUTHOR

Monica Diedrich knew she could hear animals speak ever since she was eight years old. By the age of 18, she'd also begun to share the gift of her insight and guidance with humans, helping them with their life challenges as well. Today, however, her work is devoted *exclusively* to the well being of animals.

She holds the degree of Doctor of Metaphysics and is an ordained minister. Studying Eastern traditions developed her understanding of how humans, animals and nature are all interconnected, as well as showing her the importance of attaining healing at all three levels — physically, emotionally and spiritually.

Since 1990, she's been a pet communicator, talking with animals non-stop. She also worked for a while as a veterinary surgical assistant, where she sometimes used her gift to help animals come out of anesthesia when they weren't responding readily

In addition to providing both introductory and private consultations, Monica presents seminars, teaches classes, and writes books about the art of animal communication. She's also a regular contributor to several TV shows, including one aired in South Korea.

Her first book, *What Your Animals Tell Me*, has won two awards:

- 2001 National Self-Published Book Awards from *Writer's Digest*
- 2003 Nonfiction Award, Farmer's Market Online, "Direct from the Author Book Award," first place.

It's also been translated and released in several other languages, among them, Spanish, Japanese and Croatian.

A native of Argentina, Monica has lived in Southern California for over 30 years, with her husband, and with her children, both human and pet.

She can be reached through her website at:

www.petcommunicator.com.

Order Form

Online orders: Go to: www.petcommunicator.com

Mail orders: (checks only please—no credit cards)
Fill in the information below and mail this order form to:
Two Paws Up Press,
PO Box 6107,
Anaheim, CA 92816-6107

Please send the following. I understand that I may return for a full refund (except S & H) if the book is in resellable condition.

Title:	Copies:	Price:	Total:
What Your Animals Tell Me	_____	**$16.95**	_____
Pets Have Feelings Too!	_____	**$18.95**	_____
For Pet's Sake, DO SOMETHING!	_____	**$16.95**	_____
(pre-order. Due Fall 2006)			
CA residents: Please add 7.75% sales tax			_____
S & H: $4.00 per book			_____
		TOTAL	_____

Mailing address:

Name: _____

Street: _____

City, State, ZIP: _____